Make
Your Own
Handcrafted
Doors
& Windows

John Birchard

Sterling Publishing Co., Inc.   New York

This book is dedicated to my mother (a woodworker)
and my father (a writer).

ACKNOWLEDGMENTS

I would like to give special thanks to Bill Spencer, whose generosity made the drawings and photos for this book possible.

I would also like to thank Larry Martin, Jody Evans, Paul Tichinin, the Mendocino Regional Occupational Program, Roy Underhill, Jeff Woodward, Doug Christie, Al Garvey, Terry and Cecily Klingman, Lee Josephs, and all the others who contributed to the making of this book.

Thanks also go to the following people and companies for contributing material: Rob Van Nieuwenhuizen of Furima Industrial Carbide Co., Wetzler Clamp Co., Connie Bland of Porter Cable Co., Gene Sliga of Delta International Machinery Corp., Powermatic, Inc., MacMurray-Pacific, Inc., Barry Dunsmore of Freud, Inc., William C. Feist of Forest Products Laboratory, USDA, and the many others who made this book possible.

Edited by Michael Cea

Library of Congress Cataloging-in-Publication Data

Birchard, John.
    Make your own handcrafted doors and windows / John Birchard.
        p.   cm.
    Includes index.
    ISBN 0-8069-6544-4 (pbk.)
    1. Doors. 2. Windows. 3. Doors—Maintenance and repair.
4. Windows—Maintenance and repair. I. Title.
TH2270.B57 1988   87-33701
694'.6—dc19   CIP

                3   5   7   9   10   8   6   4   2

Copyright © 1988 by John Birchard
Published by Sterling Publishing Co., Inc.
Two Park Avenue, New York, N.Y. 10016
Distributed in Canada by Oak Tree Press Ltd.
% Canadian Manda Group, P.O. Box 920, Station U
Toronto, Ontario, Canada M8Z 5P9
Distributed in Great Britain and Europe by Cassell PLC
Artillery House, Artillery Row, London SW1P 1RT, England
Distributed in Australia by Capricorn Ltd.
P.O. Box 665, Lane Cove, NSW 2066
Manufactured in the United States of America
All rights reserved

Contents

Color Section opposite page 64

Introduction

Until very recently, building doors and windows was, by necessity, a specialized area of woodworking. To be cost-effective, the craftsman had to work in a production-line setting, with large, very expensive, and specialized power tools. The demand for a functional, reasonably priced product was met, but conformity and often early obsolescence were the price we paid. Now, with improved tools (especially routers and small, low-cost shapers), glues, and the techniques available, anyone with the inclination and common woodworking skills can build his own doors and windows with results that will be long-lasting, pleasing to the eye, and very energy-efficient.

And what a joy and pride in your craftsmanship you'll experience every day living in a house with doors and windows that you have carefully thought out and designed to your own needs and tastes! Perhaps a small viewing window cut in your existing front door is all you need. While you are at it, you can also design a pretty stained glass panel to fit in your new peephole, so that your visitor will have something pleasant to look at while waiting. Be creative. Design it in a nice round or diamond shape, or maybe with an arched top to give it an Old World feeling. Though your needs may be small, your feeling of accomplishment will be great if you do it yourself and apply the best of your creative powers.

However, maybe your needs are more extensive. It might be time to finally break down and replace the stained and rotted sash with new ones made to last with rot-resistant redwood or cedar, and glazed with insulated glass to improve your home's energy efficiency. As long as you're at it, do a good job of weather-stripping them so that the family room will never be cold and drafty again. With just a router and a table saw, you can even make operable or fixed sash that will last for years.

You may be lucky enough to be starting from scratch. Perhaps you have a new house, and a chance to do it right the first time. There are so many choices to make, and doors and windows are such an important and expensive part of any building. Even if you are just going to buy factory-made doors and windows, there are many trade-offs and considerations to be made. Will the money you'll spend now on high tech, insulated, coated glass, and weather stripping really pay off in savings on your heating bills? Is it worth it to you to build an R30 front door, or would you be happier with the foyer designed to work as an air lock and coatroom to attain the same insulation rating?

Ironically, as technological innovations like coated glass, tighter weather stripping, and insulated core materials have improved the energy efficiency of many of the components of doors and windows, common, ordinary wood has remained the best material for both structure and insulation that we have. It is workable, it is beautiful, it endures, and it gives us one more reason to build doors and windows ourselves.

You may even find, as I did, that by building your own doors and windows, you've built yourself a career as well. The demand for good, well-constructed, and unique doors and windows will never be satisfied. And by dealing directly with your customer, you can sell them at prices that will be very competitive with manufactured products. Once the word gets around, custom doors and windows can easily become the bread and butter of your small woodworking operation.

An amazingly small amount of space (I've built as many as 20 doors at once in my 400-square foot shop), and a few good power and hand tools are all you'll need to start a creative and satisfying business. Of course, a love of problem solving and a flair for design will help, but even if you're more of a traditionalist there's a need for what you can produce.

To determine what to produce, ask yourself the following question: What are the particular conditions of your local environment? Do your neighbors want 4-inch-thick insulated doors to protect them from those long cold winters, or louvred or Dutch doors to let in the cool evening breezes? Perhaps what they need is someone who can come around now and again to plane the edge of a sticking door, oil a lock, replace a broken pane of glass, or hang a new set of storm windows. With the proper travelling tool kit, and the know-how that this book provides, you could easily become happily self-employed.

Doors and windows are such common items in our modern lives that we tend to take very little notice of them. Still, they quietly add their bit to the quality of our lives, helping bring warmth and light into our homes, brightening our comings and goings.

A well-designed door or window is something that both owner and craftsperson can take pride in—a combination of beauty and function that enriches both the quality of life and the pocketbook. Whether you intend to build your own doors and windows, buy them, or build them for others as a tradesman, you owe it to yourself to put some time and effort into understanding these simple but important structures.

Historical Overview

The sash window is a relatively recent invention, probably developed in Europe in the 17th century. At first, only the wealth of the nobility could afford an expensive item like a window with glass in it. Early sash joiners worked almost entirely by hand, and developed a complicated system of interlocking parts to hold several small pieces of glass in one window. Pieces larger than one square foot were hard to come by in those days.

These multipaned windows, so common to us today, were the technological wonder of their time. They let the light of day in, and kept the cold wind out. What a joy they must have been to the inhabitants of the dark and drafty castles and keeps of Northern Europe.

Wooden doors much like today's panel doors have been with us since antiquity, though in those days even a roughly made door of wooden planks must have been a luxury item. Over the passing centuries, artistic and engineering heights have been achieved with doors.

Some of the earliest, still existing doors are marble-panelled stone doors from Pompeii and Greece (200 A.D.), and cast-bronze doors from Greece and Rome of the same period. The double doors of the Roman Pantheon were 24 feet high, and cast in solid bronze. They were supported by pivots fitted into sockets in the threshold and lintel.

Wooden doors were common in both Egypt and Mesopotamia. Pompeiian murals and surviving fragments indicate that contemporary doors looked much like modern doors. They were constructed of stiles and rails that supported wooden panels, and were occasionally equipped with hinges and locks, often made of wood.

In the Orient, wooden doors usually consisted of two panels, the lower one solid, the upper one a wooden lattice backed by paper. Mediaeval castle and citadel doors were made of heavy lumber held together with diagonal bracing and iron banding. They may not have been pretty, but they were state of the art when it came to security measures.

The doors to cathedrals and other institutions of the same era were also impressive for their size and weight, and often adorned with intricate carving and relief work. The gilded cast-bronze doors to the Baptistery of Florence, constructed around 1425 by Lorenzo Ghiberti, were said by Michelangelo to be worthy of being the doors to Paradise, and have since become famous as one of the first flowerings of the Italian Renaissance.

Many other fine examples of wood carving and joinery still exist on doors which have withstood centuries of service in the harsh climate of Central Europe. Today, though the functional emphasis of doors has shifted to providing a more symbolic type of security, a more muted artistic statement, they are still as important as ever in our lives.

For most of us, it would be a rare day indeed when we didn't use a door or gaze through a window. And for those of us who love to create useful and beautiful things from wood, the time has never been better to take advantage of this wonderful opportunity for creative expression.

Basics

1
Setting Up Shop

Today, with the availability of good, low-cost power tools and cutters, as well as improved glues and the simplified techniques that they make possible, the small-scale woodworker can make high-quality doors and windows at a price that is competitive with the manufactured product. Home builders, too, can successfully construct these necessities with sturdy and unique results that are a fine expression of their creative talents.

A good deal of organization and know-how are necessary to make this possible, though, and the better set up you are, the quicker and more pleasing (less frustrating) will be the work. There is an element of risk in every undertaking, but a well-organized shop is a safer place to work, and the careful worker is less likely to waste materials and money on mistakes or misunderstandings. Though you may already have a good shop and a lot of experience in woodworking, what I am about to discuss deals with the specialized needs of the door and window shop.

Like our forefathers, you can build doors and windows with virtually no power tools. In later chapters I will describe and il-

lustrate some of the hand methods used by pre-industrial jointers for those who want to do it the way our forefathers did. But even if you use only a saw and a hammer (a tape measure would also be handy), you'll need a good, dry place to work, and a sturdy workbench that is large enough to lay a door (about 7 feet × 3 feet) out on.

You can get by with as little as 100 square feet of shop space, but as your talents and techniques grow you'll need more. I've found my 16 × 28-foot shop with storage area underneath to be quite adequate for jobs that involve as many as 30–40 doors or windows. Still, I could use a lot more storage space at times: a separate room for hand work and one for finishing would be nice.

If you find yourself, like me, in a small but adequate space, you'll have to make the best of it and organize your shop carefully so that the work flows as smoothly as possible. The shop shown in the floor plan drawings (Illus. 1 and 2) has the radial arm saw bench, table saw, and planer positioned near doors that can be opened when you are bringing in long pieces of lumber to be rough-cut, or for working with the nearly

7-foot lengths that will be required for the stiles of most doors.

Rough lumber is stored off the ground underneath the working floor, which is on posts and piers about 3 feet above the grade (Illus. 3). Posts and piers are a cheap and acceptable way to make a foundation for this type of building, and the space beneath the shop is ideal for lumber storage because it is sheltered from precipitation, but open to air circulation. You can use 2 × 4's or 4 × 4's to keep your lumber off the ground; be sure to sticker it to allow for better air circulation.

Storing your lumber at ground level is a lot easier than trying to get your uncut lumber up into the rafters or a loft. On the other hand, a storage area high in the shop in the rafters or a loft can be a great place to put lumber that is seasoned, but not quite dry enough to work yet. Heat, even the little bit trapped by your windows, if that's all you have, rises and collects at the top of your shop, and will do a good job of driving excess moisture from your wood in a couple of weeks.

If you don't already have overhead storage racks in your shop, you might want to install some, especially if you plan to season or air-dry any wood yourself. Overhead racks like those shown in Illus. 4 will also come in handy for storing assembled

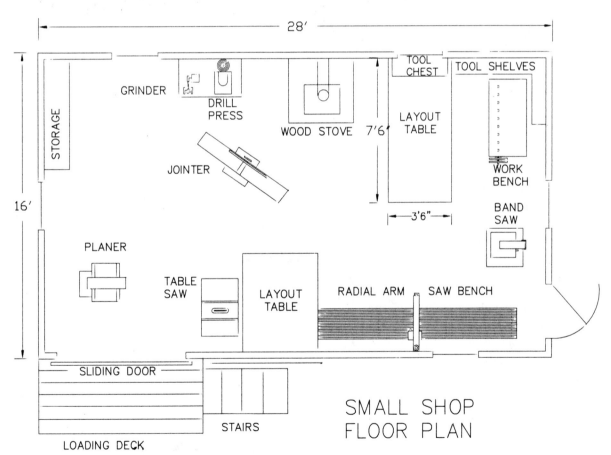

Illus. 1 and 2 (following page). A couple of alternative floor plans for a small door- and window-making shop.

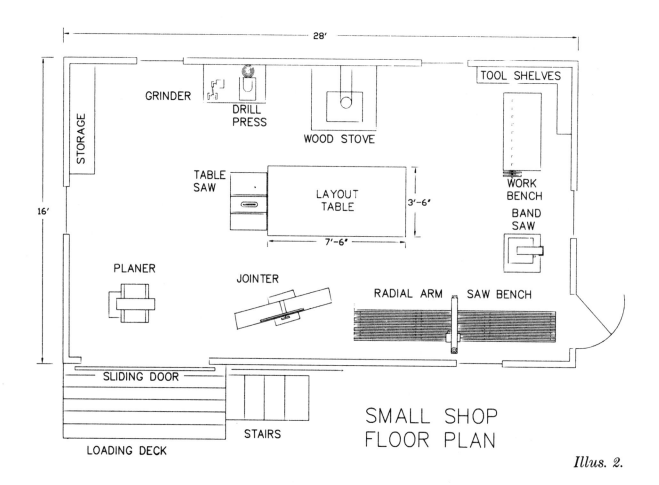

GRINDER DRILL PRESS WOOD STOVE TOOL SHELVES

STORAGE

28'

16'

TABLE SAW

LAYOUT TABLE

3'-6'

7'-6'

WORK BENCH

BAND SAW

PLANER JOINTER

RADIAL ARM SAW BENCH

SLIDING DOOR

STAIRS

LOADING DECK

SMALL SHOP FLOOR PLAN

Illus. 2.

Illus. 3. This section view of a small woodworking shop shows some areas for lumber storage and points out the necessity for at least 10 feet of clearance between the floor and the ceiling. A gambrel roof, rather than a conventional roof, will provide better clearance and more storage space.

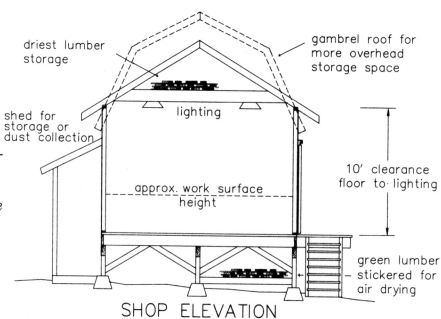

driest lumber storage

gambrel roof for more overhead storage space

shed for storage or dust collection

lighting

approx. work surface height

10' clearance floor to lighting

green lumber — stickered for air drying

SHOP ELEVATION

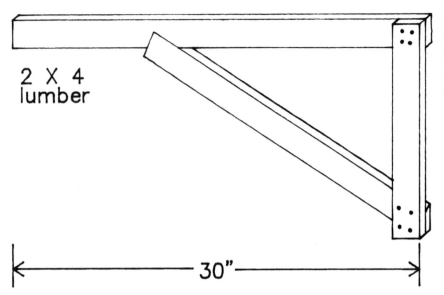

2 X 4 lumber

|← ——————— 30" ——————— →|

Illus. 4. Overhead storage racks like this one will be handy for storing window jamb or sash.

window jambs while the sash is being made.

If you don't already have heat in your shop, or even if you do, you may want to consider installing some type of wood-burning stove. There will be a lot of wood scrap produced as you work that can be used as fuel, and the heat from a wood-burning stove tends to be dry. Dryness is important, especially when you are making something that will be used in a dry place.

Exterior doors and windows will be exposed to a full range of weather conditions, and must be carefully sealed with paint or an exterior-grade stain for protection. Interior doors, on the other hand, dry out with time, causing loose panels and cracked joints if the wood was too moist when the door was assembled. Even the best kiln-dried lumber will rapidly absorb moisture from the air if stored in an environment that is too moist.

Just as lumber that is too moist will warp and shrink as it dries, lumber that is too dry can also cause problems. A panel that is already tight can swell and force the joints of the door's framework apart. Everyone is familiar with the door that is so swollen that it won't shut.

Usually these problems are avoided by properly sealing the wood of your completed doors with paint or varnish, but even the best finishes absorb some moisture, and as time and the elements work on these sealers they will eventually fail. However, a moisture metre for checking the wood, and a cheap humidity gauge for checking the relative humidity of various locations in the shop, will help take the guesswork out of seasoning your lumber and acclimating it to the type of environment that it will occupy as a finished product (Illus. 5).

Try to use only lumber that has under 7% moisture for interior doors, especially doors with panels, and lumber in the 9–12% range for exterior doors and windows. Generally, moisture content is less critical with windows than doors because the pieces are smaller and shorter. Whenever possible, get your lumber a few weeks before you start a job, and put it in a part of the shop where it will approach the moisture level you need.

Illus. 5. A moisture metre and relative humidity gauge can help you balance out the moisture content of your lumber before you work it so that it will match as closely as possible the humidity of the environment that it will eventually occupy.

Layout Table and Workbench

The two most important fixtures in the door- and window-maker's shop are the layout table and the workbench. These can be combined in one bench, but it is often helpful to have two benches, one next to the other so that a piece can quickly be clamped in the vise for planing or chiselling while the rest of the project is still laid out on the assembly table (Illus. 6).

Access to the layout table from at least three sides is necessary. This table is used both for preassembly and for the final gluing of pieces; so it is important that the

window and door maker is able to get around it and reach across it easily. Quick access to hand tools and clamps from this area is also important.

The shop shown in Illus. 1 combines a small layout table with the radial arm saw bench and table saw, and has a full-sized layout table next to the workbench, but another option that would work well would be a centrally located layout table used in conjunction with the table saw (Illus. 2). It is important that this table be wide enough to accommodate large pieces (a 36- or 42-inch door being about the widest you will usually encounter), but not so wide that you can't reach across it or get around it quickly. Seven-and-a-half feet will usually be long enough.

The layout table should be sturdily braced below, with overhanging edges for clamping pieces to it, and a smooth, flat surface. If you use this table also as a gluing table, you may want to cut a piece of ¼-inch plywood or Masonite pressed board to the same size and use it as a cover for the table while gluing. Glue build-up on your working surface can cause bad marring and scratches in your work; so wipe any wet glue off, and use a scraper to remove any dried glue.

Your workbench has to be even more sturdy than your layout table, because this is where you'll be doing all your planing, sawing, chiselling, and coaxing of stubborn joinery and other wooden-headed assemblies. There are many types of workbenches available through catalogues and woodworking suppliers. You, however, can build your own from hardwood, or even such cheap materials as high-density particle board and construction-grade lumber.

Illus. 6. Your layout table should be located so that a vise and workbench, hand tools, and clamps are as close by as possible.

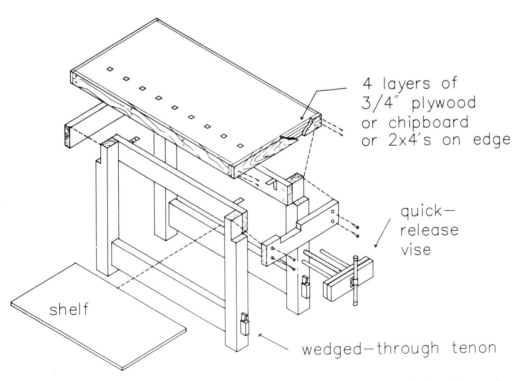

4 layers of
3/4" plywood
or chipboard
or 2x4's on edge

quick—
release
vise

shelf

wedged—through tenon

Illus. 7. This workbench can be made from construction-grade lumber and a sheet of particle board for the top, or from fine hard woods.

Illus. 7 is a plan for a small bench that can be made from whatever materials you have available. The top can be made from 2 × 4-sized pieces with their faces glued together, or from a sheet of high-density particle board cut into four pieces and laminated to form a 3-inch-thick piece. If you use particle board, be sure to band the edges with solid lumber. You may also want to veneer the top with plywood, Formica laminated plastic, or wood for a nicer work surface.

At least one good quick-release vise and a series of holes for bench dogs are essential. The old European jointer's bench usually had both an end vise and a side vise for holding windows and doors on edge as they were being planed to their final size (Illus. 9). Fixtures such as the bench support and door holder shown in Illus. 10 will also come in handy when you are working on a completed door or window, either in the shop or on the job.

Illus. 9. Some workbenches also have a side vise which can be used to hold larger pieces on edge.

A EASY-TO-MAKE BENCH DOGS

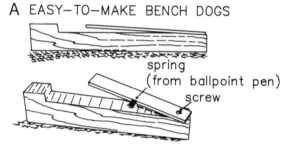

B BENCH SUPPORT

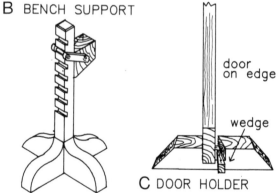

C DOOR HOLDER

Illus. 8. Work is held between bench dogs (which fit in the line of square holes on the surface of the bench) and the end vise for planing or other operations.

Illus. 10. A shows how to make a spring-loaded bench dog that won't slip back in the hole when pressure is released. B is an adjustable bench support for holding one end of a large piece, like a door, while the other end is held in the bench vise. C is a block of 4 × 4 with a slot cut in it. One side of the slot is angled, and a wedge can be driven in between it and a door to hold the door on edge.

14

Portable Tool Kit

Anyone who specializes in making doors and windows, or who makes them for himself, is going to be called upon to do some on-the-job installation or repair work. This is another area in which organization is extremely important. Making the transition from the shop to the job can be a trying experience. You may pack up all your tools and travel to the job only to find out once you're there that you forgot your tape measure or your T-square. Also, at such jobs you've got to load and unload heavy and often fragile doors or windows without marring them; and worse yet, you've got to cut big holes in your wonderful creations for locks and hinges. At times like these, the proper tool should be right at hand.

The travelling tool kit shown in Illus. 11 contains everything you will normally need when hanging or working on doors and windows, and is designed to work as a workbench. If at all possible, get a separate set of tools just for this kit, so that they will always be there when you need them.

Dust-Removal System

If you are planning on doing a fairly large volume of work in your door and window shop and have power tools such as a jointer, planer, router or shaper, you should start thinking about setting up some kind of dust-removal system as well. Dust-removal systems fall into two categories: stationary and portable. The amount of space you have, the type of foundation your shop is on, and how much money you can afford to spend are factors that will determine the dust-removal system best for you.

Stationary systems usually consist of a 12–15-inch paddle-wheel-type fan driven by an electric motor. The fan sucks the dust and chips from the machines via a series of ducts and blows it into a cyclone bag, where it is separated from the air that is carrying it (Illus. 12). This is the proper type of system to have in a large shop where several people are likely to be working at once on various machines. Ducting can be run either overhead, or below the floor, and the blower and catch bags can be

Illus. 11 A and B. This portable workbench is also a travelling tool kit that can hold everything you will need for on-the-job work. Casters make it easy to move around.

Illus. 12. A dust-collection system of some kind is essential for any serious woodworking shop. This one is a fixed blower type which traps the dust inside a large canvas bag.

placed outside the work area to reduce noise and take up less work space.

This can be a very expensive type of system to develop, and a time-consuming one to operate and maintain. A full-scale system of this type for the shop shown in Illus. 1 or 2 could cost close to $1,000 to set up. The blower-motor combination alone costs around $500, and ducting (usually 4-inch stove pipe, drainage pipe, or PVC [polyvinyl chloride] pipe), sliding dampers (to close the ducts of the tools that aren't

being used), and hoods to fit the various machines will add considerably more to the cost. The more ducting and ports you have, the more powerful your motor will have to be.

Illus. 13. A damper can be made from plywood and particle board to close off ducts that are not being used.

A cheaper alternative for a small one- or two-person shop is the portable-canister type of system based on a powerful shop vacuum, or a fan and motor mounted on a 55-gallon drum that is on casters (Illus. 14). This system eliminates the need for ducting and dampers but has the disadvantage of taking up space in the shop and never being where you want it, when you want it.

No matter which system you use, you'll still have to make hoods to go on your tools, and you'll probably find that there is no system that gets all the dust put out by every tool.

Good cross-ventilation and an exhaust fan that can move the entire volume of air in your shop every couple of minutes will also be a great help when you are sanding or applying finishes. Dust masks and organic vapor masks should also be standard equipment for the serious woodworker, as many

another area of the shop for another operation. If you have the space, a rolling dolly will do this job well. If you are short on

I—BEAM SAWHORSE

Illus. 15. A very sturdy sawhorse can be made by making an I beam out of 2 × 4's and then nailing legs on it, as shown.

floor space, you can build yourself a couple of sawhorses that can be set up where you need them and tucked away in a corner, or put outside when not in use (Illus. 15).

A portable out-feed roller on a stand is also very handy to have when you are making doors and windows (Illus. 16). It can be set up with the planer, jointer, shaper, router table, table saw or band saw to help get good, accurate results when working long pieces like the stiles of a door or a large window. To use the out-feed roller with a jointer, shaper, or router table, you'll have to adjust the height very accurately to get good results. Clamp the board that you will be working on to the table, set the roller a couple of feet away from the edge of the table, and then bring it up to where it just

Illus. 14. A large heavy-duty shop vacuum can also be used as a portable dust collector.

woods can be toxic or irritating to the lungs; many varnishes and oils also contain toxic vapors.

Sawhorses, Rollers and Dollies

Sawhorses, rollers and dollies are all useful items in the door- and window-maker's shop. Often, a whole series of parts have to be transported to a certain machine for an operation and then transported to touches the board. Setting up the roller a little low is better than setting it up too high.

You can easily make an out-feed roller out of scrap-metal parts that can be gotten at most junkyards (Illus. 16). I have one that is made of a conveyer roller about a foot wide mounted on a frame that is attached to a piece of steel pipe. This piece of pipe fits inside another piece of pipe that has a hole drilled in it and a nut welded to it for a screw-in bolt that sets the height. The base of the stand is an automobile wheel hub that works nicely because it is heavy and can be tilted up on edge and rolled around when it has to be moved.

Illus. 17 shows how to make the same type of out-feed roller out of wood. No bearings are necessary; just wax the area where the roller tenons meet the stand. If you don't have a lathe to make the roller, a common rolling pin will work fine.

Illus. 16 (above left). An out-feed roller made from an old truck wheel, a steel pipe, and a conveyer roller. Illus. 17 (above right). A wooden out-feed roller. The roller was turned on a lathe, but similar ones are available as rolling pins.

2
Hand Tools

Acquiring good hand tools and keeping them in top shape is very important in this and other areas of woodworking. It's easy to overlook the importance of good hand tools with so many wonderful power tools available, but hand tools can still do many operations faster and better than power tools.

Hand tools were used for thousands of years before the invention of the router and the belt sander, during which time generations of anonymous artisans perfected techniques that quickly and accurately got the job done. You'll be a better, more efficient woodworker if you learn to use these time-honored tools and techniques. The feeling of satisfaction that you get from completing your project will be that much more intense when you know you did it the traditional way.

Saws

Crosscut Saws

Several types of hand saws have applications in door and window making. You should have at least one good seven- or eight-point (the number indicates the teeth per inch) crosscut saw in every tool box (Illus. 18). If you do not own a good one that has been handed down to you from a woodworking ancestor, try searching at flea markets, garage sales, or anywhere that old tools are in evidence.

A sad fact of our modern age is that the quality of tools, particularly the common but important hand tools like saws and planes, is on the decline. A turn-of-the-century London Spring or Diston saw was made with the best possible steel, carefully tempered, crowned, and balanced to give a true and easy cut, and was meant to last a lifetime (or several). If you are patient and know where to look, you can often get these old saws today for a fraction of the price of a new one.

Check with your local saw sharpener if you are unsure of the quality of a particular saw, and let him put it in good working order. You won't regret it when you use the tool and it cuts perfectly, without dragging or tearing out the grain.

Your standard crosscut saw will be great for rough-cutting lumber to length and many other on-the-job tasks. I also have a smaller, finer crosscut saw with about 14 points per inch; it is known as a panel saw.

Illus. 18. Shown from top to bottom are a 7-point crosscut saw, a finer 14-point panel saw, and a 14-point backsaw, which will cover most of your coarse hand-sawing needs.

I use it constantly for trimming and finer crosscutting on nearly finished pieces where a fine, careful cut is essential. These saws are a little harder to come by, but worth looking for, as they are much less likely to cause chipped-out grain on finish work.

Backsaws and Dovetail Saws

Backsaws and dovetail saws are handy for cutting parts of joints like tenons, or for mitring or crosscutting mouldings, trim, or other pieces where perfect accuracy is essential (Illus. 19). A full-sized backsaw can be used in combination with a mitre box, which can either be made or purchased, to give you perfectly straight cuts at any angle. These saws also come in handy when doing remodelling or when changes need to be made. The backsaw, with its stiffened back, can cut right up to a 90-degree stop, and can go into places that no power saw can go into.

Dovetail saws, designed for making the most careful cuts, are also handy for working with fine mouldings or for making small stop cuts like those that are necessary when installing friction hinges in windows.

Coping Saw

One other saw that may come in handy for the door and window maker is the coping saw. A 19th-century technique for making the interlocking joints, called cope-and-stick joints, which are so common on windows and doors, employed a fine-bladed "coping" saw to undercut the ends of the rails and muntins so that they would fit over the bead and create a nice-looking mitre at the corner where the two pieces met (Illus. 21).

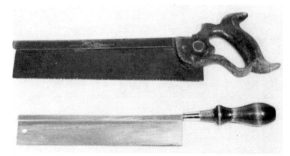

Illus. 19. Backsaws are used extensively in the shop and on the job for mitring, shoulder-cutting, etc. The smaller backsaw shown here is known as a dovetail saw.

20

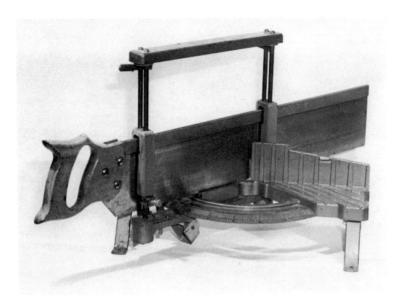

Illus. 20. Hand-operated mitre saws are pretty much a thing of the past since the advent of power mitre saws, but can still be used for moulding cutting, etc.

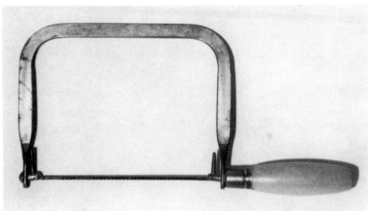

Illus. 21. Coping saws were once used to do the cope-and-stick joinery in sash-making. They are still handy for cutting inlays or appliqués.

Several other techniques now exist for achieving this same interlocking cut, but for the beginner who is short on cash to invest in power tools, or for the purist, this is still an important tool. Even if you have all the power tools you want, you may find a coping saw handy for cutting fine pieces with lots of curves for inlays or highlights.

Planes

Planes are as indispensable now as they have been for centuries when it comes to making and installing doors and windows (Illus. 22). Learn how to sharpen and use a plane properly and you will never have a need for those noisy, dusty, hard-to-control, and expensive belt sanders.

Planes are used to flatten uneven joints or warped or twisted boards, to straighten edges, smooth and finish rough wood, fit panels, cut and smooth rabbets and slots, smooth curves, and even to make mouldings or decorative beads (Illus. 23). The well-established jointer of the last century probably had upwards of a hundred different types of planes, and, when necessary, could make new ones for special tasks.

Illus. 22. Hand planes are still the quickest, most pleasant way to flatten and smooth your work.

Illus. 23. Moulding planes were once found in every cabinetmaker's tool chest. They were used in sash and door making as well as for shaping mouldings, raised panels, etc.

Illus. 24. A good, low-angled block plane (foreground) and a jack or smoothing plane will handle most of the modern woodworker's planing needs.

Illus. 25 A and B. Compass planes are great for smoothing curved surfaces. This adjustable one has a spring steel sole that you can bend to any curve, concave or convex, by turning the knob on the front of the plane.

Illus. 26. Wooden-soled planes work with less friction. The two Bailey planes on the left have metal adjustment mechanisms, while you can adjust the shop-made plane on the right by tapping on the iron or the plane body.

At the minimum , you should have a low-angle block plane—the small kind that can be held in one hand—and a medium-sized jack or smoothing plane (Illus. 24). Though metal-bodied planes are pretty much the standard these days, wooden-soled planes actually work with less friction, allowing for a smoother, easier cut.

As with saws, the older planes are often the better buy. Turn-of-the-century Bailey planes with wooden bodies and metal-adjustment mechanisms are worth the effort to find and renovate (Illus. 26). The metal-screw mechanisms can be used quick-ly and easily to adjust the depth of the cut, which is crucial to good planing.

Sharpening the Plane

The first essential for good planing is a razor-sharp iron. The standard test to determine the sharpness of the iron is to see if the blade will shave a few hairs off the back of your hand. Another test is to hold the blade so that the edge is pointing directly at a strong light. If you can see any light reflected off the edge, it's not sharp enough. Small points of reflection indicate nicks (Illus. 27); a reflection all the way

Illus. 27. If you can see the edge of a plane iron, it's not sharp. The shiny points along this one indicate nicks in the edge.

across means the iron needs to be completely sharpened.

To do a proper job of sharpening, you will need a grinding setup like the one shown in Illus. 28 and couple of honing stones—a coarse and a fine stone—for honing and touch-ups between grindings. A low-speed grinder can be made from any type of small electric motor (washing-machine motors are often easy to come by) and a mandrel, which can be bought at most hardware stores.

Illus. 28. You can make your own low-speed grinding setup like this one with a small electric motor and a mandrel. The smaller, finer stone in the background is best for hollow-grinding plane irons.

The smaller the diameter of the Carborundum stone, the better the grinder will be for hollow-grinding. Four-inch to six-inch stones work well. In hollow-grinding, the radius of the stone is ground into the bevel of the blade, so that the middle of the bevel is actually relieved slightly. This makes it easier to hone the edge and to resharpen without grinding.

The tool rest shown in Illus. 29 is made from a scrap of 1½-inch stock screwed to a base that can be clamped to the bench where the mandrel is mounted. By moving the tool rest in or out, or tilting it with wedges, you can change the angle of the grind.

The angle of the grind should generally be such that the surface of the bevel is about twice as wide as the thickness of the iron. Low-angle irons can be a little wider, but the iron will dull very rapidly if the edge is too fine. Move the iron fairly rapidly back and forth across the grinding stone without too much pressure. You will usually need to slow down a little in the middle and speed up along the edges to get a straight edge. At this stage, you want a perfectly straight and square edge (Illus. 30). Later on, you will relieve the corners slightly on the honing stone to prevent them from marring the work.

When you think you have achieved the proper grind, hone the iron a bit as shown in Illus. 31 and look carefully at the polish marks. The polish marks should be even all the way across both edges of the bevel. If they're not, take the iron back to the grinder and grind a bit more in the areas that need it. This way, you can quickly get a good, even grind and a straight edge.

A LOW—SPEED GRINDING SETUP

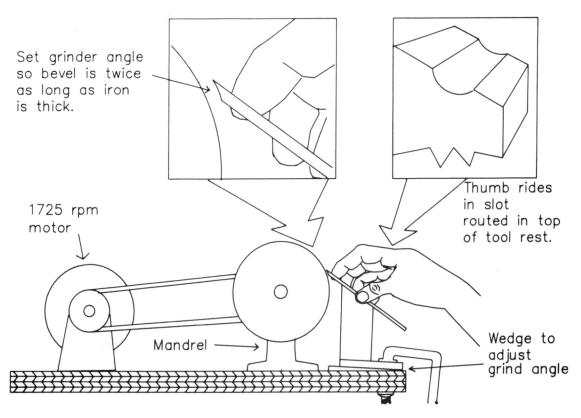

Set grinder angle so bevel is twice as long as iron is thick.

Thumb rides in slot routed in top of tool rest.

1725 rpm motor

Mandrel

Wedge to adjust grind angle

Illus. 29. How to make and adjust a tool rest for plane iron grinding.

Illus. 30. Grind your iron so that it is perfectly straight and square across the edge.

Illus. 31. Hone the iron a bit and look at the polish marks to determine if the grind is even all the way across.

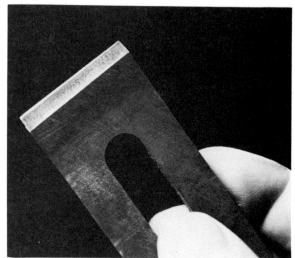

Illus. 32A (above left). Uneven grinding. Illus. 32B (above right). The proper grind.

Illus. 33. Be sure to polish the back side of the iron too. It should be kept perfectly flat.

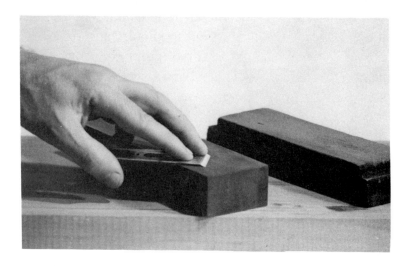

When honing, avoid rocking the blade, and don't hone too much. Also, be sure to lay the iron flat-side down on the stone and to rub quite a bit in a circular motion to remove the burr left by grinding; keep this side of the edge polished and free of rust or nicks (Illus. 33).

It is important that the honing stones be absolutely flat. If they aren't, they can be dressed on a piece of 120-grit sandpaper stretched on a flat surface, or you can use Carborundum powder and water on a sheet of glass.

Hone first on the coarse stone; then polish quickly on the fine stone. Less than a dozen strokes per stone should be plenty; too much honing will just dull the blade. By placing your fingers on the outer corners of the iron when you hone, as shown in Illus. 31, you will relieve the corners slightly so that they won't dig and mar the work.

Setting Up the Plane

After you have sharpened the blade well, the next step is to set it up properly in the plane. Most larger planes have a blade cap or chip breaker that should meet the blade just at the leading edge, all the way across. Any crack here will cause clogging.

If the cap isn't tight, file or hone it until it is. The leading edge of the cap should be about $1/32$ inch back from the edge of the iron, and should be well polished so that shavings will flow smoothly over it. The cap helps support the edge of the iron and directs the shavings up and away from the throat of the plane.

When the chip breaker has been properly placed on the iron, put the iron and breaker in place in the plane, adjust the iron so that it is just even with the sole of the plane, and take a look at the width of the throat opening. Many planes have a screw in the back, under the blade-adjustment wheel, that adjusts the width of the throat opening. Block planes usually have a sliding front section of the sole for the same purpose. The throat opening should be as narrow as it can be without clogging with shavings (Illus. 35 and 36). This will help keep the wood fibres from tearing out and breaking off as you plane.

Now adjust the iron for a light cut. When possible, plane with the grain of the wood so that the fibres don't tear out. Often the grain will switch directions, making this impossible. Also, when flattening the joints of a newly assembled door or window, you will find it necessary to plane across the grain on some of the parts (Illus. 37). A really sharp plane will cut almost as well across the grain as with it, and you may have better luck planing across the grain on difficult woods.

Under ideal circumstances you can get a finer finish with a plane than with sandpaper or other abrasives, but generally your wood won't allow a perfect finish with just a plane. This will usually mean that you must go over the wood with a cabinet scraper and then an orbital sander to smooth torn-out grain or other imperfections.

The proper use of the hand plane, then, is for flattening, smoothing, and straightening. It works especially fast when removing milling marks left by jointers and planers, or any other kind of gouge, scrape, or scratch.

When flattening, don't be afraid to work at right angles to the grain of the wood. When straightening, or removing wood from the edges of doors or windows, take long, even strokes, and check the wood frequently with a straightedge and square.

Later chapters discuss in more detail the many applications of planes in door and window making.

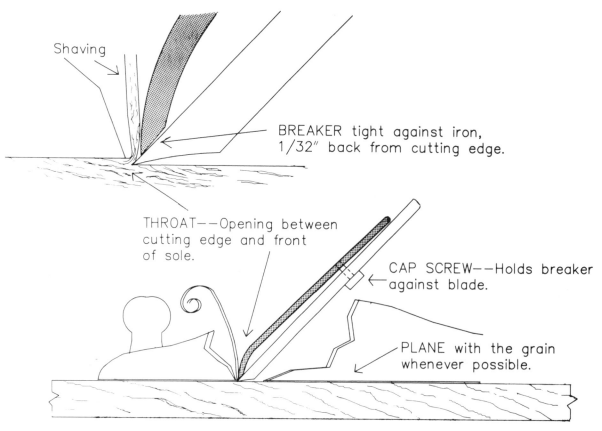

Illus. 34. The proper alignment of breaker and iron in the throat of the plane. The breaker must be tight against the iron all the way across, or it will clog with shavings.

 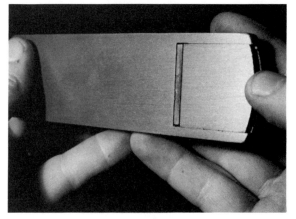

Illus. 35 (above left). For fine work, adjust the throat opening to make it as narrow as possible. Illus. 36 (above right). Open the throat up a bit for coarser work.

Illus. 37. With a sharp plane, you can plane across the grain to smooth and flatten joints.

Cabinet Scraper

One of the handiest and least understood of wood-finishing tools is the cabinet scraper, which is simply a flat, usually rectangular piece of medium-hard steel. Many brands of scrapers are available through specialty shops or from companies through catalogues, and you can easily make your own from an old hand-saw blade.

On hard woods, cabinet scrapers work more quickly than sandpaper, and give better results when it comes to final smoothing and finishing (Illus. 38). They are real time-

Illus. 38. Cabinet scrapers are quick and work better than fine sandpaper on hard woods.

savers. Softer woods such as pine, redwood, fir, and cedar don't scrape as easily and can usually be finished more rapidly by flattening with planes and smoothing with an orbital sander.

The scraper can be used to smooth the areas where the plane tends to tear out the grain, by removing the surrounding wood without further tearing out the grain (Illus. 39). A scraper is also much easier to control than a plane. You can work right up to a joint or an edge and stop without tearing the wood where it changes grain direction.

Illus. 39. Scrapers will smooth unruly grained woods where planes tend to tear out the grain.

To get the proper cutting edge on a scraper, start by jointing the edge flat and square with a mill file (Illus. 40). Also, make sure that the flat sides of the scraper are well polished, especially near the cutting edges. This can be done on a honing stone.

After jointing the edge, also polish it carefully on a honing stone (Illus. 41). The objective is to create perfect right-angle corners between the edges and the sides.

29

Illus. 40. To sharpen a scraper, start by jointing the edge perfectly flat and square.

Illus. 41. After filing the edge, polish it on your honing stones. Once again, keep the scraper perfectly square to the stone.

Be careful not to round these corners when you are polishing the sides and edges.

Now, with a round or three-cornered burnishing tool, also carefully polished, turn a little hook out from the corners that will be the actual cutting edge (Illus. 42). Place the scraper in a vise, and draw the burnisher along the edge with an even stroke and a fair amount of pressure. Several light strokes may work as well as one heavy one. The burnisher should be held nearly perpendicular to the sides of the scraper for the first stroke, and at a slight angle for following strokes. Draw the burnisher away

from the edge as you draw it across the scraper, thus helping to pull the metal out to form the hook.

You won't be able to see the hook with the naked eye, and the only way to tell if you've gotten a good edge is to try it. It should actually make nice thin shavings if it is working right.

Sharpening scrapers is more of an art than a science. Experiment with different angles, pressures, and scrapers until you find the combination that works for you. When your scraper starts to dull, you can give it a new edge just by laying it flat and

30

using the burnisher to turn the edge up, and then putting it in the vise and turning it back down again. If your scraper and burnisher are nicely polished, you can do this several times before it is necessary to rejoint and repolish the tool.

Chisels

These unimposing tools have many uses in door and window making and installation, from helping to cut mortise-and-tenon joints to installing hinges and locks. You will need several different sizes and at least a couple of different types of chisel; as with plane blades, they must be kept razor-sharp.

The best all-round type of chisel for the type of work you will do is a heavy-duty or socket type of chisel, with a blade that is not too long and either an impact-resistant plastic handle or a metal-ringed wooden

SHARPENING A CABINET SCRAPER

1. Jointed and polished scraper with perfectly 90° corners.

2. Begin burnishing with awl flat to edge of scraper.

3. Angle awl about 10° for final 2 or 3 strokes.

4. Hooked cutting edge is invisible to naked eye.

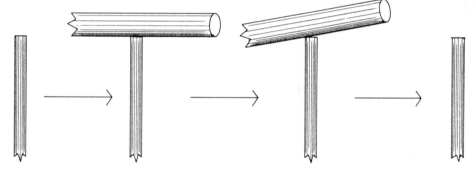

Illus. 42. A rounded awl can be used to burnish the scraper edge and turn the square corners into a slightly hooked edge.

Illus. 43. A triangular awl can also be used for burnishing.

handle that can withstand plenty of pounding (Illus. 44). The sizes most needed would be ¼, ½, ¾, 1 and 1½ inch. It's nice to have two complete sets of these sizes if you can afford it—one set to keep in the shop, and one for your travelling tool kit. Keep your favorite ones in the shop; the on-the-job chisels will take more abuse, and will be more likely to get lost.

Another type of chisel that will be necessary if your prefer handwork over machine work is the mortising chisel (Illus. 45). These chisels have long, thick blades, and are designed for cutting the deep mortises that are often made to join rails to stiles. Even if you bore out most of the waste of your mortise with a drill, you will still need to use a chisel to trim the edges.

One with a ⅜-inch or ½-inch blade will be sufficient for most mortises.

The chisels mentioned above should be sufficient to cover most of the needs of the door and window maker, unless, of course, you intend to do some serious carving as a decorative technique. They are sharpened with the same techniques shown for sharpening plane blades, with the bevels at about the same angles.

The major difference between a plane and a chisel is that you can get cut very seriously with a chisel, but not with a plane. Always be sure to work carefully, with finesse rather than with brute force. By remembering never to cut towards any part of your body, you'll decrease the chances of an accident considerably.

Illus. 44. A set of heavy-duty socket chisels are part of the door and window maker's standard equipment.

Illus. 45. You will find a long, thick-shanked mortising chisel like this one handy when cutting deep mortises.

Measuring- and-Marking Tools

Besides the usual tape measure, the door and window maker will need a few special tools for marking and measuring his work. Marking gauges with either one or two spurs, like the ones shown in Illus. 46, are very handy for mortising, slotting, or finding the middle of a piece of lumber.

Several types of squares are also essential (Illus. 47). A sliding T square will be very handy on the job or in the shop, and can be used like the marking gauge to draw a line a certain distance from the edge of a piece of lumber. I also have a small machinist's square, which I use around the shop whenever I need a very accurate right angle, such as on the end of a rail or when I am setting the fence on my jointer.

A larger framing square will also be very helpful when you are squaring up the tops and bottoms of doors or windows, or installing jambs on the job.

A couple of different-sized levels are also essential. I have a two-foot level with factory-fixed tubes and a six-foot level

Illus. 46. Marking gauges are used for marking lines parallel to an edge.

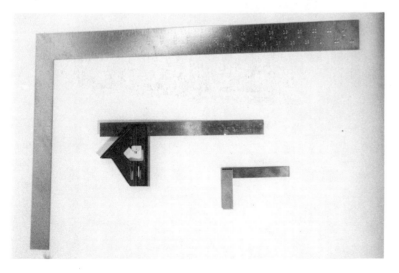

Illus. 47. Several sizes and types of squares are a necessity both in the shop and on the job.

which I use more as a straightedge when trimming edges or installing jambs for doors. Often, I'll hold the two-foot level against the six-foot one and double-check my readings to make sure they are accurate (Illus. 48). The six-foot level is essential for doing a quick, accurate door installation job.

Clamps

No matter how many clamps you own, it always seems as though there are never quite enough (Illus. 49). One fairly complex door can need as many as eight bar clamps for assembly, and C-clamps will be used by the dozen if you get into bent laminations or veneering.

Be prepared to invest several hundred dollars in clamps if you intend to make more than a few doors or windows. You will especially need several ¾-bar clamps at least 4 feet long, and a couple of bar clamps at least 8 feet long for clamping doors from top to bottom. A few smaller, lighter-weight bar clamps will come in handy for edge-joining wood to make wide rails or panels. Jorgensen or C-clamps will be handy for all sorts of operations, from holding down a router guide to clamping a fence to a table saw.

There are, of course, many other hand tools—screwdrivers, files, etc.—which you will need, but the above-mentioned ones will be the center of your collection. Buy the best tools you can afford, maintain and use them properly, and you will receive a sense of pride from owning them and good results when using them.

Illus. 48. A 6-foot level is used with a smaller one to check a window jamb for plumbness and straightness.

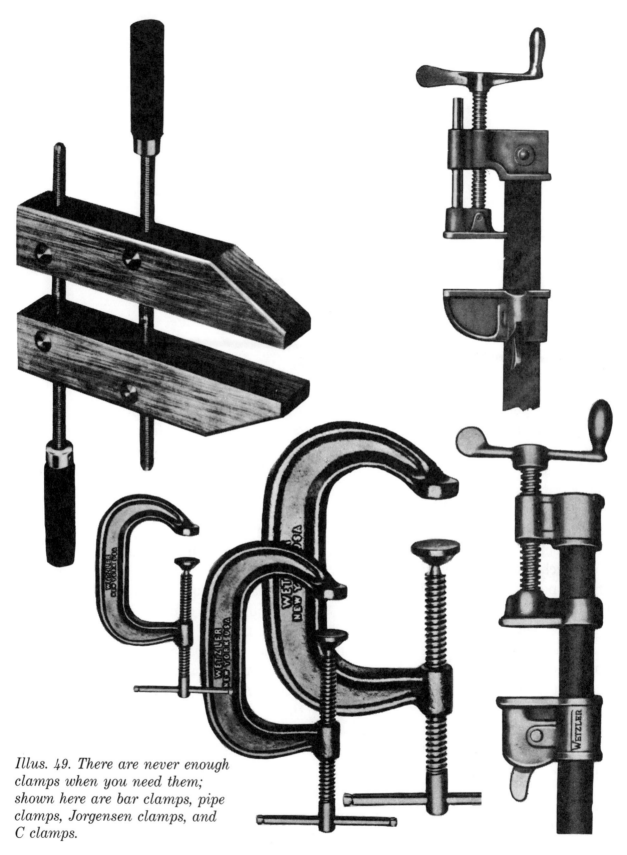

Illus. 49. There are never enough clamps when you need them; shown here are bar clamps, pipe clamps, Jorgensen clamps, and C clamps.

3
Power Tools

Several major power tools are of great value to the modern door and window maker, and yet it is surprising how small an investment in equipment is really necessary to develop a productive shop. The key is in learning to be creative within the limits of the machinery that you have, to adapt it when possible to better fit your needs, and to always keep it in proper running order. If you know the limitations of your machines and keep your cutters sharp and properly adjusted, you'll avoid much frustration and waste.

Another important key is to learn to work safely! Develop proper safety habits and don't get sloppy or lazy; it's just not worth the price you may have to pay. Take a moment to think about every power-tool operation before you do it. Consider the possible risks, and if they seem too great, find another way to do it. Remember that dangers to the eyes, ears, and lungs are equally as serious as the injury you can receive from working with sharp steel.

Take the proper precautions and enjoy your work.

Most of the machinery discussed in this chapter can be found in most well-equipped home woodworking shops, but I'll also discuss some special jigs and fixtures for window and door making, and some important maintenance tips.

Let's assume that you are just starting to put your shop together. You only have so much to spend, and you want to get the tool that will do you the most good first. Never buy a second-rate tool just because it's cheap. It will wear out quickly and you'll just have to buy the expensive one eventually. Always save your money until you can afford professional-quality tools. Here, then, are the major tools you will need in order of importance.

Table Saws

A good, heavy-duty, floor-model table saw would be my pick as the most indispensable power tool for both the professional door and window maker and the hobby craftsman or owner-builder who wants to make his own doors and windows (Illus. 50). With just a table saw, a hand plane, clamps and glue, you could make some very impressive frame and panel doors.

A table saw can rip, crosscut with great accuracy at various angles, resaw, cut slots or dadoes, make raised panels and mouldings, and perform other special operations (Illus. 51). In this day and age, it would be hard for most woodworkers to get along without one.

Table saw prices range from under $100 to over $2,000. There are two general types of saws available: small bench-model saws and larger floor-model saws. The smaller bench-model saws work well as portable tools that can be moved onto a job site for light work such as ripping trim or siding (Illus. 52). The cheaper saws often have underpowered direct-drive motors and inferior blade-adjustment mechanisms, as well as small sheet-metal tables that will make them most frustrating to work with when trying to cut large, thick pieces for doors or windows.

For the door and window maker's shop, a heavy-duty floor-model saw with a 10-inch or larger blade capacity, and at least a two-horsepower motor is essential. If you are considering buying a particular saw, check it over carefully for cracked castings or excessive blade wobble (Illus. 53), and be sure to compare prices of old standard models with some of the newer imports. Also consider whether replacement parts for the saw (especially if it is used) and accessories that you may want to add later can be obtained easily.

Some of the better-quality table saws are designed to accept a mortising attachment on the side of the saw (Illus. 55). This can be great help to the door and window maker, because mortising is difficult to do but essential for door and window making. Some other major accessories for the table saw are ball-bearing-mounted sliding tables, and wide extension tables.

A large, smoothly finished table and easily adjusted blade inserts are important for accurate crosscutting of large pieces (Illus. 54). The only other tools that come close to the table saw's accuracy for crosscutting are the power mitre box, or "chop" saw, and

Illus. 50. A heavy-duty floor-model table saw with at least a 2-horsepower motor will be one of the most necessary and versatile power tools for the door and window maker.

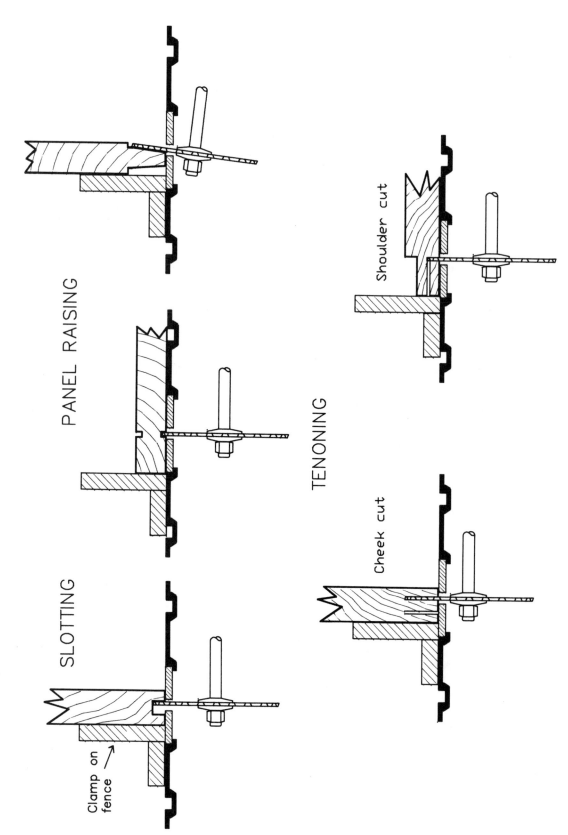

SLOTTING

PANEL RAISING

Clamp on fence

TENONING

Shoulder cut

Cheek cut

Illus. 51. Slotting, tenoning, and panel raising can all be accomplished with just a table saw. Some saws also come with an optional mortising table on the side, making it possible to do all the cutting for a door with just the table saw.

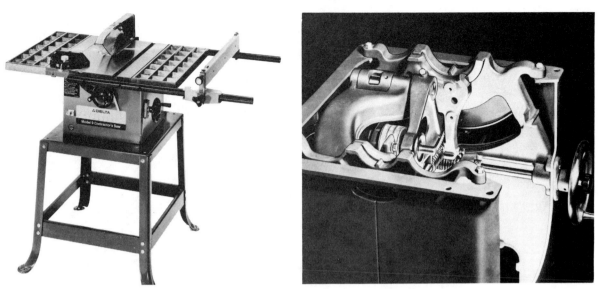

Illus. 52 (above left). Smaller bench-model saws are handy for on-the-job work, but will be frustrating to work with in the shop. Illus. 53 (above right). Carefully examine the castings that carry the arbor and motor, and check the blade for excessive wobble when considering the purchase of a particular saw.

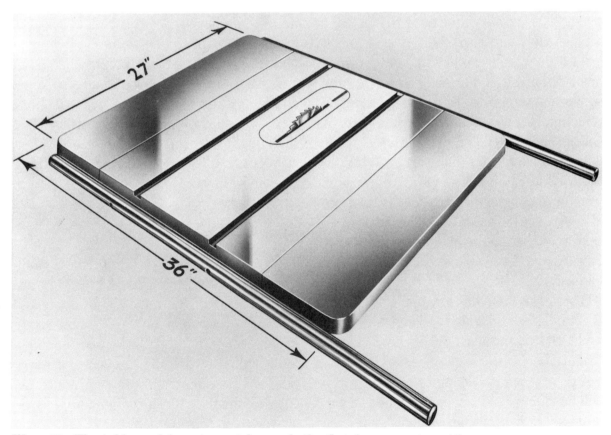

Illus. 54. The table and insert must be perfectly flat for accurate cutting.

Illus. 55. This table saw has a mortising attachment on its side.

these saws are very limited as to how wide a piece they can cut.

As a door and window maker, you may need to make a perfectly straight and square cut across the ends of a kick rail up to 18 inches wide and 30 inches long. A special jig like the one shown in Illus. 56 will allow you to do this with ease if your table is big enough. The more clearance in front of the blade, the better. At least a foot of clearance is essential. The amount of clearance behind the blade is not as important. An out-feed table or roller can be added easily.

Often, saws are designed so that extension tables can be added to the sides. A saw table that is at least 36 inches wide is essential.

A good fence is also important, since you will be ripping at least as much as you will be crosscutting. The fence should slide easily, adjust accurately to an easily readable

gauge, and have a positive lock to prevent creeping while you are doing long runs of identical cuts. The blade height and angle-adjustment mechanisms should also work smoothly and easily, and be lockable (Illus. 57). Nothing is more frustrating than finishing a long series of supposedly identical cuts and discovering that something slipped while you were working.

Special Fixtures

You can make a large sliding cutoff table like the one shown in Illus. 56 for accurate 90-degree cutting of rail ends for doors and windows. Rail ends have to be absolutely square in both directions to avoid open joints. Most of the small, one-track mitre guides that come with saws are not accurate enough or large enough for the type of work you will be doing.

A tall, accurately squared clamp-on fence

40

CROSSCUTTING JIG FOR TABLE SAW

The back rail must be carefully jointed so that it will screw down squarely to the sliding plywood table. The front rail merely serves to keep the plywood flat, and can be removed for cutting extra wide pieces. The runners, which ride in the slots on the saw, must fit the slots exactly.

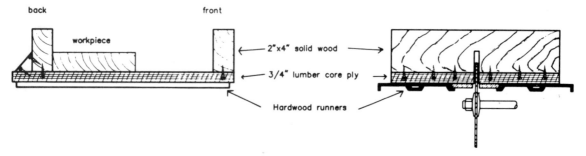

back   front

workpiece

2"x4" solid wood

3/4" lumber core ply

Hardwood runners

Illus. 56. A very accurate sliding cutoff table can be made with ¾-inch plywood and 2 × 6 hardwood lumber.

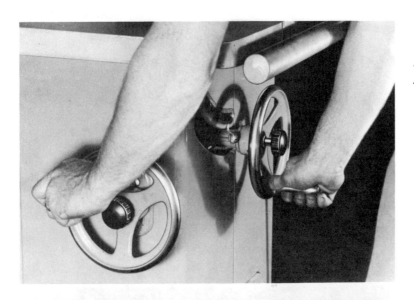

Illus. 57. You should be able to lock the height and angle adjustments to prevent creeping from vibrations while you are working.

Illus. 58. You can easily make a very accurate, tall clamp-on fence for cutting tenons, panels, or other large work where accuracy is critical.

is another fixture that you can make for your table saw that will help when cutting raised panels and tenons, and for other table saw operations that require large pieces to be cut very carefully (Illus. 58).

Be sure to make or purchase at least two push sticks, and keep them within arm's reach of your saw at all times (Illus. 59). Push sticks should be used whenever you are ripping anything that will bring your hands closer than 6 inches from the blade. Other hold-down devices like those shown

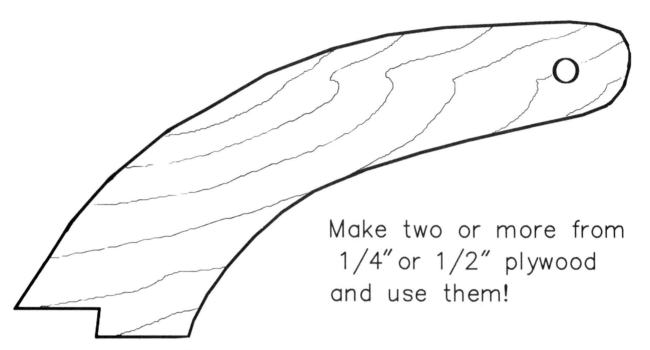

Make two or more from 1/4" or 1/2" plywood and use them!

Illus. 59. Keep your push sticks where you can reach them easily from the saw.

Illus. 60. Holding devices that clamp to the table or the fence will help prevent kickback or injury when you are ripping short or narrow pieces.

in Illus. 60 will help keep the workpieces tight against the fence and table when you are cutting. They can either be made to fit the job or purchased.

Avoid pinching the blade or pinching a workpiece between the blade and the fence. This can cause the saw to kick the piece back with enough force to cause serious injury (Illus. 61). Table saw blades should always be lowered so that they are just high enough to make the required cut.

Blades

Because you will be using the table saw for at least two different functions—ripping and crosscutting—you will have to change blades occasionally to get the best results (Illus. 62 and 63). High-speed steel blades with between 10 and 20 teeth work well for ripping, though they don't last as long between sharpenings as carbide blades. Still, they are cheaper to buy and sharpen, and will make a thinner cut than most carbide blades. Use your best ones only on clean, dry, knot-free lumber, and they will stay sharp a surprisingly long time. A carbide rip blade with between 10 and 20 teeth might be a good investment if you are using especially hard or dirty lumber.

For crosscutting with the table saw, nothing works better than a 60- to 100-tooth alternate-top bevel carbide blade. The prices and quality available in these blades varies greatly, and if possible, the blades should be inspected carefully by eye to determine whether the workmanship is worth the price.

Length and thickness in the carbide cutting chips will ensure a long-lasting blade, good for many sharpenings. The faces of the carbide cutting chips should be polished to mirror brightness. Look closely at the brazing that connects the teeth to the blade. It should be uniform and free of pitting. If possible, set it gently down on a flat surface and check for any sign of warpage.

Besides regular cutting blades, dado cutters and moulding heads can also be run on table saws (Illus. 64 and 65). Dado cutters are primarily used for cutting slots wider than the normal width of a blade. Two types are available: wobble cutters, which are infinitely adjustable through a range from $\frac{3}{16}$ to $\frac{15}{16}$ inch, and stacked cutters, which consist of several cutters of different widths that are stacked together on the arbor. Stacked cutters will give an exact and repeatable sized slot, but they lack infinite adjustment. Moulding heads accept various types of knives for making mouldings, rabbets, tongue-and-groove cuts, etc.

Table Saw Maintenance

As with all tools and machinery, proper maintenance is the key to smooth, accurate work. Whenever you change blades on your table saw, you should look the saw over and follow a few procedures that will keep it in perfect running order. The cleaner it is, the safer it will be to use.

Start by wiping down the blade you just removed with mineral spirits. This will remove any pitch that has started to build up on the blade, and also help protect it from rust (Illus. 66). Pitch is one of the main enemies of blade sharpness on all high-speed cutting tools. As it builds up, it acts as an insulator, which makes the blade run hotter and wear down faster. If you already have a build-up of pitch on your blade, you may

Illus. 61. Kickback, caused by pinching a workpiece between the blade and the fence, is one of the major hazards of the table saw. Also remember to never raise the blade higher than necessary.

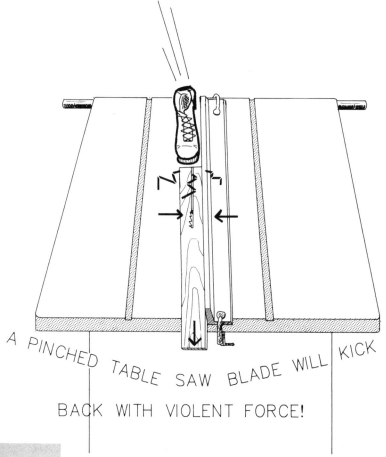

A PINCHED TABLE SAW BLADE WILL KICK

BACK WITH VIOLENT FORCE!

Illus. 62 (above left) and 63 (above right). Many types of blades are available for table saws. At left is a 60-tooth alternate top bevel carbide blade designed for very fine cutting in sheet stock, plastic laminates, and hard wood that will give fine results when used to crosscut. A combination blade may be better for ripping. At right, shown from left to right, are the rip, crosscut, and combination blades. Both photos from Table Saw Techniques, *by Roger Cliffe (Sterling Publishing Co., Inc., Two Park Avenue, New York, New York 10016).*

Illus. 64. A wobble-cutting dado head can cut any size slot from ³/₁₆ to ¹³/₁₆ inch wide.

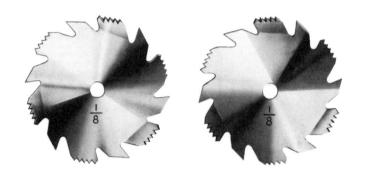

Illus. 65. Stacked dado cutters are limited to certain exact cutting widths.

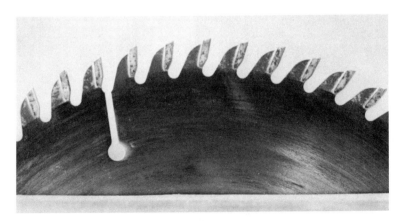

Illus. 66. Clean blades periodically to prevent pitch buildup.

45

need a stronger cleanser like oven cleaner with lye in it to remove it. Let it soak for an hour or two; then wipe it off with paper towels.

Place the blade you have just removed on a storage rack with wooden or cardboard discs between the blades to prevent them from touching each other (Illus. 67). This rack can also be made portable for transporting your blades to and from the saw shop for sharpening. (Saw-sharpening shops also vary in their quality and pricing. Examine your blades carefully again when they come back newly sharpened, and try different shops until you find your favorite).

After removing the blade, clean the table and the table-insert hole carefully with a brush or compressed air and check the table-insert adjustment to make sure it is perfectly flush with the top of the table (Illus. 68). Then polish the table top with paste wax and either fine steel wool or a rag. If there is any rust or caked-on pitch or dirt, you may have to use a buffer and rubbing compound to remove them.

Now check the inner working parts of the saw for build-up of dust and pitch. If you don't remove it frequently, sawdust can get packed into the gears and cause them to jam or break. Finally, inspect the electrical connections for loose connections or worn insulation.

Troubleshooting Advice

If you have trouble getting a good, clean cut, especially when ripping, start by checking the alignment of the blade with the milled slots on the table (Illus. 69). They should be perfectly parallel. The fence should also be parallel to both the slots and the blade. Most saws can be adjusted so that the blade is parallel by loosening the table bolts and rotating the table slightly.

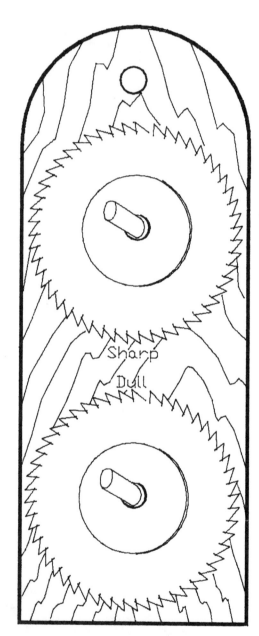

Illus. 67. A portable storage rack for your blades will help protect them from damage when you transport them to and from the saw-sharpening shop.

46

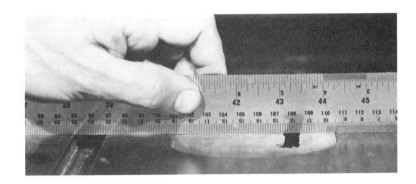

Illus. 68. Remove sawdust from the blade insert hole before making it flush with the top of the table

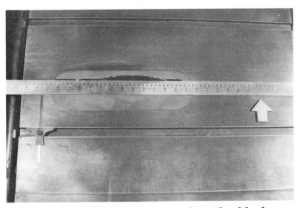

Illus. 69. Check to be sure that the blade is parallel to the table by measuring the distance from the straightedge to the channel at both ends of the table.

If the blade wobbles or is excessively noisy even when it is not cutting, it may be warped. Lay it down on the table and check it for flatness. If the blade is true, then the wobble could be caused by worn blade collars, a bent arbor shaft, a bent motor pulley, or a worn belt. If the arbor is not running true, you may have to take it to a machinist to be fixed. If you have a saw with a table insert that won't adjust properly so that it's flush with the top, you can easily make one out of hardwood or plywood, complete with adjustment screws to do a better job.

Routers

Your next power-tool investment after a good table saw should be in a router, which, for the money, is the most versatile power tool available (Illus. 70–72). A good heavy-duty plunge router can be used for mortising, cutting curved pieces from templates, rabbeting, slotting, cutting moulding, and making cope-and-stick joints to name just a few cutting techniques. It can be used freehand with bits that have their own guides to follow a curved or irregular edge in a table like a mini-spindle shaper, or on the job to cut hinge mortises quickly and easily.

As you expand your investment in power tools, you will probably want to buy more than one router. If you intend to use them for making doors and windows, then your first one should probably be a plunge router with a $\frac{1}{2}$-inch collet (which can be reduced to $\frac{1}{4}$ inch also) and at least $1\frac{1}{2}$ horsepower. With this type of router, you can cut mortises for mortise-and-tenon joints quickly and accurately without having to invest in any other special equipment. Make sure that the plunge router you buy comes with an adjustable fence attachment.

Illus. 70 (above) and 71 and 72 (below). For the money, routers are among the most versatile of woodworking tools. A heavy-duty plunging router, shown above on the right, will make a good mortiser. One-half-inch spiral fluted bits that will cut up to 3 inches deep are available. Other routers can be used on a table for various moulding operations or on the job for hinge mortising and grooving.

Illus. 71

Illus. 72.

A smaller, lighter router is also very handy for on-the-job work and all the lighter cutting tasks like rounding over edges and making mouldings (Illus. 72). Though for tasks like these the emphasis is on lightness (you'll appreciate the advantage of a light router when you are bending over the edge of a door, making repeated cuts for hinge mortises), other qualities like ease of adjustment, ease of bit changing, positive locking, and the ability to take a fence attachment are also important. I also put a premium on quietness of operation. Routers tend to be noisy, which can be very fatiguing. The quieter the better.

Not all routers are designed for use in the inverted position, as they are used on a router table. Since using a router in an inverted position is such a handy way for window and door makers to work, you may want to consider buying yet another router to be used mainly on the table. This router should also be heavy-duty, at least 1½ horsepower, with a ½-inch collet, but it should not be the plungeable type.

A router with a detachable base is best used on a table. This type of router can easily be pulled out of the base (which is screwed to the table top) for changing bits or for use with another base in the normal upright manner.

Router tables can be purchased through suppliers, but many are of inferior quality in that they tend to sag from the weight of the router. The table shown in Illus. 73 can be built from scrap lumber. Formica-covered sink cutouts, ideal for the table top, are available from building-supply dealers or cabinetmakers, or you can make your own table top from plywood and a scrap of

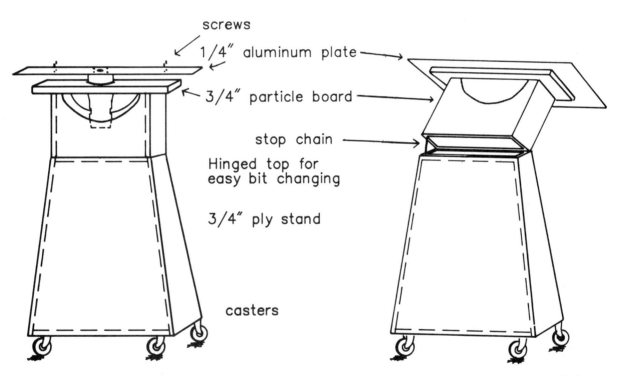

Illus. 73. A router table that can be easily built from scraps. The table base is attached to the rolling stand by hinges and a stop chain that makes changing the bits much easier. A hole is cut through the plywood sub-table that's large enough for the router base to fit through. The plastic base is removed from the router and used as a template to mark the positions of the screw holes on the ¼-inch aluminum plate that is used as the table top. The router is screwed to the plate, and the plate is screwed down near the corners to the sub-table.

Formica. Other materials such as ¼-inch Plexiglas (acrylic plastic) or sheet aluminum also work well. Here, again, the tendency of the table to sag from the weight of the router is great. To adjust the flatness of the table, drive screws through from the underside of the sub-table, near the router. Hinging the table and attaching it to a stand on rollers will also make changing bits easier and allow you to position the table easily.

Maintenance

As with other tools, it is important to keep routers clean and free of dust and pitch build-up. Most good routers have permanently lubricated and sealed ball bearings that never need attention. The electrical brushes, however, need occasional replacement. Check them now and then and replace them if you see that they are wearing away. Running them until they are totally worn away and "die" can damage the armature (Illus. 74).

Do not take excessively heavy cuts, especially when mortising or rabbeting, and be especially careful not to damage the electrical cord or switch, as these are some of the most vulnerable parts of the router. The bases can also be damaged by overtightening the fence or face plate screws. Also, be careful not to mar the plunging sleeves on plunge routers, as this will cause them to jam when plunging.

Jointers

A standard fixture of most professional woodworking shops, the jointer is nearly in-

Illus. 74. Two large plastic screw-ports near the tops of most routers hold the spring-loaded carbon brushes. Do not let the brushes run until they are totally worn away.

dispensable when it comes to quickly and accurately straightening the edge or face of a piece of rough stock (Illus. 75).

It is, of course, possible to straighten boards with hand planes, and before the Industrial Revolution, this is how it was done. A long, narrow jointer plane was used for straightening edges, and a shorter, wider jack plane could be used for flattening the face of a board. A very light pass with a jointer plane can still be used to improve the fit of an edge joint by removing the scallop marks left by a jointer, but generally a well-adjusted and properly used jointer will give you a perfect joint without having to hand-plane.

For door making, a six-inch-wide jointer with the longest possible bed is a minimal requirement. Once again, you'll be happier if you save your money and get the best tool

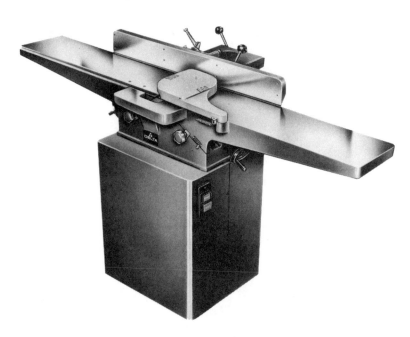

Illus. 75. A six-inch or wider jointer with the longest possible bed is one of the standard workhorses of most small woodworking shops. Careful tuning and proper use will produce straight and true surfaces in seconds, every time.

the first time. If you can't afford a good six-inch or larger jointer, find a cabinetmaker who has one and pay him to straighten your stock until you can get the right one. Having perfectly straight stiles is essential for making doors that are flat, and trying to straighten a seven-foot 2 × 6 on a short-bed jointer is unsafe as well as frustrating.

When buying a jointer, look first at the tables. They should be precision-ground and nicely polished. Jointer tables can be made either from rolled steel or cast iron, but cast iron seems to be generally favored today. Use a precision straightedge to check the tables for warps. In today's highly competitive manufacturing market, the table castings are not always allowed to cure properly, and have been known to come from the manufacturer with noticeable warps.

Both the front and back tables should have height-adjustment mechanisms (Illus.

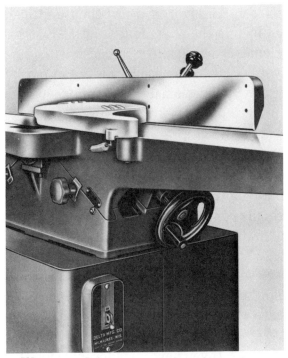

Illus. 76. Jointers must be adjusted very precisely to work properly. Before buying one, make sure that the table-adjustment mechanisms for both height and levelness work well.

76) and positive locks to prevent creeping from vibration when the tool is in operation. An independent system for levelling the tables is also essential on larger jointers. Some have four adjustable points of support on each table so that it can be adjusted for twist as well as sag. Others have gib adjustments to take up any wear in the dovetail ways on which the tables move up and down.

Finally, look at the cutterhead. The diameter of the cutterhead is a good indication of the quality of the tool. Smaller-diameter cutterheads, especially those with only two knives, should be avoided.

Maintaining the proper alignment between the tables and the cutters is essential to getting good results from your jointer. An error of a few thousandths of an inch in the alignment of either of these elements will make it impossible to get a perfect cut, and nothing less than perfect is acceptable when it comes to edge-jointing or flattening.

Start by setting the knives properly in the cutterhead. As with other tools, they should be removed frequently for sharpening by a reliable sharpening service. They should come back absolutely straight with a well-polished bevel and balanced in weight to avoid vibration.

Several methods of reinstalling the knives can be used, and most modern machines have a built-in system for setting the knives that will give you perfect alignment in minutes. If you have an older machine that doesn't have a built-in setting mechanism, try placing two bar magnets on the out-feed table so that they project over the cutter-head (Illus. 77). Make two index marks on

Illus. 77. If your jointer doesn't have a built-in knife-setting mechanism, use bar magnets to hold the knives in place while you are tightening the gibs.

each magnet—one at the edge of the table, and one where the top dead center of the blade arc will be.

Now, remove the magnets and place the blade and its backer in position in the cutter-head. Replace the magnets and allow them to hold the blade in position while you lightly tighten the setscrews that hold it. Do this for each of the knives; then check them carefully near both ends with a

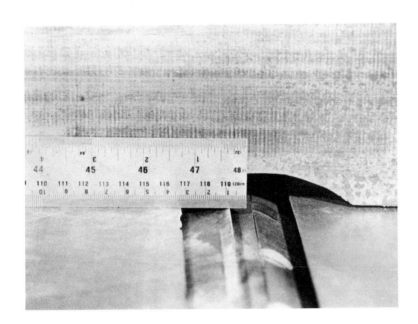

Illus. 78. When the knives are properly installed, use a straightedge to set the out-feed table so that it is at exactly the same height as the tops of the knives.

straightedge or dial indicator gauge before and after you tighten them fully.

If the blade placement is perfect, you can avoid the necessity of jointing the knives once they are in place. Jointing the knives in place is another way to improve the accuracy of the cutting circle, but it tends to dull the blades. They will last longer if you can set them so exactly that they don't need to be jointed.

Now check the alignment of the out-feed table with the cutting knives. Use a good-quality straightedge for this (Illus. 78). The knives should just "kiss" the straightedge without lifting it off the out-feed table. If the knives are too low, you will get a slightly tapered or bowed edge when you attempt to straighten a board; if they are above the level of the table, the ends of your boards will be "snipped," meaning that a slight dip will be cut in the ends of the boards.

When you think you have it right, lock the back table and make a final test by jointing two fairly long boards and holding them against each other. If the two boards meet perfectly all the way along, you've gotten it right. If there is space at the ends, try raising the out-feed table a bit. If there is space in the middle, lower it a bit.

Proper Operating Procedure

Even when you have the jointer set up perfectly, you can still get frustrating results if you don't know how to feed the lumber correctly. Safety should also be uppermost in your mind at all times when operating the jointer. Shop accidents most commonly occur on the jointer and table saw. Use push sticks on anything that brings your hands closer to the table than the top of the fence, and never try to joint anything less than one foot long.

Feed your stock slowly and evenly. The jointer will work best on a concave surface; so always "eyeball" your stock by closing one eye and sighting down the length of it to check which way it warps (Illus. 79).

Whenever possible, straighten the con-

TO STRAIGHTEN WARPED BOARDS:

1. Sight down board to determine concave side.

2. Straighten concave side on jointer (several passes may be necessary).

3. Run straightened edge against table saw fence to trim convex side.

Illus. 79. The proper procedure for straightening a warped or rough board is to run the concave side on the jointer until straight, and then use the straight side to rip a parallel straightedge on the table saw. To straighten the wider surfaces of a board, once again joint the concave side, and then run it through the thickness planer with the straight side down.

cave side. Never take more than an ⅛-inch-deep cut. Start your cut with enough downward pressure to hold the board flat on the in-feed table, and as soon as the end of the board has passed onto the out-feed table, keep your downward pressure near the beginning of the out-feed table (Illus. 80). Pushing down on the in-feed table can also cause a warped cut.

Shapers

You know you've become a serious woodworker when you start to consider purchasing a shaper for your shop. A shaper is a very versatile and useful tool for the door and window maker, but it may be low on your list of priorities if you are just getting started (Illus. 81). Though you can make quite a variety of doors and windows without it, you won't be able to quickly and accurately make cope-and-stick joints, which are the preferred joint for sash or frame-and-panel doors. Shapers are a virtual necessity for production work.

Shaper sizes are generally referred to by the diameter of the spindle: ½-, ¾-, and 1-inch shapers are common in smaller shops. Some shapers can take interchangeable spindles of different sizes, and cutters often come with bushings that allow them to fit on several different-sized spindles. Even larger spindle sizes are used for high-speed production work.

Prices can vary greatly in the ½-inch to 1-inch range from under $500 to several thousand dollars for one machine. Half-inch shapers are becoming more popular, and

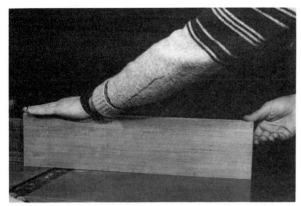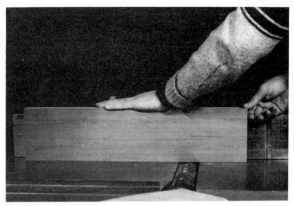

Illus. 80A and B. To get good results on the jointer, it is also important to apply downward pressure in the proper places. The pressure should be applied near the beginning of the out-feed table at all times.

Illus. 81 A and B. Shapers are high-production tools that allow quick and easy cutting of cope-and-stick jointery, mouldings, and raised panels. Sizes and prices of shapers and their cutters vary widely.

good-quality ones are acceptable for most door- and window-making tasks, but look around carefully for a good deal in a larger used machine before getting committed to a smaller one.

Once you have one shaper, you will immediately want more. The well set-up production shop needs at least two shapers so that both the cope and the stick sides of the joints can be run without having to change bits. The two shapers, working in tandem in the making of the cope-and-stick joint, are nearly essential for smooth production work. However, a third, heavy-duty shaper for making raised panels would be ideal.

A shaper works much like a large router, except that the bits are hollow-centered and are stacked on a spindle, rather than fitted into a collet as on a router (Illus. 82 and 83). This allows several bits and spacers to be stacked in such a way that complex cuts can be made in one pass. Allowances can also be made for the thickness of the material or the panels that will fit into the slots.

When shopping for a shaper, be sure to check the spindle bearings and the trueness of the spindle carefully. A dial indicator placed near the top of the spindle will show you any runout or crookedness in the spindle. The flatness of the table is also important, and the fence mechanism should be tested for ease of adjustment and general workability. The spindle should travel up and down easily, and have a positive lock to prevent it from slipping while it is working (Illus. 84).

Give the machine the nickel test. Place a nickel on edge on the table and turn the machine on. If the machine vibrates enough to topple the nickel, the pulleys may be unbalanced, or the drive belts worn. Excessive noise may indicate worn bearings.

Also check the horsepower rating of the motor. One horsepower may be enough for a light-duty ½-inch shaper, but larger shapers meant for panel cutting and other heavy tasks commonly run up to five-horsepower motors.

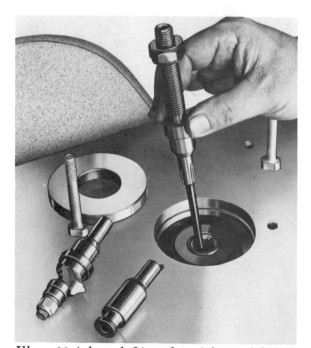

Illus. 82 (above left) and 83 (above right). Some shapers can take interchangeable spindles of different sizes. Shapers work like a large router table; multiple hollow-centered cutters stacked on a spindle (Illus. 83) allow you to make complex cuts in one pass.

Illus. 84. The spindle should have a positive lock to prevent it from slipping while you are working.

Cutters

Cutters can also be quite expensive. And the larger the shaper, the more expensive they can be. A matched set of door-making cutters for the smallest spindle size can cost over $300. High-speed steel cutters, on the other hand, are relatively cheap, and can be easily resharpened and reshaped on a small grinding stone.

Steel cutters are not easy to find anymore, but several companies still offer them in various patterns. An alternative is to buy a head that will hold changeable knives that you can buy as blanks and grind yourself.

A series of different-sized spacer collars will also be necessary for use with your cutters. Look around carefully before investing in knives that you are unsure of, and, if possible, visit other craftsmen and find out what they are using before you buy.

Planers

A thickness planer will eventually become essential to any door- and window-making operation (Illus. 85 and 86). Like jointers,

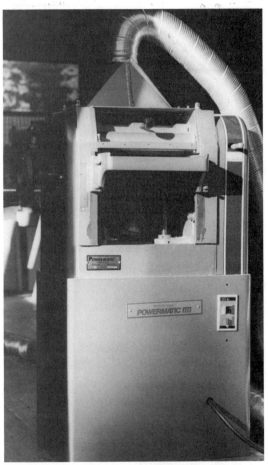

Illus. 85 and 86 (following page). Thickness planers come in various sizes. Twelve-inch-wide planers are the most common, and will be adequate for most door and window makers.

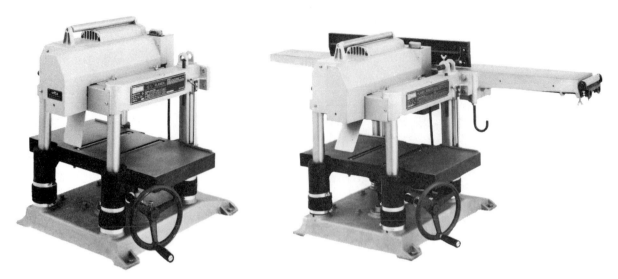

Illus. 86A and B. Jointer/planer combinations are also possible.

they remove wood with a series of knives held in a rotating head, but unlike jointers, most planers have built-in power-feed rollers. The thicknesses of doors and windows vary from 1 to 2 inches, and panels must often be planed down from thicker stock. The planer allows you to buy rough lumber and custom-surface it to fit your exact needs.

Most smaller shops have planers that will handle lumber up to 12 or 15 inches wide and 4 to 6 inches thick. These will be fine for door and window making, as wider stock is not often needed. Even these smaller planers are quite expensive machines, and may be one of the last major purchases you will make for your shop.

You can get by without a planer by ordering your lumber from a yard that will custom-plane it for you, or by taking your lumber to a shop that will plane it for a reasonable price. Be sure to have one side of your lumber jointed straight before planing, and then plane off the other side. Planers will not straighten warped or twisted wood. That is the job for the jointer.

When shopping for a planer, carefully inspect the head, head bearings, feed rollers, table rollers, and especially the roller-adjustment mechanisms. At least a two-horsepower motor is advisable for a good-quality 12- or 15-inch planer. Planer-jointer combinations and the lightweight, high-speed imported planers work well for small shops or for home builders and hobbyists, but they won't take more than $\frac{1}{32}$-inch at a pass; so they can't be hurried during a job.

To get the best results from your planer, make sure the rollers and the chip breaker are properly adjusted, the knives carefully set, and the moving parts occasionally lubricated. A badly adjusted or dull planer will leave defects in your materials like end snipe or chip-out that must be dealt with later by hand.

One of the most important adustments on most planers is the height of the chip breaker. It should be just above the cutting height of the blades. If it is too tight, the board will jam in the planer. If it is too loose, end snipe results. Many modern planers are factory-adjusted, and include a precision knife-setting system that will save much time.

Other Power Tools

A good band saw is a handy tool for any shop (Illus. 87). It is not essential in door and window making unless you are making curved shapes, but you will find that if you have one you will use it constantly for all sorts of little cutting jobs. A good one should have at least a 12-inch blade capacity and at least a 1½-horsepower motor so that it can be used for resawing wide stock to be used for panels.

Some horizontal boring machines can be used for both dowelling and slot-mortising, while others are designed only for quick, effortless dowelling. Machines meant just for dowelling are generally of lighter construction and have a cam clamp or pneumatic ram which holds the piece flat against the stationary table while it is being

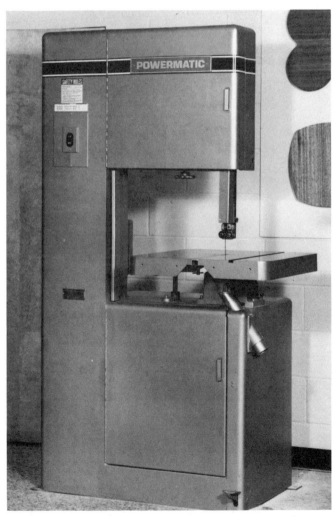

Illus. 87A and B. Band saws are not essential for door and window making, but are always handy for quick free-hand cutting, resawing, and various other shop functions.

Illus. 88. Horizontal boring machines can be used for both dowelling and mortising. Lighter-weight models should only be used for dowelling. Heavier machines with sliding cast-iron tables can accept end-milling bits for mortising.

The drill press is another all-around shop machine that is not really needed, but which will be used very often if it is around (Illus. 89). A good-quality drill press can be used for drilling, mortising, routing, shaping, and sanding. Mortising is done by

Illus. 89. The drill press is another standard shop machine that can perform many functions.

bored. Some other machines with sliding tables, usually of heavier construction, can use a variety of end-milling or routing bits to cut slot mortises.

Dowelling can be accomplished with several different kinds of dowelling jigs, and mortises can be made in other ways too, but the horizontal boring machine is definitely the quickest and most comfortable way to do these operations.

using a hollow chisel attachment and a fence-and-hold-down attachment that bolts or clamps onto the table to hold the work in place. An adjustable out-feed roller will have to be used to support the ends of long pieces like door stiles.

Drill presses come in both bench models and floor models. Some have tiltable tables, and most have stepped cone pulleys for changing the speed of the bit's rotation. Higher speeds are used for shaping, sanding, and drilling operations in wood, and lower speeds generally for metal working.

In recent years, hand-held electric planers have become very popular among light, electric tools (Illus. 90). These tools have a rotary head and an adjustable in-feed table just like a miniature jointer, and will plane wood up to 3½ inches wide. They are great for on-the-job work or trimming and straightening large pieces in the shop. With one of these tools, you could almost get by

without a jointer or planer if you did not have to rush your work. They can also be used to surface and flatten wide pieces as long as perfectly uniform thickness is not important.

A radial arm saw is handy to have for rough-cutting long pieces of lumber to workable size, and can be used for many other operations if nothing else is available (Illus. 91). They are generally not as accurate for crosscutting as a table saw or chop saw, but a good-quality radial arm saw can be made to work quite well. A good

Illus. 90. Portable electric hand planers, especially those in the 3½-inch size, are great for on-the-job work or for trimming finished pieces in the shop.

Illus. 91. Radial arm saws can perform many of the same functions as table saws, and are great for the rough-sizing of long lumber.

hand-held circular saw will also perform well most of the jobs the radial arm saw does.

The power mitre box, or chop saw, is a very handy tool for both on-the-job work and for quickly and accurately cutting precise angles in the shop (Illus. 92). It is especially useful for mitring moulding, or stops for multipaned windows, and is much easier to adjust than most radial arm saws. I generally leave my radial arm saw set at 90 degrees, and use the chop saw for cutting angles.

A couple of different hand-held electric drills will be handy for the door and window maker (Illus. 94). A good-quality, variable-speed reversible drill can be used for dowelling, boring the waste from hand-chiselled mortises, and other general work. A cordless electric drill will be ideal for on-the-job work like installing hinges and locksets.

Illus. 93. Orbital sanders make quick work of final surface preparation.

Illus. 92. Power mitre boxes can quickly and cleanly cut angles.

Orbital sanders also have a place in the modern door maker's cabinet. The smaller ones that fit in the palm of the hand are great for making quick work of the final smoothing of a door or window.

Illus. 94. Hand-held electric drills are especially useful on the job. The cordless drills make great screwdrivers for installation work.

Door Making

4
Designing a Doorway

Whether you are starting from scratch or replacing a door in an already existing home or building, you should start by considering the many factors that can influence the design of a doorway. A doorway is a variable barrier. An entry door easily admits those who are welcome to enter, while providing protection from both the elements and unwanted visitors. Most buildings also have many interior doors which help to separate the functions of the various rooms within. Some merely provide a visual barrier, hiding from view the clutter in the closet, while others help keep living areas warm or provide for privacy and quiet.

A secondary function of the doorway is less obvious, but perhaps just as important. A doorway must work with the other elements of a building, both interior and exterior, to provide a pleasing aesthetic living environment (Illus. 96 and 97). It would be a bleak outlook that did not imbue the doorway of a home or building with a symbolic statement about the building, its inhabitants, and the surrounding environment.

So often, cost factors dictate the easy ap-

Illus. 95. A door functions as a variable barrier, easily admitting those who are welcome to enter.

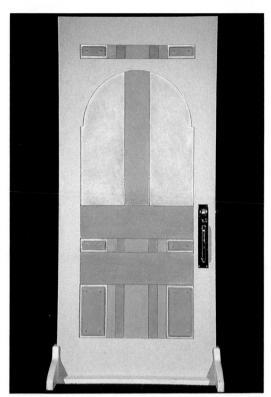
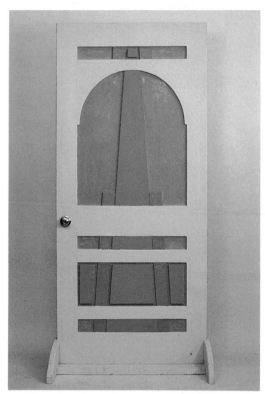

These eye-catching doors by Al Garvey combine interesting lines and bright colors.

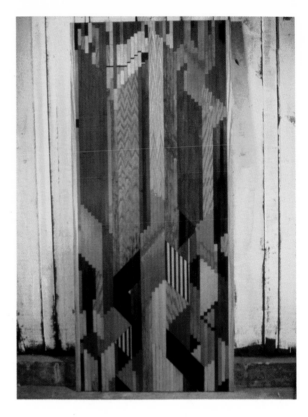

*Carved and laminated doors by Jeff Wood-
ward illustrate some of the more exotic
door-making possibilities. Door on upper
right was made by laminating strips of
contrasting wood; the other doors were
made by laminating strips and carving the
resulting flaps.*

B

Painted appliqué carefully glued to a large plywood panel creates stunning effects (doors by Al Garvey).

Left: Glass-walled solarium. Right: Victorian entryway. Bottom: Solarium windows need not always be rectangular.

Left: Intricate moulded frame-and-panel door. Right: Stained glass and detailed millwork. Bottom: Dormers can add floor space and light to upstairs rooms.

E

Right: The window tower serves as a hallway and office and reflects the splendor of this home's forested setting. Below left: A collage of exotic woods and halved brass tubing give this door its unique character. Below right: Small touches enhance beautiful vistas.

F

Above left: Trimwork need not always follow the lines of doors and windows.
Right: Appliqués can greatly enhance a plain door. Below left: Door with
Victorian millwork. Right: Building adorned by liberal use of unique doors and
windows.

G

The warmth of redwood enhances clean traditional lines.

H

Illus. 96 (above) and 97A and B (below). Aesthetically, an entry door is one of the most important elements in creating a harmonious design for any type of building.

Illus. 97A and B.

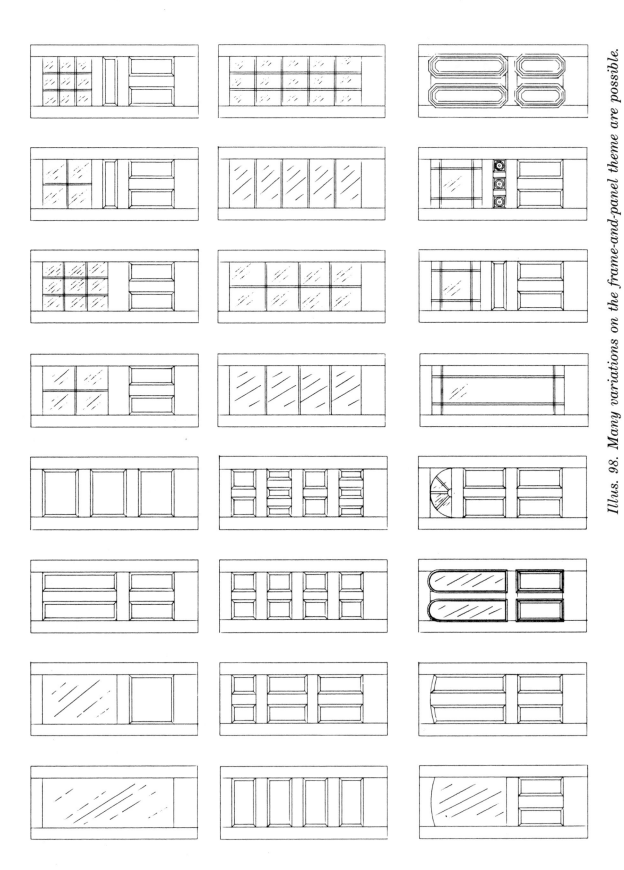

Illus. 98. Many variations on the frame-and-panel theme are possible.

proach, which is to buy a nice door and get it installed as quickly as possible. But for those who are willing to go a step further, this is an ideal chance to share their creative energy with the world. A doorway is like a painter's blank canvas—a well-defined space waiting to be filled with something beautiful and unique. It is important to consider some of the factors that define that space.

In designing, there are many compromises that have to be made. If you are starting a completely new structure, you have a chance to make the choices that will serve you best all down the line. Still, you may have to choose between such desirable assets as energy efficiency or light, security or beauty, and elaborate design or affordability. After you have finished reading this section carefully, you may want to list, in order of importance to you, the design considerations that will shape your doors.

Technical Requirements

Standard manufactured doors are usually 6 feet, 8 inches high, and come in widths from 1 foot, 6 inches to 3 feet (Illus. 99). Exterior doors are available in $1\frac{1}{2}$-inch or $1\frac{3}{4}$-inch thicknesses. Interior doors may be thinner. Often, doors can be purchased "pre-hung," meaning that they are already mounted in the jamb, on the hinges. Some will even have a lockset, or holes for the lockset, pre-cut for easy installation.

Building codes vary from one locality to another, and should be consulted by the custom builder so that he can make sure he is meeting the local requirements (Illus. 100). Many areas now require the use of tempered glass in doors where the glass

panes are over a certain size, and some require at least one 3-foot or wider door in any public building for wheelchairs. "Panic hardware" is also required for quick exit in case of fire in many public buildings.

For the custom builder, the sizes and thicknesses listed are mere guidelines. A call for a 7-foot or taller door is not uncommon for commercial buildings or even homes, and a 42- or 48-inch-wide entry door can add a touch of grandeur to a private entryway. Insulated doors up to 4 inches thick may be important energy savers for your part of the country, and you can obtain a feeling of stateliness by using extra-thick lumber for your panel doors. However, building code requirements should be taken seriously as a question of liability could easily develop, especially in a commercial setting that could involve you as the builder.

Door Swing

The direction in which a door swings is generally determined by the layout of the room, the position of light switches, and whether or not it is an interior or exterior door. Inward-opening exterior doors are considered more secure by some because the pins on the hinges cannot be pulled and the door removed. In places where outward-opening exterior doors may be necessary, special screws are available that prevent a door from being removed in this way, but the lock bolt is still more vulnerable to tampering on an outward-opening door. Outward-opening exterior doors are easier to seal against the weather, and might be a better bet in a place that is exposed to gusting winds and wind-blown

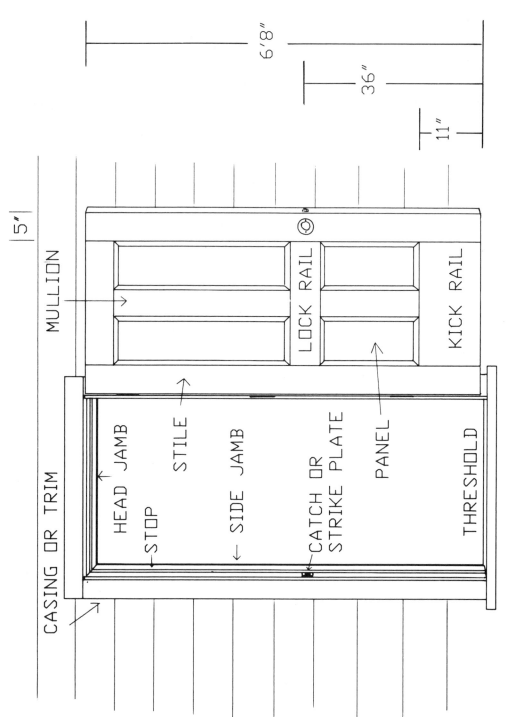

Illus. 99. Standard doors are usually 6 feet 8 inches high and can vary in width from 18 to 36 inches. Custom door makers should only use these sizes as guidelines for creating unique and beautiful doors. Shown here are common terms used when referring to parts of doors and door frames.

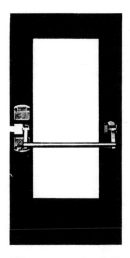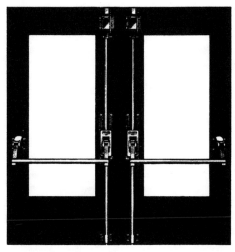

Illus. 100. Building-code requirements for doors vary greatly according to locality and the type of building involved. Some of the more common requirements are as follows: panic hardware in public buildings, tempered glass, and fire-resistant doors. Check with your local building inspector to find out which requirements apply in your situation.

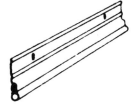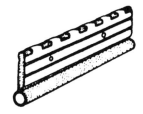

Illus. 101A. Various types of weather stripping are applied along the edges and top of the door to make it airtight.

Aluminum
with Vinyl Bubble

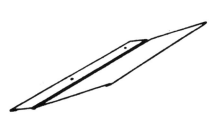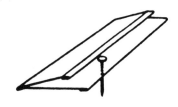

Spring Metal

Bronze
Cushion Metal

VINYL SEAL DOOR SWEEP

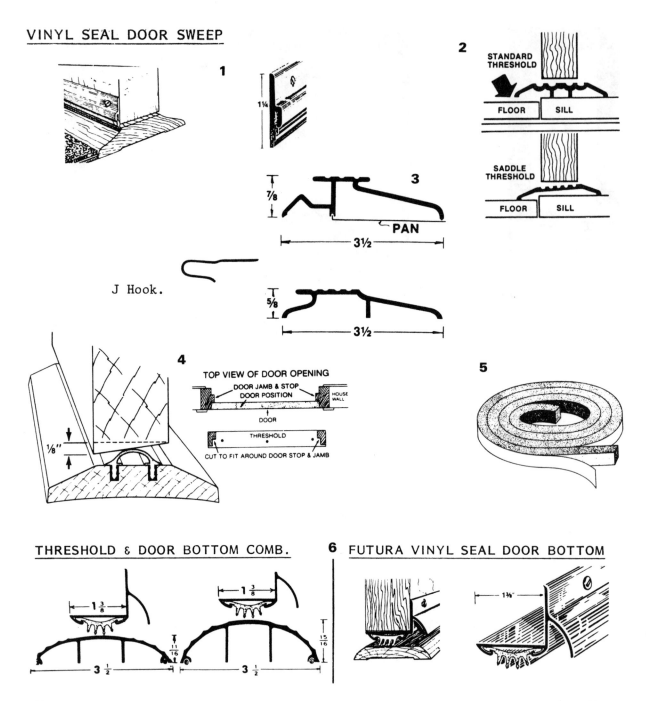

1

1¼

2
STANDARD THRESHOLD
FLOOR SILL
SADDLE THRESHOLD
FLOOR SILL

3
⅞
PAN
3½

J Hook.

⅝
3½

4
⅛"
TOP VIEW OF DOOR OPENING
DOOR JAMB & STOP
DOOR POSITION
HOUSE WALL
DOOR
THRESHOLD
CUT TO FIT AROUND DOOR STOP & JAMB

5

THRESHOLD & DOOR BOTTOM COMB.
1 ⅜
1 ⅜
11/16
15/16
3 ½
3 ½

6 FUTURA VINYL SEAL DOOR BOTTOM
1¾"

Illus. 101B. Various systems are available for sealing the bottom of the door from outside air and wind-blown rain. As shown in the drawing, they are as follows: 1, a simple screw-on seal may work for outward-opening doors; 2, a saddle-type threshold is used where changes in floor levels occur; 3, a special extruded threshold with an interlocking J-hook extrusion on the bottom of the door will stop wind-blown rain in difficult places; 4 and 6, flexible vinyl strips can be applied to either the threshold or the bottom of the door to stop air infiltration; and 5, various types of foam rubber or neoprene stripping with adhesive backing can be used to seal the edges and tops of doors.

70

rain. The bottom of the door is usually the problem area (Illus. 101B). In difficult places, special thresholds and J-hook weather stripping can be used.

Security

One of the main functions of a good door is security; so don't forget to include this in your design. Security is more important to some people than to others. Thick lumber for both the door and the jamb, a small, high window, and a good double-lock-and-dead-bolt system will provide adequate security for most people. Side lights should be avoided if security is a concern and no alarm system is being used. Special locks may have to be ordered from the manufacturer for extra-thick doors such as insulated doors. Commercial installations will also require special security considerations in many cases.

Climate

One of the most important factors in determing the nature of any exterior doorway is the climate in which it will serve. Obviously, a cold-winter, hot-summer climate will dictate different entryway considerations than a more moderate or tropical climate. A solid-core wood door $1\frac{3}{4}$-inch thick has an R factor, or resistance to heat loss, of 2.90, just slightly better than a panel

THREE—LAYER INSULATED DOOR CONSTRUCTION

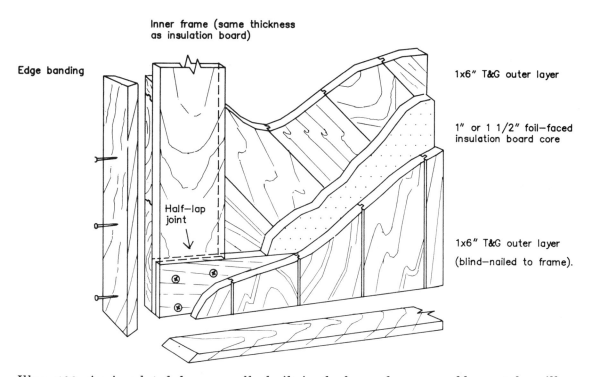

Illus. 102. An insulated door, usually built in the layered, or assemblage, style, will provide an R factor of up to 10.

door of the same thickness at 2.79. A hollow-core door of the same thickness, which may look just like the solid-core door but weighs half as much, has an R factor of 2.18.

You can easily build a door with an insulated core that will provide an R factor of 10 (Illus. 102), but perhaps even more important than the R factor of the door are factors such as the direction it faces, the care with which it is hung and weather-stripped, and structures such as an overhanging roof, protective walls, or storm doors that help to shelter the doorway and prevent the influx of cold outside air.

Another factor to consider in your design is the room that the door enters into. If you have an alcove or "mud room" in the entry-way that combined with another interior door to the living area forms a sort of air lock, you may be willing to sacrifice a little energy efficiency for more glass area (the R factor of insulated glass is 1.61 [a single layer of glass has an R factor of 1]), since the alcove will act as a buffer in maintaining the temperature of the living area.

In any climate, but especially in harsh northern climates or in areas that have distinct wet and dry seasons, the longevity of the door itself will depend greatly on the direction it faces and the amount of exposure it gets to sun and rain. Sunlight destroys finishes and discolors wood with amazing rapidity, and constant changes in temperature and moisture will cause rapid expansion and contraction of the wood that will loosen panels, delaminate even the best exterior grades of plywood, and force joints apart in short order (Illus. 103).

Paint or varnish is your main defense

Illus. 103. The bottom of this unprotected door has been bleached and cracked by ultraviolet radiation and moisture.

against weather damage to your doors, but the more you can protect your doors from the elements, the longer this finish will last. For your own comfort as well as the longevity of your door, always try to protect your entryway from exposure by sheltering it with a porch roof (Illus. 104) or a secondary storm-and-screen door combination. This is especially true if you want a varnished or oiled finish that will show the natural color and beauty of the wood. There are exterior-grade varnishes and stains available that provide some protection from ultraviolet light, the most harmful part of the spectrum, but even these finishes will have only a limited life in direct exposure.

You can also lessen the likelihood of major damage from the elements by keeping in mind that the wider a panel or frame member is, the more it is going to expand and contract. Even the best finishes pass some moisture. Plywoods and well-built laminated doors are cross-bonded to prevent expansion and contraction (Illus. 105), but solid wood will move with enough force

Illus. 104. The best protection for a varnished exterior door is an overhanging roof.

CROSS BONDING

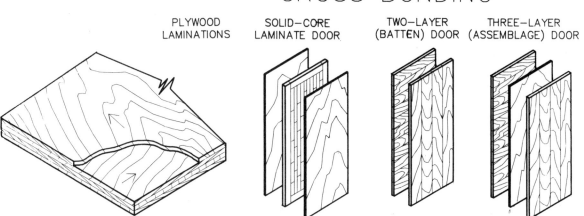

PLYWOOD
LAMINATIONS

SOLID–CORE
LAMINATE DOOR

TWO–LAYER
(BATTEN) DOOR

THREE–LAYER
(ASSEMBLAGE) DOOR

Illus. 105. The cross-bonding of thin layers of wood prevents expansion and contraction. Exterior-grade plywood should be used for all panels wider than 12 inches, and laminate doors should be carefully sealed to prevent delamination.

to break even the best glue joints. Laminate doors often delaminate when the core is exposed to moisture because the thin outer veneers cannot hold the expansive force of the solid-wood core in check.

Limiting solid-wood panel and rail widths to about 12 inches and avoiding large expanses of edge-joined lumber will help prevent problems from expansion and contraction. It is conceivable to build a door simply by edge-joining enough 2 × 6's to span the width of the doorway. It might work for an interior door, but it is a perfect example of what you wouldn't want to do for an exterior door.

Materials

Your choice of materials will depend on the type of construction technique you plan to employ and the way in which you intend to finish your door, as well as the availability of different woods in your own locality. If you intend to paint your finished door, then you will be more concerned with the strength and workability of your wood than the beauty of the grain. Fir is a very strong and stable wood for paint-grade doors, but a bit difficult to work. Pine and redwood are easier to work, but are more easily damaged by bumps and scrapes because of their softness. If you are going to use plywood for panels or laminate doors, be sure that it is of a good enough grade for your situation, and of equal quality on both sides if both will show.

Your Abilities

Another major consideration if you are designing your own doorway is your own resources and abilities. A well-planned job that's within your capabilities is bound to be a winner, but trying to do more than you are ready for will only cause you grief and frustration.

There are many ways to build solid, nice-looking doors. Some methods are simpler than others, especially if you are working with a limited amount of equipment. Even the simplest methods can be adapted to many different architectural styles. Consider carefully, and don't bite off more than you can chew.

If you are replacing an existing door with something more to your liking, you will have to make a choice between working with the size and shape of the opening that already exists or making fairly major structural changes. The rough opening, the hole in the framing and siding of the building, can be enlarged, but it will usually mean removing a considerable amount of siding, and reworking the structural support system around the doorway (Illus. 106).

Also of major importance are the flashing, trim, and sill, which serve to channel moisture outward and away from the interior of the house (Illus. 107). Note how these factors work on your existing doorway, and seek the advice of an experienced house carpenter during the design stage of your project if you are unsure of the consequences of the changes you intend to make.

Closing down, or decreasing the size of a rough opening is also possible. You may want to consider turning part of the doorway into sidelights or adding a wider, more elaborate trim detail to avoid having to reside areas adjacent to the doorway that is being narrowed. This is easier than enlarging the opening, but still must be done with care to avoid leaks and to blend the change in, so that it doesn't stand out from the rest of the doorway.

Door Structure

Doorway

Aside from the door or doors themselves, a doorway is composed of several distinct parts. In new construction, a doorway begins its existence as an opening left in the wall framing. This opening, called the *rough opening*, is framed on either side by double studs which capture and support an upper beam called the *header*. The header must be strong enough to carry the load across its span, and will vary in size accordingly. If there are sidelights in the doorway, they may be framed as separate

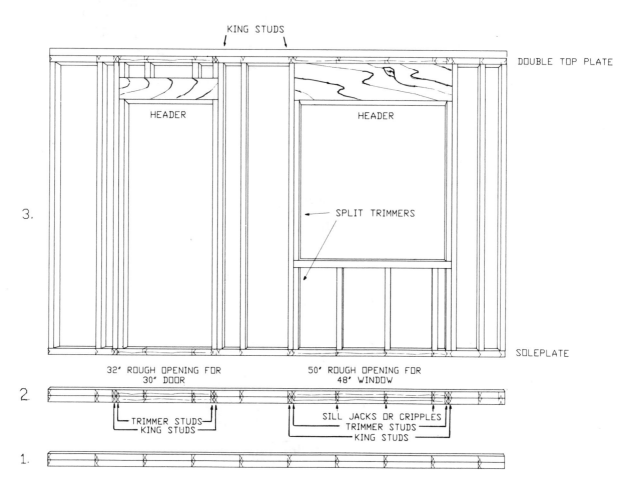

Illus. 106. In new construction, holes are left in the wall framing for doors and windows. These are called rough openings. A header spans the rough opening, or several rough openings at once if a series of doors or windows occurs, and the studs on either side of the header are usually doubled to help carry the load. Short studs below a window are called cripples or sill jacks. Enlarging an already existing rough opening will call for reworking of the framing, which may mean removing a considerable amount of siding. You can usually close in a rough opening by adding more framing and a wider trim detail.

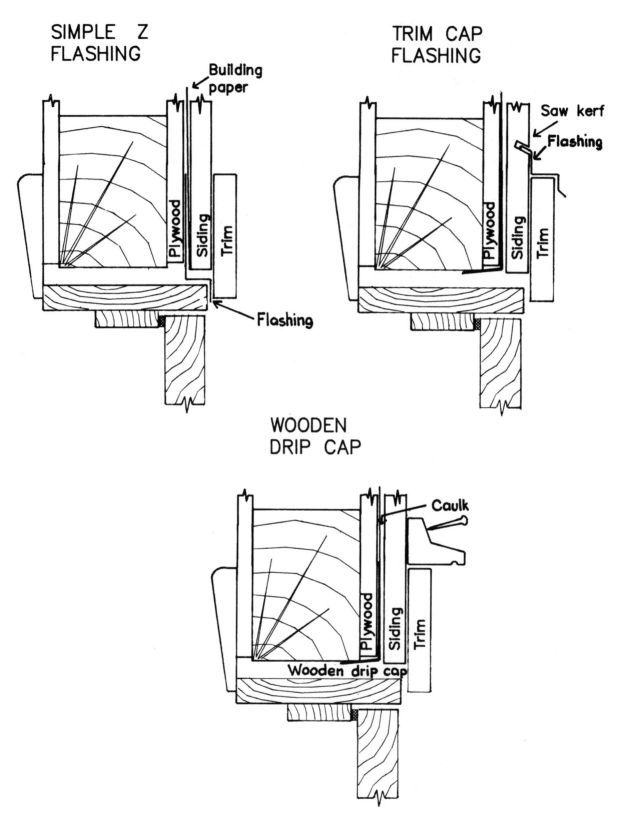

Illus. 107. Flashing and trim help to prevent leaking around doors and windows.

Illus. 108. The header must be strong enough to carry the load across the entire span.

openings under a single header. Separate jambs are then installed in each opening. Careful consideration should be given to the trim details that will be used when windows and doors are made close together, or in rows.

When planning rough openings, remember that a door of any given width will require a rough opening of that width plus twice the thickness of the jambs plus 1 inch (to be divided into ½ inch on either side for shimming the jamb). For a 3-foot-wide door, this means that a rough opening of at least 38 inches is necessary (assuming that the jambs are made from ¾-inch material). The height of the rough opening will depend somewhat on the thickness of the finished floor material. If an 80-inch door is to be used, the rough opening will have to be high enough to accommodate the door, the upper jamb piece, and a sill. The sill may vary in thickness and in type, depending on whether the door is interior or exterior and what the finished floor treatment will be. As with the width of the door, allow ½ inch at the top for shimming, and remember that it is easier to fill in too large an opening than it is to increase its size. Often, doors end up being cut down a bit at the bottom to accommodate the threshold and floor treatment, but this can easily weaken a door, and can be avoided with good planning.

Doorframe

The doorframe, or jamb as it is sometimes called, lines the rough opening and provides attachment for the door hinges themselves.

These days, jambs are usually made from ¾-inch material, with thinner strips applied after the door is hung in place to provide stops for the door. (Decorative, plain, and hidden stop details are shown in Illus. 109.)

Illus. 109. Decorative, plain, and hidden stops.

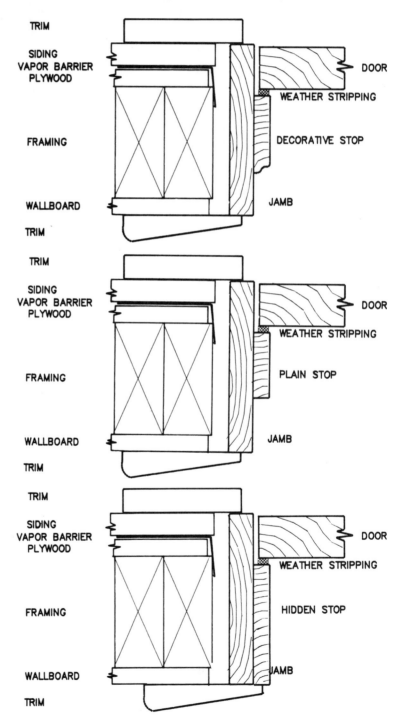

TRIM

SIDING
VAPOR BARRIER
PLYWOOD

FRAMING

WALLBOARD

TRIM

DOOR

WEATHER STRIPPING

DECORATIVE STOP

JAMB

TRIM

SIDING
VAPOR BARRIER
PLYWOOD

FRAMING

WALLBOARD

TRIM

DOOR

WEATHER STRIPPING

PLAIN STOP

JAMB

TRIM

SIDING
VAPOR BARRIER
PLYWOOD

FRAMING

WALLBOARD

TRIM

DOOR

WEATHER STRIPPING

HIDDEN STOP

JAMB

JAMB CONSTRUCTION DETAIL

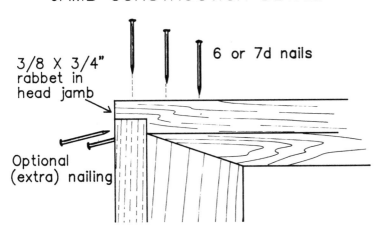

3/8 X 3/4" rabbet in head jamb

6 or 7d nails

Optional (extra) nailing

Illus. 110. The head jamb should be rabbeted to receive the side jamb, and nailed from the top before you install the jamb in the rough opening.

The stops literally stop the swing of the door, and provide a surface against which the door seals to prevent air infiltration. Weather stripping is often applied to the stops.

The side jambs are rabbeted into the top or head jamb, and nailed through from above with three or four 6d galvanized nails (Illus. 110). The threshold is generally installed after the door jamb is in place and the door is hung, but if it is wooden it can also be attached to the jambs by nailing from the outside before the jamb is installed in the rough opening.

The width of the jamb material will vary with the thickness of the wall in which it is installed. Generally the jamb must be as wide as the full thickness of the wall except where hidden stops or special treatments like a brick or stone veneer or shingling are applied to all or part of one side of the wall (Illus. 111). The placement of the door in the jamb will depend on the direction of swing of the door. The door will usually be positioned so that it is flush, or nearly flush, with the surface of the wall on the side towards which it will open.

An alternative method for building jambs,

called stop-rabbeted jambs, is more in line with old-fashioned door-framing methods (Illus. 112). For this method, begin with 1½-inch stock and cut a rabbet about ½ inch deep and wide enough for the thickness of the door. The head and side jambs are attached in the same manner as with the previously described method, but more care must be taken to see that the stops line up perfectly. At first glance, this would seem to be a more weather-tight method of construction, but if your door or the wall in which it is installed is not perfectly straight and true, it will be more difficult to get a tight closure. With applied stops, as in the first method, it is quite easy to adjust the run of the stops to the natural shape of the door, and as long as a bead of construction adhesive is used, as well as nails, every foot or so to attach the stops, there should be no problem with air infiltration between the stops and the jambs.

Door Types

Let's discuss three basic kinds of doors: batten doors, laminate doors, and frame-and-panel doors. Some doors are combinations

Illus. 111. The jamb usually runs from the outside to the inside of the wall, unless hidden stops are used or you are working on shingled walls. Here, an extra-thick exterior trim is used, and shingles are applied up to it. Brick or masonry can also be applied right up to the lower part of a jamb.

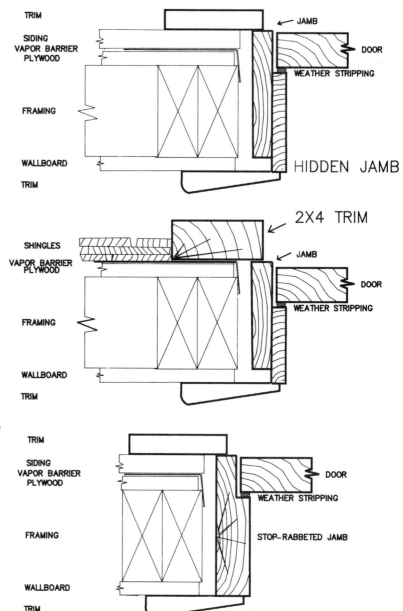

Illus. 112. Stop-rabbeted jambs are cut from one piece of 2-inch-thick lumber. It will be difficult to get a tight closure with this method if there is any warpage in the door or the side jambs.

of these techniques, and it is possible to build doors that don't fall into any of these categories, but these will be the main techniques discussed in this book.

The batten door is one of the simplest and oldest techniques (Illus. 113). It is familiar to nearly everyone as the "old barn door," and can indeed be found commonly on sheds, outbuildings, and in other rustic settings where air infiltration is not a critical concern. The battens, or "ledges," as the old English jointers called them, which run across the top and bottom (and often across the middle, as well) hold the vertical boards together, while the diagonal battens or "braces" prevent the door from sagging and

Illus. 113. The batten door is one of the oldest and simplest methods of making a door.

falling out of square. Clinched nails or screws applied carefully in a neat pattern attach the two sets of boards together.

You can elaborate on this technique by making the battens into a frame around the door or into a solid layer (Illus. 114). Usually the grain of one layer is run in opposition to the other layer, a form of cross-bonding that gives the door a reasonable amount of stability. You can add a vapor barrier of building paper, a layer of plywood, or even rigid insulation between the two outer layers of 1-by material, creating a three-layer lamination. If a solid middle layer is used, the outer layers can be applied in interesting patterns, and the result is a simple yet beautiful assemblage technique. This is essentially a laminate door, though nails or screws are usually used, in addition to glue or construction adhesive, to bond the thicker 1-inch material to the core. Make sure you use only straight, dry lumber with this technique, as the potential for warpage and shrinkage is great.

Laminate doors are more often built by laminating two layers of thin plywood to either a core of solid wood or, thin strips of wood, or cardboard as in hollow-core doors. In production work this is done with large, pneumatic veneer presses that rapidly apply pressure and dry the glue with radio-frequency generators. There are other clamping techniques that we can use that do not require such massive equipment.

The laminate or flush door has the advantage of being very stable dimensionally, and, again, various techniques can be used to increase the visual appeal of the door. Irregular-shaped windows can be included in the design, and appliqués or routed designs can be used to break up the flatness that is inherent in the technique (Illus. 115). Sometimes a flat, unobtrusive door is what's needed, in which case laminated doors fit the bill perfectly.

The third technique, the frame-and-panel door, is perhaps the most common and venerated of door-making techniques. This technique was developed so that lumber could be joined in a way that would allow for the constant movement caused by the contraction and expansion of the wood. The

Illus. 115. Windows, appliqués, and various types of hardware can be used to dress up laminate doors.

frame members are joined rigidly to each other usually with either mortise-and-tenon joints, dowels, or splines. The panels, which are usually made from either wood, plywood, or glass, float in slots or rabbets in the frame members. Never attempt to glue wooden panels into the slots. Flexible caulk can be used to help seal either the glass or the wood panels where they meet the framework, but rigid glue would cause problems.

By varying the sizes and shapes of the panels, and using different mouldings, different woods, stained glass, appliqués, carvings, or inlays, you can obtain an infinite variety of pleasing designs with any of these techniques. One of the greatest joys of building doors is making something totally unique each time.

These techniques can be applied to both interior and exterior doors. Interior doors are not exposed to the harsh climatic changes that exterior doors must endure, and so can be built with much less concern for the strength and permanence of the joinery. The standard thickness for interior doors is 1⅜ inch or less. You can really get more creative with interior doors because you have less to worry about. As long as you start with good, dry lumber and use reasonably sound joinery, an interior door is likely to hold together quite well no matter how it's designed.

Double Doors

Double doors are often made with frame-and-panel type construction with glass. They are a beautiful way to open up the favorite rooms of your home to the outdoors (Illus. 116). Generally, barrel bolts are attached to the top and bottom of one of the doors to fix it in place. They can be applied to the face or hidden on the edge of the door. The other door is used for coming and going, and has a lock-and-catch mechanism that catches on the fixed door. An astragal or T-moulding can be applied to either door, depending on the swing of the doors. This acts as a weather sealer where the two doors meet.

The main difficulty with double doors is getting them to meet properly in the middle. It is especially important with double doors that they be perfectly flat and true. If one of the doors does show a slight twist or warp, use it as the fixed door. The bar-

Illus. 116. Double doors are beautiful and functional.

rel bolts can then be used to hold it straight, and a good, straight installation will result.

Pocket Doors

Pocket doors are generally used on the interior of a building (Illus. 117). The doors themselves can be constructed in any manner, but the wall in which they are mounted must be built with 1-inch-thick framing material with the flats to the wallboards, or be made extra thick so that a pocket results into which the door or doors slide when opened. A track is mounted above the door so that it hangs and slides easily. You can build your own pocket wall and buy the track, or often you can buy the wall and track prefabricated, and build your own door for it. Double-pocket doors are a nice way to separate two rooms that will sometimes function as one, such as a dining room and living room, or a solarium and living room.

Illus. 117. You can slide pocket doors into a wall pocket that you have created by framing the wall with 1 × 4's laid flat to the wallboard.

Design

After giving thorough consideration to all the factors mentioned and the way they affect your particular situation, you will most likely want to draw out your ideas with pencil and paper. If you don't have a drafting table and the proper tools, you can use graph paper and a ruler as a straightedge. Use a large enough scale so that you can indicate details such as mouldings or inlays.

Remember that locksets are usually placed about 36 inches above the floor, but may be affected by a step up or down, or by the placement of a deadbolt. Most locks are offset $2\frac{3}{8}$ inches from the edge of the door, which would center them on a $4\frac{3}{4}$-inch stile, but you can also get locks with $2\frac{3}{4}$-inch offset for doors with wider stiles. The drawing stage is the time to play with the visual effects and proportions of your design. Only when you are happy with your drawing are you ready to head for the shop.

5
Constructing Doors with Hand Tools

The methods by which a door can be built consist of many variations on a few basic themes. A mortise-and-tenon joint, a raised panel, or decorative moulding can all be cut entirely by hand or with various types of power tools. For the custom builder, a thorough understanding of the possible approaches to a problem is as important as the speed with which it can be done. Large, expensive machines lock you into certain methods—you've got to use a $500 set of shaper cutters quite a bit to justify the expense.

Uniqueness has its own value, and you can often make more of a "profit" working carefully by hand than you can through the production approach. Also keep in mind that those who built by hand out of necessity developed the most efficient methods possible with their limited tools. By discovering the fine points of our predecessors' craft, we will certainly profit greatly (Illus. 118).

As explained in the previous chapter, doors fall into three basic types—batten doors, flush or laminate doors, and frame-

Illus. 118. The time-honored methods of hand construction bring their own rewards to the careful and patient craftsperson.

and-panel doors. Batten doors are layered doors built with solid lumber, and flush doors are built from plywood laminated to a solid or hollow core. Frame-and-panel doors include all doors built with a framework of solid lumber that supports panels of either glass or wood. The framework is rigidly glued together, while the panels "float" in slots or rabbets to allow for expansion and contraction.

Over the centuries, various methods of bringing the lumber from its rough state to its finished form have evolved. Since so many varieties of dimensioned lumber are available today, I will not always start the door-making descriptions with the squaring-up of rough lumber that a 19th century jointer would have done, but will assume that dimensioned lumber is at hand.

In this chapter, I will describe a series of doors that can be built entirely with hand tools. In a few places, methods for using a table saw, Skilsaw®, or a router, which speed up the process greatly, are discussed, but for the sake of the purist, old-fashioned methods will also be explained. These doors are not all simple (though assemblage doors require very few tools to build, they can be as intricate and beautiful as any frame-and-panel door) but they would be a good place to start if your tools and experience are limited.

The second series of doors, described in Chapter 6, will be used to illustrate more conventional modern methods suitable for the small custom builder, and the final series in Chapter 7 will convey more production-oriented methods, including the use of spindle shapers.

Note: Before moving on to the types of doors, I want to discuss two words that will appear throughout this book. The words muntin and mullion have been considered in other sources to be interchangeable terms. I make a distinction in this book and classify muntins as horizontal pieces and mullions as vertical ones.

Batten Doors

Batten doors are perhaps the simplest method of door construction, usually consisting of a layer of vertical boards with horizontal battens nailed across them top, bottom, and middle to hold them together (Illus. 119). Diagonal braces are also applied between the battens to help keep the door from falling out of square, and to give the door more visual appeal.

To build a batten door, begin by cutting your vertical pieces to rough length about an inch longer than the finished door. The door will be trimmed to its finished length after it is assembled. Tongue-and-groove or ship lap-edged lumber is best used to prevent cracks from opening up between the boards during the dryer parts of the year. Tongue-and-groove boards can be blind-nailed to the battens if there are enough battens, but ship lap-edged boards will have to be surface-nailed or screwed.

If your lumber is not already milled on the edges, carefully check the boards for straightness with a straightedge or by fitting them one to the other, and plane them where necessary to achieve a tight fit. After you have gotten the boards good and straight, you can mill alternating rabbets on the edges, if necessary, with either a rabbet plane, a table saw, or a router to create a ship lap-edging.

BATTEN DOOR VARIATIONS

Illus. 119. Many variations of batten doors are possible. Generally, batten doors consist of two layers: one solid layer and one layer made up of battens and sometimes diagonal braces screwed or nailed to the solid layer.

Illus. 120. When laying out a batten door, trim the two outside boards to approximately equal width to avoid narrow or different-sized edge pieces.

Rip the edges off the two outside boards so that you'll have equal-sized boards with square edges on both sides of the finished door (Illus. 120). Lay the boards out where they will go, and position the edges of the door so that the two outside boards will be of approximately equal width. Use a straightedge or marking gauge to mark one edge. Cut this line with your ripsaw or table saw, and plane the edge straight and

smooth. Now measure across from this finished edge near the top and near the bottom of the door to the widths you will need. Be sure to check both the top and bottom of your jamb, as the opening may vary in width. Mark the second line with a straightedge, and cut about ⅛ inch outside it, so that you can plane to it after the door is assembled.

When you have the vertical boards the

way you want them, lay them out on 2 × 4 sleepers on your workbench or across two sawhorses, and clamp them with pipe clamps to hold them tightly together. One clamp in the middle, underneath the boards, and one on top on either end will prevent the boards from bowing and popping apart. Now cut the boards for the battens to length. Be sure to take the hang and swing of the door into account at this point. You may want to leave the ends of the battens back from the edges of the door if they will be on the side that will close against the stops.

A nice touch is to bevel the edges of the battens all around on the side that will be away from the door (Illus. 121). It will be easier to do and less likely to mar your door if you bevel the edges of the battens before the battens are applied. For an especially large door, or for an extra touch, you may want to notch the ends of the braces into the battens, thus seating them and further strengthening the door. If so, the notches

should be cut and the braces fitted before the battens are nailed to the door (Illus. 122).

Illus. 122. If you are going to cut notches in the battens for the braces, do it before nailing the battens in place.

When you are ready to nail on the battens, check them for squareness to the door, and then tack each one in place with one or two small finish nails. Now, flip the door over, mark your nailing lines across the vertical boards, and nail through into your battens. A 6d or 7d galvanized nail is usually used with ¾-inch material so that the nails can project through both layers and be clinched to give them extra holding power (Illus. 123). You can also nail from the batten side if you don't mind the clinched nails showing on the flush side of the door.

Screws will also work for applying battens, but they should be carefully counterbored, and be the exact length to hold the board without going through. If you are using nails, be sure to set the heads of the nails below the surface of the wood before flipping the door over again to clinch the nails. A large nailset can also be used to set

Illus. 121. Soften the edges of the battens by chamfering them with a hand plane before nailing them in place.

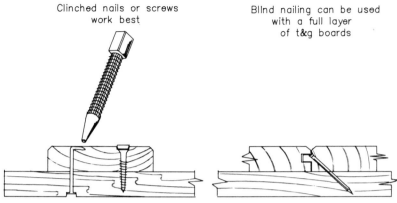

Clinched nails or screws work best

Blind nailing can be used with a full layer of t&g boards

Illus. 123. Either clinched nails or screws can be used to attach battens to the vertical boards. If nails are used, the heads should first be set below the surface; then they should be clinched and the set should again be used to curl the tips down into the wood.

the clinched parts of the nails below the surface of the battens. If your wood is hard or tends to split easily, you may want to predrill the nail holes with a bit that is slightly smaller than the nails.

Once the battens are permanently in place, the braces can be carefully marked and cut. If you have a long enough board, lay it the full diagonal length of the door between the upper and lower battens, and mark on both it and the battens to indicate where it is to be cut and its exact placement. Use a sharp block plane on the ends of the braces to adjust the fit, if necessary; bevel the edges as you did on the battens, and nail them on in the same manner.

Finally, check the dimensions of the door again, and trim the top and bottom as necessary for a perfect fit. Bevel or sand the edges to soften them, and the door is ready to hang.

Many variations on the batten door are possible, from using rough, heavy lumber and wrought iron nails and hinges to very refined and nicely painted designs (Illus. 124 and 125). By adding vertical battens along the edges and placing the horizontal battens at the ends of the door, you can create a door that looks and feels more like a frame-and-panel door. For larger doors

like barn or garage doors, you may want to build the frame first, out of 1½-inch material, with half-lapped joints at the corners; then nail on the ¾-inch boards either vertically or diagonally. The use of long, metal strap hinges, bolted or screwed onto the battens, will also greatly improve the strength of the door (Illus. 126).

Illus. 124 and 125 (next page). Many variations, both refined and rustic, are possible with the batten method of construction.

Illus. 126. Long strap hinges can be used in place of battens to hold a door together.

Assemblage Doors

This intermediate form of construction between batten and laminate doors requires only very simple tools, and yet offers an unlimited range for your creative expression (Illus. 127). Instead of just two layers, as in the batten door, this door will have three. The inner layer, or core, is usually made from ½- or ¾-inch exterior-grade plywood, but can also be made from solid lumber if the design permits. This layer gives stability to the two outer layers, and supports them so that you can assemble them any way you like.

Make a pencil-and-paper design for this type of door. If you don't have drafting tools, just use graph paper, a sharp pencil, and a ruler. You will make a frame or trim around the edge of the door to cover the core and help protect the edges; this frame will be made from ¾-inch material, so plan your design to be 1½-inch smaller in both directions than the finished size you need.

1 x 6 core

Plywood core

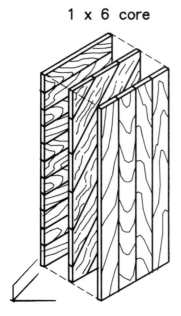
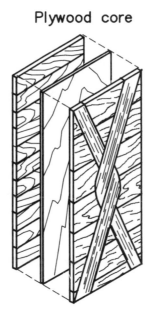

Illus. 127. Assemblage doors rely on a third layer, or core, to stabilize the two outer layers.

Often, the interior side of a door of this type is done with plain or V-grooved T&G boards in a simple vertical or diagonal pattern, but since we have the plywood core to give the door stability you can use any type of board. Make it as simple or as complex as you like. Let your imagination run wild, and consider various materials as well as designs (Illus. 128). Using clear epoxy or polyester resins, you can inlay half pieces of brass tubing, stones, flat brass wire, or anything else at hand.

If your design is a complicated one, you may want to enlarge it to full size by laying out a grid on a piece of brown paper that will be cut up and used as patterns for cutting your pieces. If your original drawing was at a scale of 1 inch = 1 foot, and your graph paper had ¼-inch grid lines, then your full-scale grid will have lines every 3 inches. Transfer your drawing to the full-sized grid, and use an X-acto knife or scissors to cut it out.

Illus. 128. Many interesting visual effects and complex graphic designs are possible using this method.

Begin building your door by cutting your core piece to size, 1½ inch smaller in both directions than the final dimension (assuming you are using ¾-inch material). If you are building an exterior door, apply first the side of the door that will be exposed to the weather.

Cut the boards to the sizes and shapes you want and lay them out on the core. Work from top to bottom or from one edge to the other, and, where you can, use one piece as a pattern for the adjoining piece. A sharp block plane will work well for adjusting straight pieces, and can also be used to trim the outside of a curved piece. You can trim and adjust the concave, or inside, curves with a rounded rasp, a coping saw, or coarse sandpaper (Illus. 129). Be sure that the outer layer will totally cover the core and, if anything, overhangs it just a bit around the edges. The edges of the assembly can be trimmed and planed after the outer two layers are applied.

It will greatly improve the longevity of your door if you seal the edges of the pieces on the exterior side, especially on the end

Illus. 129. Use a rounded rasp to adjust the inside curve of a piece for an assemblage door. A drum sander would also do this job well.

grain. You can either soak in the same varnish or oil you will use to finish the door or use a clear glue. If you use varnish or oil, apply it and let it dry before applying the pieces to the core. If you are using clear epoxy glue, the edges can be sealed as the pieces are glued and nailed to the core.

For the construction of this type of door, you may be able to get by without the use of nails if you use the gluing methods decribed in the section on laminate doors (pages 94–98), but if you do nail, use small galvanized finish nails that won't penetrate the plywood core. Be sure to set them well below the surface before applying the second outer layer. You may be able to nail all your pieces around the edges only, so that the nails won't show.

A thick, viscous glue such as F 26 construction adhesive or some type of marine epoxy should be used as well as the nails. Cover the inside of each piece as it is applied with a fairly thick but even coat. A toothed trowel does this job well. Be sure you are working on a good, flat surface, as any bow or sag now could well become a permanent feature on your door.

Let the first side dry well before applying the second side. Be sure your nails won't go through the outer layer even after you set them well below the surface. Many people don't realize that the swelling and shrinking action of wood will actually force nails to back out of the wood over the years if they are not set below the surface.

When both outer layers of wood have been applied and the glue is allowed to dry, trim the edges carefully with a hand plane, Skilsaw, router, or electric planer. By clamping and tacking a straight piece of lumber to the door and using it as a guide for your Skilsaw or a router, you can get a perfectly straight and square edge without planing. Use a fine-toothed blade such as a plywood or combination blade if you are using a Skilsaw.

Illus. 130. When trimming the bottom of a door, use a sharp, fine-toothed blade and cover the edge with masking tape to help prevent chip-out.

You will need to rip or plane the pieces that will cover the edges to exact thickness before applying them with nails and glue. For an even stronger edge-banding that won't need nailing, you can rout a slot around the edge of the door after it has been trimmed to size, and make a T-moulding that, when glued in place, will greatly strengthen the edges of the door (Illus. 131). Check your dimensions again before applying the edge pieces. If you nail them on, you won't be able to plane the edges much, so care here is important.

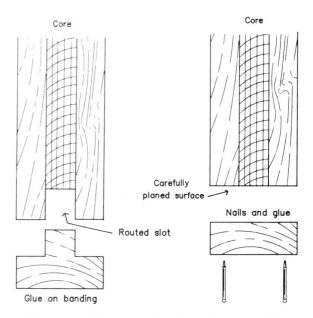

Illus. 131. The edge-banding for assemblage doors can be nailed on or a T moulding can be cut and glued into a slot that's routed around the edge of the door.

If you do nail the edge-banding on, longer nails can be used, and ring-shank nails will be even better for gripping. Be careful not to split the boards in the surface layers if you nail into them. Just nailing into the core will be adequate if it is good, solid material. You can use large nails such as 8d galvanized finish nails to nail into the core, but you should predrill the edge pieces to avoid splitting them.

A small window can easily be cut into this type of door, or you can plan your layout from the beginning for a larger or irregular-shaped window or windows. The easiest way to treat the window hole is to line it with ¾-inch material, just as you did for the outside of the door, and then apply a ¾-inch or slightly smaller stop both inside and out to hold the glass in place. Window installation that is much more weatherproof can be obtained if the interior stop is incorporated in the window frame itself by cutting a rabbet in the material before applying it to the door. The corners of the frame can either be mitred or rabbeted so that the stop rabbet is continuous. If your door is really going to be exposed to terrible weather, you could even slope the bottom piece and project it out from the surface of the door, as with a window sill, to drain moisture away from the door.

Laminate Doors

Laminate doors are a sort of reversal of the assemblage method. The plywood is applied on the outside, while the core somewhat resembles the assemblage door style.

Nearly everyone is familiar with the hollow- and solid-core laminate doors that have proliferated in recent years as a cheap alternative to the frame-and-panel door. Hollow-core doors, often nothing more than two $\frac{1}{8}$-inch sheets of plywood on a 1 × 1 $\frac{1}{4}$-inch wooden frame with cardboard reinforcement strips, are very lightweight, and usually suitable only as interior doors.

A good solid-core laminate door, on the other hand, can be a substantial door. It has the advantage of good dimensional stability, and will hold up well if proper gluing

Illus. 132A and B. Windows, appliqués, and applied moulding patterns can be used to dress up laminate doors.

techniques are used. Cheaper grades of lumber, end cuts, and scraps can be used to build up the core, and the outside can be either left very simple or decorated in any of a number of ways.

Building your own solid-core door will take quite a bit of setting up. In factories, the core is first assembled and edge-glued, and then finished with large drum sanders to the desired thickness. The outside plywood laminations are then glued in place with a large veneer press, a huge machine that can apply tons of pressure evenly over a large area. In high-production industrial shops, radio-frequency generators are used to dry the glue within minutes, greatly speeding production.

You can build your own veneer press if you intend to do a lot of veneering, or you can rely on the following: glues that work well even without heavy clamping pressure, a very sturdy work surface, plenty of clamps, and a crude, but effective, method of applying pressure in areas where clamps cannot reach.

Materials

The type and thickness of core material you use will depend on the intended thickness of the finished door and the thickness of the plywood used for the outside layers. Three-quarter-inch stock can be used with $\frac{1}{8}$- or $\frac{1}{4}$-inch plywood to make a thin but solid door, or with thicker plywood to make a door that has a greater, nearly standard, thickness. Various types of $\frac{1}{8}$- and $\frac{1}{4}$-inch veneering materials are available for use with a thicker core to produce a standard thickness door. One-eight-inch "door skins" can sometimes be bought from lumberyards.

Be sure to check the type of glue used in bonding your veneers. Unless it specifically says exterior grade, it is most likely made with a non-waterproof glue. Other materials such as Formica, sheet metal, or pressed board can also be used to veneer interior solid-core doors.

Assuming that your core material is all the same thickness, you can begin your construction by edge-joining your core material. This can be accomplished in just about any manner you have at hand, and in any direction so long as a few guidelines are followed. Don't use any boards wider than approximately 4 inches. If you have wider stock, rip it to 4-inch widths, and separate pieces from the same board to prevent warping caused by radial tension.

It may be helpful to assemble the rough lumber into boards that are still narrow enough to be run through a thickness planer as the first stage of your core assembly (Illus. 133). These "boards" can then be edge-joined after machine planing in order to avoid a lot of hand planing. Also assemble the core in such a way that the minimal amount of end grain is exposed along the edges.

If you rip your stock narrow enough, you can simply nail the boards together along the edges, applying glue to each as you work, or you can use bar clamps for a more traditional glue-up. A urea resin glue should be used for this operation because it is easily cleaned up with a wet rag. Be sure to remove excess glue from the outside surfaces before it dries.

If you plan to have a window or windows in the finished door, cut out the spaces now to simplify cutting and avoid waste. If the window is irregular in shape, you may want

Illus. 133. To build up a core for a solid core door, begin by joining your pieces into boards narrow enough to go through your planer; they should be as long as your door. Next, join the three central boards, being careful to keep the joints very flat. When these joints are dry, trim the ends about 3 inches shorter than the height of the door and apply end caps to cover the end grain. Finally, join the two outer pieces to complete the core lamination.

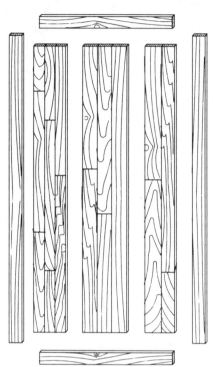

to cut it out with a jigsaw after the core is assembled. Do any smoothing or shaping work with rasps, chisels, or spokeshaves before the veneers are applied to minimize the risk of damaging your veneers while working.

The easiest way to cover up your end grain is to join all but the last piece on either side; then trim about 1½ inch off each end of the core with a Skilsaw, and, in a second operation, glue and nail a cap on each end. Now cap the edges in the same manner so that only a 1½-inch square of end grain shows at each corner of the door. This will greatly improve the stability of any exterior door of this type.

When the core is dry, use a cabinet scraper to remove any glue that may have oozed to the surface and dried. Then use a hand plane and work across the boards

to flatten out any places where the boards do not come together evenly. You are now ready to apply the veneers to the core. A veneer press can be constructed as shown in Illus. 134 by combining a series of clamping frames to apply pressure about every 10 inches. If enough pressure is distributed over the door, urea resin glue will work well.

Another clamping method using 2 × 4's to distribute the clamping pressure is also possible, but for this method an epoxy resin glue or panel adhesive is recommended because of its superior strength even when tight contact is not made between the two pieces of wood (Illus. 135). Approximately one quart of glue will be needed for a 3 foot × 6 foot 8 inch door like the one shown. A good, sturdy worktable or clamping stand that is no wider than the door you are build-

Illus. 134. You can make a veneer press to apply thin plywood veneers to solid core doors by using ten of the veneer press frames shown here. These Jorgensen-brand press screws are commercially available. Urea resin can be used if you have enough clamping pressure evenly distributed over the entire lamination. Photo from Gluing and Clamping, *by Patrick Spielman (Sterling Publishing Co., Inc., Two Park Avenue, New York, New York 10016).*

Illus. 135. If you don't have a veneer press, you can apply pressure to the central area of a large veneer by applying pipe clamps to a grid work of 2 × 4's, as shown in Illus. 136. Epoxy or a thick viscous glue like panel adhesive should be used in this case because it has better holding power and does not have to be tightly clamped.

ing will also be a necessity for the second method. Two by fours will do for both the horizontal sleepers and the pressure beams. The horizontal sleepers should all be about 12 inches longer than the width of your door. Lay them out on edge on your worktable, no more than 12 inches apart for the sleepers, and then lay three 2 × 4's, their flat sides up, the length of the door on top of the sleepers. The door will be sandwiched between these pieces and an identical layout on top, and bar clamps will be used to clamp the overhanging ends of the sleepers and the beams together to develop pressure in the central area of the door. C-clamps will be your best bet around the edges, which are the most critical part of the glue-up. The more, the better.

If your door has windows in it, mark them carefully from the core onto the inside of the veneers, and cut them out before applying the veneers. A jigsaw or keyhole saw can be used to accomplish this, but be careful not to tear out the grain. When you are ready, place the first veneer face down on the pressure beams, and apply glue evenly over the whole surface with a toothed trowel. Carefully position the core on the veneer, and then apply glue to the upper side of the core. Finally, put the upper veneer in place, and use a brad or two at each end to hold it so that it doesn't slide out of place. Now put the three 2 × 4's vertically on top of the door, and matching horizontal pieces over these. Clamp the ends of the horizontal pieces together, and drive wedges (shingles) between the horizontal pieces and the center vertical piece to even out the pressure. C-clamps should be applied as close together as possible around the edges (Illus. 136).

Once the door is dry, the edges can be carefully trimmed and sanded so that they are smooth and slightly rounded. If you have a router, you can use a rabbeting bit to cut rabbets for the glazing. If not, you can use applied moulding on both sides of the glass to hold it in place. (See the section on curved mouldings in Chapter 11.) A door of this type is easy to finish and maintain, very durable and secure, and

gives slightly better thermal protection than a frame-and-panel door.

Old-Fashioned Frame-and-Panel Door

Let's use a 2-foot 6-inch × 6-foot 8-inch four-panel door to illustrate some of the working methods that were employed for making frame-and-panel doors during the last century (Illus. 137). Alternate treatments for moulding the edges of the framework around the panels will be discussed. Of course, this same type of door can be built much more quickly with power tools, and methods for doing so will be revealed in Chapter 6.

The 17th- or 18th-century jointer would have begun his work with rough boards that had been cut by a crew of sawyers working a pit saw, or perhaps even with lumber that had been riven (that is, split with a froe and mallet) from very straight-grained material when it was still green. If he were very prosperous, or lived in a community that had been settled for many years, his lumber might have been cut by

Illus. 136. The edges of a laminate door are the most important part of the lamination, and should be clamped every 3–6 inches.

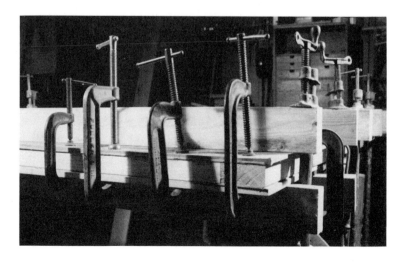

a water-powered mill. The boards would have been air-drying for a couple of years by the time he pulled them off his carefully stickered drying stack and began sawing and planing them to the dimensions he needed.

First, one face would be hand-planed flat and straight with a short, but wide, jack or

A HANDMADE FOUR-PANEL DOOR

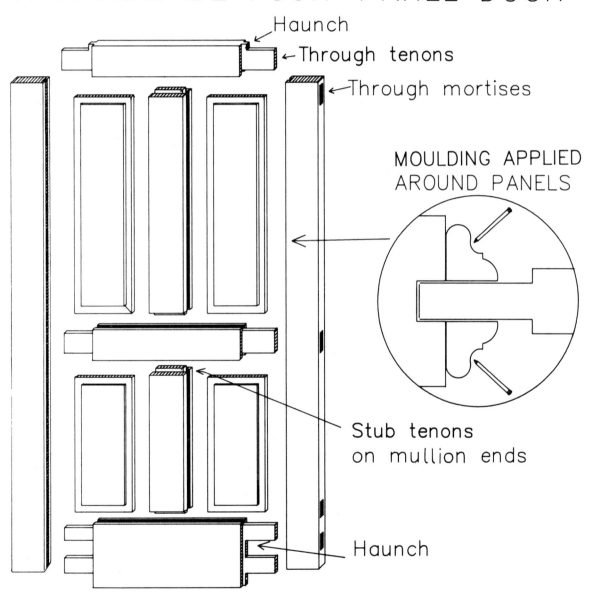

Haunch

← Through tenons

← Through mortises

MOULDING APPLIED AROUND PANELS

Stub tenons on mullion ends

Haunch

Illus. 137. This four-panel door can be made by the patient craftsperson without the use of power tools.

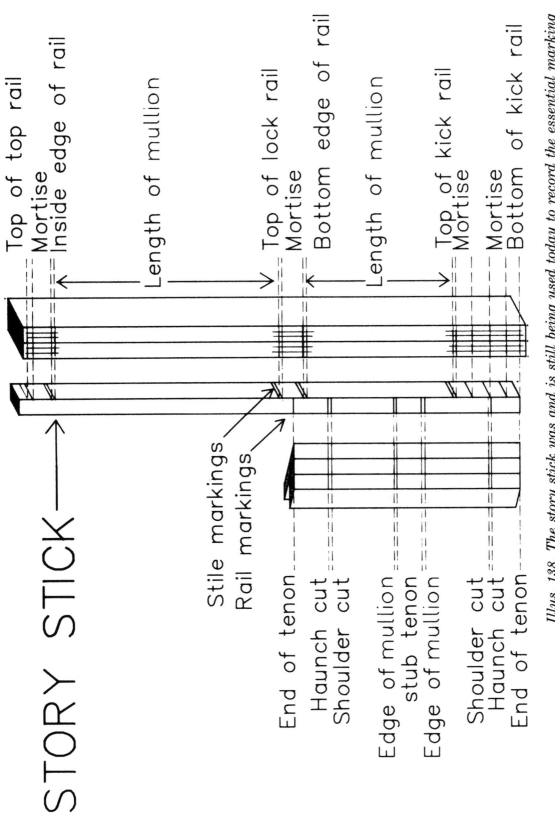

STORY STICK ⟶

Top of top rail
Mortise
Inside edge of rail

Length of mullion

Top of lock rail
Mortise
Bottom edge of rail

Length of mullion

Top of kick rail
Mortise

Mortise
Bottom of kick rail

Stile markings
Rail markings

End of tenon
Haunch cut
Shoulder cut

Edge of mullion
stub tenon
Edge of mullion

Shoulder cut
Haunch cut
End of tenon

Illus. 138. The story stick was and is still being used today to record the essential marking points for the various cuts on both the stiles and rails.

smoothing plane. Two sticks layed across the wood at opposite ends could be sighted to check for twist. By sighting from one end, he could detect the slightest bow or warp. Next, an edge would be straightened and checked for squareness to the side. Most likely, a jointer plane would be used on the edge. When one side and one edge were true, the marking gauge could be used to scratch a line parallel to a true face or edge that would determine the thickness and width of the board. The jointer would then plane or saw to these lines, and at last, a true, dimensioned board would be at hand.

Once the dimensions of the lumber had been determined, the jointer could begin the process know as setting out. For this, a stick of scrap as long as the height of the door was used to make a story stick (Illus. 138). The placement of all the important cuts and joints on the stiles was marked out with square lines across one side of the stick, including both ends of each mortise and haunch, the shoulders of the rails, and the depth of the grooves. On the other side of the stick, or on a separate, shorter stick for convenience, the essential information about the rails, including the shoulder and haunch of the tenons, the placement of mullions and the depth of their grooves, and any other features were indicated. In this way, the essential information about a door could be stored and referred to quickly and easily without possible confusion caused by trying to calculate dimensions, etc.

Now to the serious door building. Assuming you've made your marking stick to the dimensions shown in Illus. 138, use it to mark the top and bottom of the stiles, and make all the intermediate marks indicated for the mortise cuts, etc., along what will be the inside edges of your stiles. Leave an extra inch on your stiles top and bottom for now. This "haunch" will be trimmed off when the door is completed.

Transfer the marks from the stick to one of the stiles; then lay the stiles face to face, inside edges up, and use a small square to extend the marks across the inside edges of both stiles. Our door is based on the sizes of lumber that are commonly available today; so hopefully you won't have to do any ripping or adjusting of the dimensions. If you are using different widths, rip your lumber or adjust your marking stick accordingly.

Use the width side of the stick to mark the overall length of your stock for the rails, and cut them to length. If you are using a hand saw, square the mark across the face and one edge of the board, and cut it carefully, staying to the outside of the line. We will be making through-mortises, as was common in times past, so that the length of the rails will be equal to the full width of the door. Note that the bottom or kick rail is 11 inches wide, while the other two are $5\frac{1}{4}$ inches wide. Again, these are commonly available dimensions, but if you can't get a good, wide board for the kick rail, you can edge-glue two pieces of 2 × 6's and adjust your marking stick for the slightly narrower kick rail that will result.

When you have your rails cut to length, use the marking stick to mark the shoulders of the tenons and the placement of the mullions on the edges. The top and bottom rails will be marked only on the inside edges, while the middle, or lock rail, will be marked on both edges. Check the layout on your marking stick as you do this, by flipping it end for end and making sure that the marks still line up with the ones you just made on the edge of a rail. If the mullion is not perfectly centered,or one or the other of the tenons is longer, you could end up with a strange-looking door if it is not corrected now.

Now extend the tenon shoulder marks all the way around each piece, using a square and a sharp knife and marking very carefully. If the shoulders are not perfectly square and even, your joint will not close on one side.

After you have squared around all the pieces, set your marking gauge to mark the thickness of the tenons. Ideally, your tenons and mortises should be the same width as the grooves you will plow to hold the panels. This should be approximately one-third of the total thickness of the door, but in practice it will depend on the tools you are using to cut both the mortise and the groove and the thickness of the material you intend to use for your panels. Half-inch-thick tenons will work for almost any door up to 1¾ inches thick. For panels, you may want to use ¾- or 1½-inch-thick solid wood or plywood, which comes in a variety of thicknesses. The width of your panel groove will depend on the thickness of your panels, and the treatment you intend to give them in terms of raising them, applying moulding around them, etc.

If you are using a double-pointed marking gauge, you will want to work from the same side on all the pieces; so it will help to lay them all out as they will go, and mark one side of each piece. If you are using a single-pointed marking gauge, you will have

Illus. 139. When cutting tenons by hand, mark the shoulder line and the thickness of the tenon all the way around the workpiece.

to mark from both sides, but you can be assured of having your tenons exactly centered. Mark the slots for the mortises in the same manner.

The order of cutting is up to the individual craftsperson. One old English jointer recommends cutting the mortises first, and then the shoulders of the tenons, but not the long cut until after the grooves have been plowed. Another well-known hand worker likes to cut the tenons first, then the mortises, and finally the grooves. Certainly, it makes sense to cut the mortises before the grooves if there is a difference in their width or placement, as can happen if thin panels or panels offset to one side of the door are used; everything else can be done the way you prefer to do it.

Much of the waste can be removed from the mortises by boring a series of holes down their length with a drill bit of the same size or slightly smaller than the width of the mortise (Illus. 140). Don't drill all the

Illus. 140. Mortises were generally bored out before being squared and trimmed with a wide, flat chisel (to flatten the cheeks) and mortising chisel (to chop across the grain).

way through. Work from both sides towards the middle to avoid chipping out as you come through, and to minimize any error in the squareness of your boring. After boring, use a chisel the same width as the mortise to chip away between the holes, and possibly a wider chisel to pare the walls or cheeks of the mortises down flat and true. Again, work from both edges towards the middle.

Now you are ready to plow the grooves that will hold the panels. In the old days, a special plowing plane, much like a narrow rabbet plane with a fence and a depth stop, was used to do this work. Today, it is almost always done with a dado blade on the table saw, but it can also be done with a slotting cutter on a router or on a spindle shaper.

Illus. 141. A swan's-neck chisel will work well for deep mortises.

Whatever your method, plow them all the way through on all the pieces, once again being careful always to work from the same side of the door on each piece, so that the grooves will all line up with each other. As indicated before, the grooves may not always be perfectly centered on the edges of the framework. You can, if you want, be assured of centering them perfectly by cutting twice, working from both sides of the pieces. It will be quicker though to carefully set your tool for the placement you want and work from just one side.

When you are ready to cut your tenons, use a sharp chisel and cut in lightly from the tenon side towards the shoulder line to get a shallow groove in which to start your saw (Illus. 142–144). Then with the work clamped flat to the table, use a sharp backsaw or dovetail saw to cut the shoulders; make sure you cut squarely, and, if anything, undercut them, so that the outside of the joint will close tightly (Illus. 145 and 146). Now put the work in the vise, and cut down the outsides of the lines made with

Illus. 142–144. To start the shoulder cut on the tenon, use a sharp knife to score the grain (Illus. 142, right) and then a shallow, paring cut with a chisel (Illus. 143) to cut a shallow groove in which to start the saw (Illus. 144).

Illus. 143.

Illus. 144.

HAND CUTTING A TENON

1. Shoulder cut

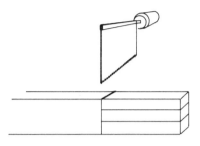

2. Cheek cut

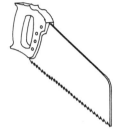

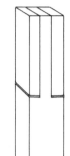

*Illus. 145 and 146 (below).
Start the shoulder cut (1) first
with a fine backsaw. The cheek
cut (2) can either be sawn with
a ripping or panel saw or the
waste can be split away with a
chisel (Illus. 146, below) and
the cheek cleaned up with a
rabbet plane.*

3. Completed tenon

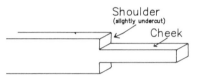

Shoulder
(slightly undercut)

Cheek

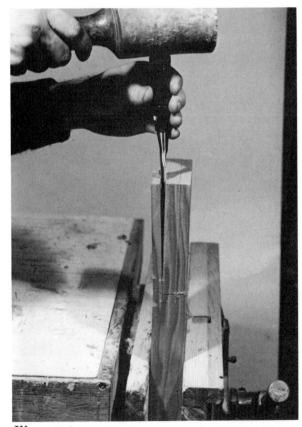

Illus. 146.

the marking gauge to complete the tenon. Leave it thick if anything. It's easy to plane and pare the tenon down from here to the proper thickness. You may have to use a different saw to make this cut because of its depth. If the grain is very straight, you can also split the bulk of the waste away and flatten the cheeks with a rabbet plane. Calipers will be very helpful in determining when you have attained the right thickness.

Once the waste on either side of the tenon has been removed, you can "haunch" the tenons by cutting away the waste at both ends with a small backsaw (Illus. 147). Be sure and leave enough of a haunch to fill the groove at the end of the stiles. The large tenons on the kick, or bottom, rails are usually divided into two smaller tenons by removing a part from the middle of the tenon. This eases the strain of contraction and expansion that would be considerable over such a large surface. It also adds meted panel to expand and force a joint apart, not to mention the trouble it will give you when you are trying to assemble the door; so resist the temptation to fit the panels too tightly.

Special panel-raising planes were used before the advent of power tools to cut a raised panel (Illus. 148). The plane typically left a bevelled profile where the panel fit into the groove, so that it would make its tightest contact along the outer edges of the grooves. Often in older doors, only one side of the panel was raised.

Another method of raising panels by hand is to cut a saw kerf around the area that

Illus. 147. Mark the haunch from the story stick after cutting the cheeks, and cut it with a small backsaw.

Illus. 148. Before the advent of power tools, raised panels were made with special panel-raising planes that had a spur to score the grain and a skewed blade to cut cleanly across the grain.

chanical strength to the joint. The parts of the tenon that are to be removed can be sawn into wedges and used at assembly time to wedge the joint tight.

When all the mortises, tenons, and grooves have been cut, the door can be dry-assembled, and measurements taken for the panels. The panels should be about $\frac{1}{16}$ inch smaller in both directions than the distance from bottom of groove to bottom of groove. It is possible for a too tightly fit-

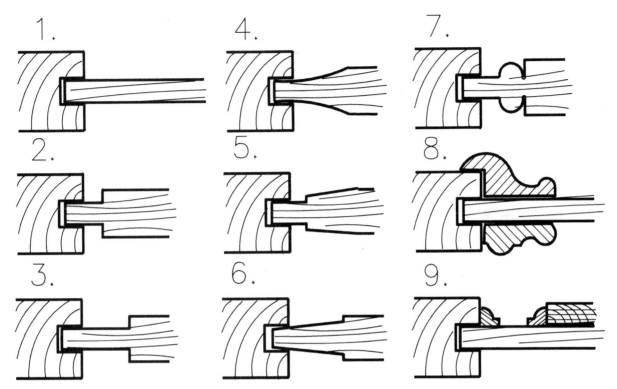

Illus. 149. Various panel and moulding details are possible, even when you work entirely by hand. The simplest, #1, is a flat panel with no frame moulding; 2 and 3 are rabbet-cut panels set at different distances from the frame. The rabbets are cut with a back saw, and the waste removed with a rabbet plane. Number 4 is made with a round-bottomed plane; 5 and 6 are combinations of rabbet cuts and bevelled planing with either rabbet planes or special panel-raising planes. Number 7 is made with a beading plane, and 8 and 9 show some designs possible with applied mouldings and plywood glued on to give the effect of a raised panel.

is to be removed with a backsaw and a clamp-on guide, and then use a rabbet plane to plane this area down to the thickness of the groove. This can be done either flat or at a shallow bevel. When hand-planing raised panels, a short section of frame stock with the groove cut in it, called a mullet, is used to check the thickness of the panel edges as the work progresses.

The visual effect of raised panels can also be obtained by using flat stock and laminating pieces to form the raised part in the middle of the door. Mouldings can also be applied after the door is glued up both around the framework and around the raised part of the panel to dress up the appearance of the door.

Special moulding planes were often used on both the edges of the raised part of the panel and the edges of the framework to soften and decorate these areas. These moulding cuts need not run around all four corners of the panel, nor must they meet in a mitre at the corners of the framework. Handmade panels were often moulded only along two edges, and mitred corners on the framework were avoided by stopping the moulding just short of each corner.

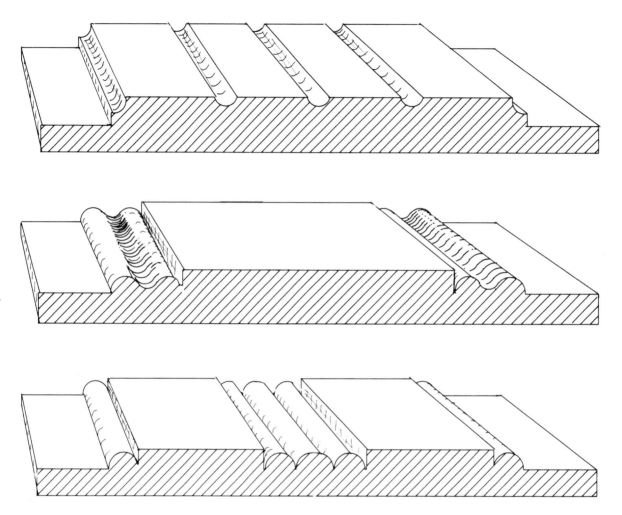

Illus. 150. One alternative to hand-made raised panels is grooved panels, in which grooves, coves, or beads are cut with the grain, and the ends of the raised part are simply bevelled off.

Panels should be completely smoothed and sanded, and at least one coat of sealer applied before the door is assembled. The end grain should be carefully sealed with several coats of oil soaked in, or with a carefully applied coat of glue that is allowed to dry before assembly. It is possible for moisture to work its way into the grooves, and be taken up into the panels, causing excessive expansion and contraction and lessening the life of the door by many years.

Make one final dry fit, to make sure that everything will go together tightly before the final assembly. Be sure to mark the proper position of the upright mullion on the rails. Since it has only stub tenons that can slide back and forth in the grooves, it is important to be sure that it is carefully positioned.

Urea resin glue is recommended for panel doors, even if they aren't exterior doors, because of its longer working time.

Aliphatic resin glues, which are fine for simple assemblies like cabinet doors, begin to "set up" within minutes, and can freeze joints before they can be fully tightened. Cover both sides of all the joints with glue, but don't get carried away. A very thin, brushed-on coat is all that's necessary if your joints are nicely fit.

Assembly

A four-panel door can be tricky to assemble. One approach is to begin by first assembling all the rails, panels, and mullions flat on your assembly surface. Then use long bar clamps to hold them together while working the stile into place along the sides (Illus. 151).

Another method is to stand one stile on edge, held firmly in the vise, and supported at the other end, and to build up from one edge to the other, using gravity to help you. With this method it will be easier to get clamps on both sides of the door as needed, but you will still have to do some fancy clamping to get both the joints where the mullions meet the rails and the joints where the rails and stiles tightly meet.

When the joints are all nearly tight, remove the clamps from all but one of the horizontal joints, and then using two long bar clamps on one side of the door, clamp the door from top to bottom; then check the measurements from top to bottom on each end of the rails, and tighten one clamp or the other until they are the same. When the mullions are tight on the rails, and the rails are perfectly parallel, another clamp can be placed across the other end of the door and tightened.

Now the two horizontal clamps will hold the stiles tightly against the rails, which will keep the joints on the ends of the mullions tight. The long clamps can now be removed, and more clamps can be placed across both sides of the door to tighten all the joints.

When this is done, check with a straight-edge to be sure that the stiles are not being cocked to one side or the other by uneven clamping pressure (Illus. 152). Usually two clamps, one on either side of the door, at each rail will be sufficient.

A more traditional way of assembling a four-panel door is to use pegs, bored through the mortise-and-tenon joints, with the holes slightly offset so as to draw the joint tightly together when the pegs are driven home (Illus. 153). This is done by dry-assembling the door, and boring through from one side just far enough to pass through the cheek of the mortise and mark the tenon without actually boring through it. The door is then disassembled and the holes in the stiles are bored on through to the other side. The tenons are then bored, but with the holes offset by about $\frac{1}{16}$ inch, so as to draw the joint up tight when pegs with tapered ends are driven through.

On through tenons, an alternate method is to drive wedges in from the outside to hold the joint and prevent it from working loose (Illus. 154). For this method, cut kerfs in your tenons, and widen the mortises a bit towards the outside. The wedges must be of a very shallow angle, and glue should be applied to prevent them from working loose. Don't drive them in until after the joint is clamped up tight, as they won't do much to draw the joint up. Once they are in, they can be trimmed, and the clamps can be removed.

109

Urea resin glue should be cured in temperatures above 75 degrees F. for at least eight hours. After the glue is dry and the clamps are removed, the door should be planed flat, especially around the joints, with a sharp smoothing plane. Use the plane to remove any other defects; then scrape and sand to finish.

ASSEMBLING A FOUR-PANEL DOOR

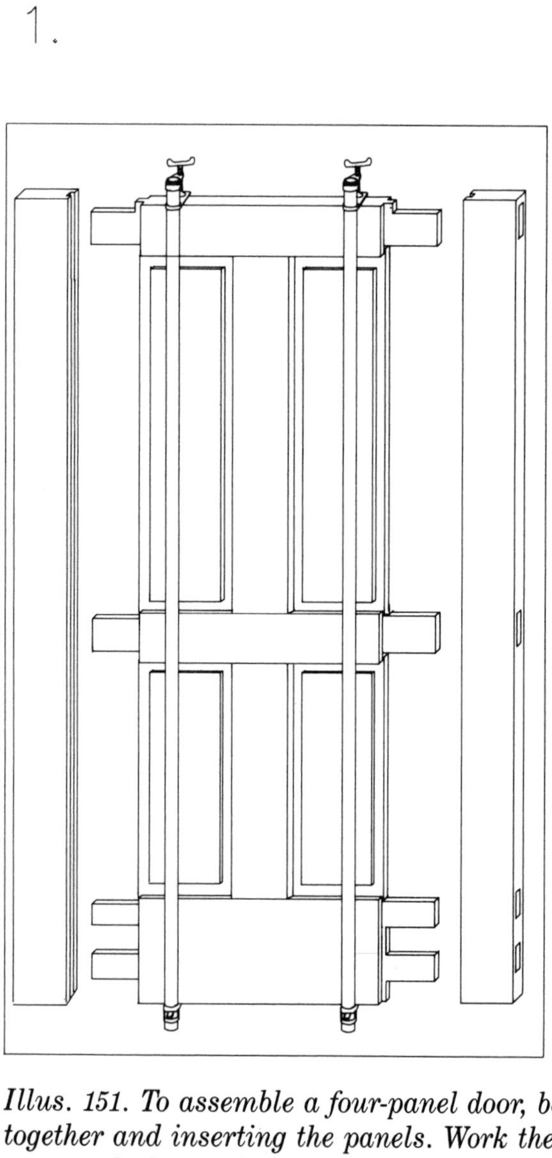

1.

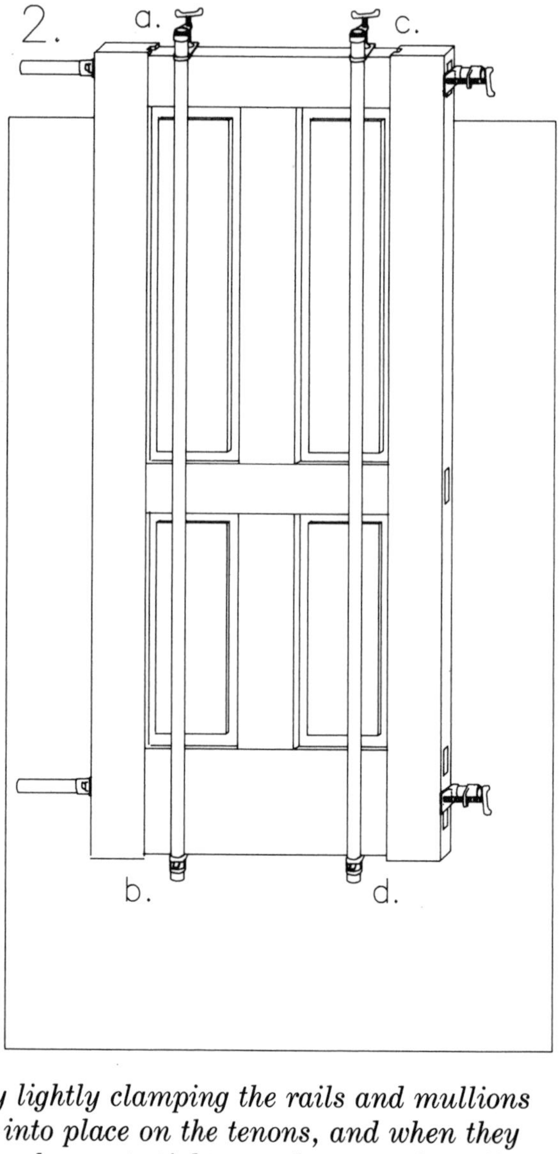

2.

Illus. 151. To assemble a four-panel door, begin by lightly clamping the rails and mullions together and inserting the panels. Work the stiles into place on the tenons, and when they are nearly home clamp one end tight; use the long clamps to tighten and square the rails on the mullions. Be sure the mullions are centered on the rails, and that the distance from A to B and C to D is the same. Then apply another cross clamp at the other end and remove the long clamps.

110

Illus. 152. Always check with a straightedge that the stiles are flat with the rails.

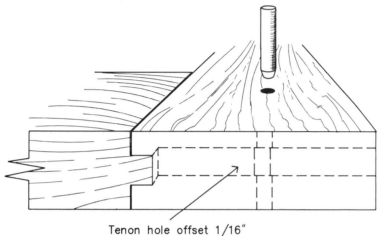

Tenon hole offset 1/16"

Illus. 153. A traditional method of tightening mortise-and-tenon joints is called draw-pegging. The offset hole in the tenon draws the joint tightly together when the peg is driven in, and holds well even without glue.

A WEDGED TENON

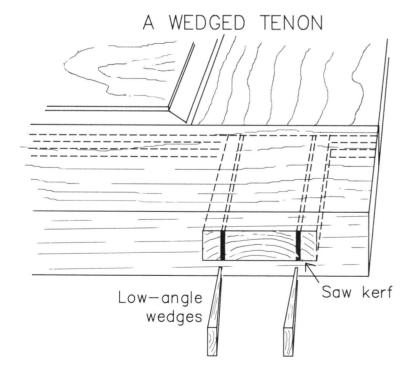

Low—angle wedges

Saw kerf

Illus. 154. Wedged tenons can also be used to keep the joint tight, even if the glue doesn't hold.

6
Small-Shop Door-Making Techniques

In this chapter I will discuss a wide variety of techniques for making doors with a few of the common power tools found in most modern amateur woodworking shops. Layered and laminate doors could, of course, be built by anyone with these tools, but since they have already been discussed in the previous chapter, they won't be mentioned here.

A good table saw and a half-inch-collet plunge router or a drill press are the only power tools that are absolutely necessary for most of these techniques. A band saw would also be handy for many of these doors, but a jigsaw could be used instead in most cases. If you don't have a planer, you will have to buy your lumber dimensioned or take it to someone to have it done. If your jointer is not big enough to handle a 6-inch by 7-foot stile, then be sure to choose your lumber carefully for straightness.

Other handy tools for these techniques include a cutoff or chop saw, a hand-held electric planer, an orbital sander, a hand-held electric drill, and, of course, a complete array of good hand tools. You may want to review Chapter 1 to make some of the important jigs and fixtures that will be needed. I'll begin by discussing a couple of ways to make the mortise joints between the stiles and rails of panel doors, how to make tenon, spline-tenon, and dowel joints, and then describe the construction of several doors using these and other techniques.

Making Mortise-and-Tenon Joints

The mortise-and-tenon joint has from time immemorial been the main structural joint of the frame-and-panel door. In Chapter 5 I described its construction without the use of power tools. Here I'll discuss a couple of methods of making these joints with modern power tools.

Generally, it is best to make your mortises first. It is much easier to adjust the position or thickness of the tenon by setting the cut, or later by hand after the machining is done, than to change the mortise. Cut the mortise first; then cut the tenon to fit it, leaving it slightly larger than needed, if anything, so that it can be planed or pared to the perfect fit.

Whenever possible, position the mortises in the exact center of the edge of the stiles. Even if the panel slot is offset for one reason or another, the mortise should be centered. This will save time and effort in the cutting of the tenons, because once the saw is set, the pieces can simply be run through twice—once on each side—to make a perfectly centered tenon.

The best method for centering the mortises is to use a machinist's calipers to carefully check the thickness of the cheeks on either side of a test piece that is exactly the same thickness as the frame stock you are using (Illus. 155). Set the guide fence on your drill press or router as close to centered as you can get it by lining up the cutter on the marks you have made with your marking gauge; then make a test cut, and check it with the calipers. When the cheeks are exactly the same thickness, the mortises are centered. Keep the calipers handy while you are cutting the mortises, and check every couple of cuts to make sure the mortises stay accurate.

Using the Drill Press or Mortise Machine

Until very recently, the most common method of machine-cutting mortises was with a drill press or mortising machine and a square chisel-boring attachment (Illus. 156). These attachments come in sizes from

Illus. 155. Use a machinist's calipers to center your mortises. The cheek on either side of the mortise should be exactly the same thickness.

Illus. 156. When using a hollow mortising chisel, make a series of holes spaced about ¼ inch apart along the mortise, and then come back and remove the wood between the holes.

¼- to ½-inch thickness and will usually cut no deeper than 3 inches in one cut. The twist bit inside the hollow chisel bores the middle of the hole and removes the waste; the square chisel is advanced by downward pressure and squares out the hole. Care must be taken not to overheat the chisels, thus ruining the temper of the steel. The bits and chisels can be purchased separately, and are quite expensive. A special quill attachment is also necessary for this type of mortising, as well as a fence and hold-down attachment that is bolted to the drill-press table.

If you plan to mortise this way, you will have to mark out the positions of your mortises in the same manner as that described on page 113. If you are making several doors with the same configuration, you can mark out the positions of the mortises on one of them; then lay them out side by side with the inside edges up, and use a square to transfer the position markings from one to the other (Illus. 157). You won't have to use the marking gauge to mark the sides of the mortises because they will be automatically positioned by the fence once it is set up.

When you are using this method, an out-feed roller or table extension of some kind will be necessary to support one end of the stile while you are working on the other end. If you have carefully centered the mortise on the edge of the piece, you will be able to work from either side, which will eliminate having to move the support roller from one end to the other.

When everything is properly lined up, cut one hole at the end of your mortise; then move down and make the next cut about ¼ inch away from the first one. Continue

Illus. 157. You can use a square to mark the ends of several mortises at once.

in this manner until you have covered the entire length of the mortise. Leaving this space between your cuts will prevent the chisel from deflecting towards the hole you have just cut, which can cause damage to the cutters. Now, go back and center your cutter on the areas between the holes, and remove the remaining waste.

Mortising with the Plunge Router

In the last few years, the plunge router has become a popular tool for cutting mortises. For this method you need a ½-inch-collet plunge router with a rating of at least 1½ horsepower and a fence attachment. A spiral-fluted ½-inch by 2½-inch carbide cut-

114

ter will give you the best results and last the longest in both hard and soft woods (Illus. 158).

Illus. 158. Either a straight or spiral-fluted router cutter will work well for plunge-routing mortises. One-half-inch shank bits are available in lengths up to 4⅛ inches.

Mark the positions of the mortises on the edges of the stiles as already described; then put a trial piece that's the same thickness as your frame stock in the bench vise, and carefully set the fence on the router base so that it cuts a slot that is perfectly centered on the edge of the piece. Make as many test cuts on the trial piece as you need to be sure it is right. Plunge the bit into the wood and move it slowly along the work until you find the depth of cut that works well without overloading the router or causing the bit to chatter. You will note during these test cuts that when you cut in one direction, the rotating bit holds the fence tightly against the work, while in the other direction it tends to "wander." Make all your cuts in the direction that holds the fence to the work.

Once you have the fence set right, tighten the setscrews as tightly as possible by hand. A pair of pliers can be used to get them a little tighter, but be careful not to crack the castings of the router base. Now, take your marking gauge and set it for the exact center of the edge of the workpiece. Mark the center of the edge at the end of the mortise where you will be starting all your cutting passes, and bore a half-inch hole here to the depth that the mortise will be cut (Illus. 159). This is to ease the entry of the router bit into the wood. Most straight-cutting router bits do not bore well (though they will if enough pressure is applied), and will last considerably longer if you bore the starter hole separately.

Once you have bored all the starter holes, you can begin cutting the mortises. Drop the bit into approximately the right depth, lock the plunge mechanism, and draw the router slowly along the work until you reach the other end. When you reach the other end of the mortise, release the plunge lock, and pull the bit all the way out of the mortise before moving it back to the starting hole. A 3-inch-deep mortise can be made with 4 to 10 passes, depending on the hardness of the wood.

Through mortises can be made in stiles up to 6 inches wide simply by marking carefully on both edges and cutting in from

Illus. 159. Preboring a ½-inch or smaller hole at the starting end of the mortise before routing will ease the entry of the bit and prevent overheating.

both edges to the middle. Deeper mortises can be routed, and then bored, and finally chiselled with a mortising chisel of the proper width.

Generally, a board 1½ inches thick, or thicker, will provide a wide enough surface to stabilize the router while doing this type of mortising, but for narrower stock, or for windows where the mortises must be very close to the ends of the stiles, a mortising jig like the one shown in Illus. 160 can be

made. The jig holds the stiles or rails firmly and triples the width of the surface that the router base rides on. Adjustable end stops can also be incorporated in the jig.

It is also possible to make your own horizontal mortiser using a plunge router and a sliding table mechanism that is sold as an accessory for Inca table saws (Illus. 161). Once again, an outboard roller will be necessary to support one end of a stile while the other is mortised.

Making Tenons

The other half of the mortise-and-tenon joint, the tenon, must be cut with equal care (if you elect to use this method) so that the joint will be as strong as possible and close tightly on both sides. Most older doors have tenons that run all the way through the stiles, and can be seen along the outer edge of the door. This appears at first glance to be a stronger joint than a blind tenon, but it exposes end grain that can soak up moisture and become rotted quicker. It also weakens the stile somewhat, and requires more time in the cutting of the mortise; so it has fallen out of fashion. More common today is a blind tenon, cut about 2½ inches to 3 inches deep.

The shoulder cut is the most critical part of the cutting sequence for the tenon. It must be perfectly square both across the rail and when viewed from the edge. It may help to set your saw blade so that it actually undercuts the shoulder a bit, ensuring that the outer edges of the joint will close tightly. The most accurate way to do this is with a table saw and a clamp-on fence that is square and parallel to the blade. If you are cutting a through tenon, you can use

JIG FOR ROUTER MORTISING

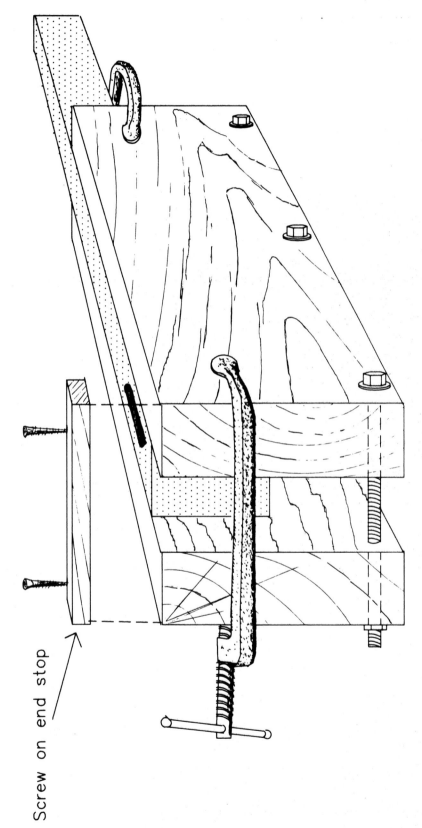

Screw on end stop

Illus. 160. A jig like this one, used for plunge-routing mortises, will help steady the router on narrow stock. End stops can be screwed on as well.

A SHOP—MADE MORTISING MACHINE

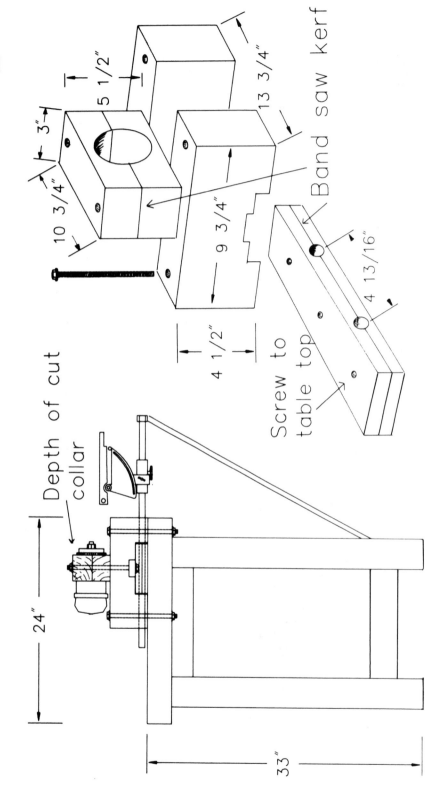

Depth of cut collar

24"

33"

10 3/4"

3"

5 1/2"

13 3/4"

9 3/4"

4 1/2"

4 13/16"

Band saw kerf

Screw to table top

Illus. 161. For under $300 in materials, you can make a horizontal mortiser. The table, which slides in and out and from side to side, is an accessory for the Inca table saw, and is available separately.

Illus. 162. You can use the stile to help get the fence perfectly parallel to the blade if you are making a through tenon.

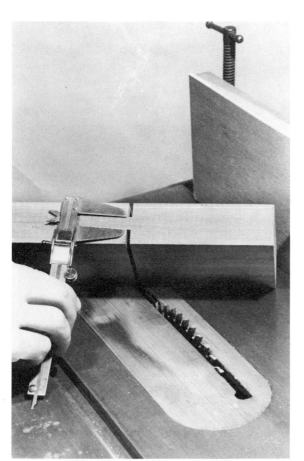

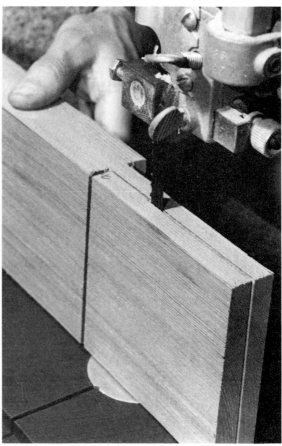

Illus. 163 (above left). Use the calipers again to check the shoulder cut you made on a piece of scrap to be sure that the tenon will be just the right thickness. Illus. 164 (above right). The band saw can be used to remove the waste from the cheeks of the tenon, but be sure to cut to the outsides of your lines, and hand-plane to the final thickness.

the stile to get your fence set at the right distance and parallel to the blade, as shown in Illus. 162.

Use a scrap piece of wood the same thickness as your frame stock to test the height of the cut until it leaves a tenon that is just right for your mortise. As you make the cuts, keep the end of the workpiece tight against the fence and be careful not to cock it one way or the other. This method is safe as long as the end of the piece is at least 4 inches wide. For narrower pieces, use a sliding cutoff table with a clamp-on stop. The haunch cuts can usually be made with the same saw setup as was used for the shoulder cuts.

The waste can now be removed from the cheeks of the tenon by any of several methods. If your tenon is fairly short, you may be able to do it with two more cuts with the table saw by raising the blade as high as the length of the tenon, and resetting the fence closer to the blade. Now stand the rail on end and run it against the fence so that it will remove the waste from each side in one cut.

Other options for longer tenons that can't be cut with the table saw include repeated cuts across the length of the cheeks, splitting, and, finally, planing the tenon to the desired thickness and band-sawing carefully along lines drawn with a marking gauge. If you band-saw, be sure to stay outside the lines, and use a plane to get the tenon to its final thickness.

Spline-Tenon Joint

The spline-tenon joint is a variation on the mortise-and-tenon joint in which mortises are cut both on the edges of the stiles and the ends of the rails, and a long spline is glued into both pieces to hold them together (Illus. 165). With the plunge router method of cutting mortises, it is quite easy to cut a mortise into the end of the rail (an operation that would be nearly impossible on a drill press). A piece of 2 × 6 clamped to the bench surface as shown in Illus. 166 or a mortising jig like the one shown in Illus. 160 will help steady the router and keep it square to the edge while working the shorter rail ends. This method can save considerable time and materials because the splines can be made from scrap or end cuts, and because you won't have to take the time to carefully set up the table saw for at least two different cuts for the tenons. The same setting of the router fence is used on both the stiles and the rail ends. This method is also helpful when making cope-and-stick joints because there is no tenon to get in the way of the cope cut.

Dowelling

Dowelling is an acceptable method of joining stiles and rails for interior doors, but it is not recommended for any exterior doors because it lacks the strength to hold the joint firmly through years of weather-induced swelling and shrinking, as well as general use (Illus. 167). The good gluing-surface area between the dowel and the stile is minimal because much of the wood in the stile that comes in contact with the dowel will be end grain. End grain does not hold well when glued to edge grain. Dowelled joints will often begin to separate in just a few years if the door is not well protected from the elements.

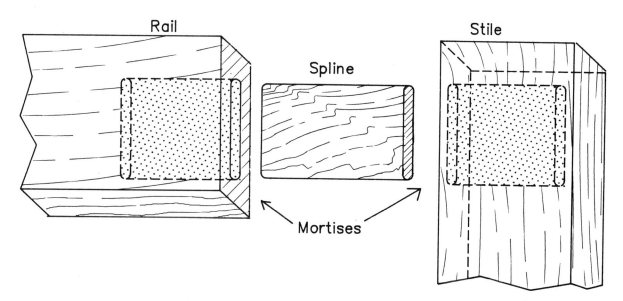

Illus. 165. The spline–tenon joint is a variation on the mortise-and-tenon joint that works well with modern weatherproof glues, and greatly simplifies door and window joinery for small shop builders.

Illus. 166. To plunge-rout the mortise on the ends of the rails for the spline–tenon joint, use a jig like the one shown in Illus. 160 or hold the workpiece in the vise and clamp a piece of thick stock to the table top to provide a surface for the router to ride on.

Illus. 167. Dowelled corner joints are acceptable for windows and interior doors, but should not be used for exterior doors.

Illus. 168. Drive all dowels through a sizer to prevent splitting caused by swollen or oversized dowels.

If you are going to use dowels in a door, be sure they are at least ½ inch thick and as long as possible. You can make your own dowels by ripping stock to ½ × ½-inch sticks; then rounding them off with four passes of a ¼-inch round-over bit on the router table. Finally, drive them through a dowel sizer to groove and size them (Illus. 168). Space them about 1½ inches apart, and coat both the insides of the holes and the dowel itself with glue before assembly. Avoid hammering the dowels into their holes, as the sudden blows can cause your lumber to crack. A slot or kerf along the length of the dowel will allow the glue to flow out of the hole without building up enough pressure to cause cracking. Bevelling the tips with a pencil sharpener or disc sander will also ease the assembly.

Either a dowelling jig and electric hand drill or a horizontal boring machine can be used to bore the holes for the dowels. Dowelling jigs can be slow and tedious to use, but they are accurate, and are cheap compared to a horizontal boring machine.

Custom Door-Making Techniques

The door designs and descriptions discussed on pages 123–155 illustrate the wide variety of structural and decorative techniques that are available to small-shop builders who are working without shapers. Strong, beautiful, and unique doors can certainly be made without the use of large production equipment, but you will have to make your design decisions carefully, and work efficiently to build a product that is competitive in price. Still, there's a lot to be said for taking your time and doing it right. Even if it is more expensive, people will appreciate your work if it shows skill and a concern for the lasting quality of the product.

Preparing the Frame Stock

The preparation of the frame stock will be basically the same for all these doors. The only major variable will be in determining the length of the rails. This will depend on the type of joint used where the rails meet the stiles. If you are using the spline-tenon method, the rails will be cut to the total width of the door, minus the combined width of the stiles. A 36-inch-wide door with 5¼-inch stiles would have 25½-inch rails. If the tenons will be cut from the rails, you will have to add twice the depth of the mortises to the figure. So a 36-inch-wide door with integral tenons and 3-inch-deep mortises in 5¼-inch stiles would need rails 31½ inches in length. A 36-inch-wide door with through tenons would need 36-inch-long rails to begin with.

It is always helpful to sit down before you begin cutting material (but with the lumber at hand so that you know the widths you can get) and make a cutting list. List the number of pieces of each length and width that you will need. Now, rough-cut the stiles to about ½ inch longer than the height of the finished door, and cut the material for the rails to about an inch longer than the length you will need for them.

At this point you can carefully joint an edge, and, if necessary, a face of each board, and use these perfectly straight and flat surfaces to rip and plane the stock to uniform widths and a uniform thickness. The minimum width for the stiles and rails is 4¾ inches, except for the kick rail, which should be at least twice that width. If you are making an especially wide door, or using a moulding that will overlap or take up part of this width, you may want to increase this width to 5¼ inches or more. Mullions and other interior frame members are often narrower.

If you don't have any stock that is wide enough for the kick rail, you can carefully edge-join two or more pieces to get the desired width. You may want to do this before planing the lumber to thickness, but it can also be done afterward, as long as you are very careful in aligning the pieces. Some hand planing along the joint will remove any squeezed-out glue or unevenness.

When all the stock is ripped, jointed, and planed, the rails should be carefully cut to the exact length necessary. Whichever joinery method you use, remember that this is one of the most critical operations in making your door. The rails must all be exactly the same length, and the end cuts must be perfectly square in both directions. You will be using these cuts as a reference later when you make the all-important shoulder cuts for the tenons (if that is the method you choose); so they must be perfect.

One of the best methods for cutting the rails to their exact length is the crosscutting jig used for the table saw (Illus. 56). A carefully tuned and sharpened radial arm saw will also give good results. A 60- to 100-tooth alternate-top-bevel carbide blade, or a fine-toothed plywood blade, should be used for best results.

When you have prepared the stock and cut all the pieces to length, you are ready to make the joints that will hold the framework together. Refer to pages 112–122 for a description of the various methods.

Doors

Victorian Screen Door

This is really a very simple door to make, but it requires strong joinery because of its

A VICTORIAN SCREEN DOOR

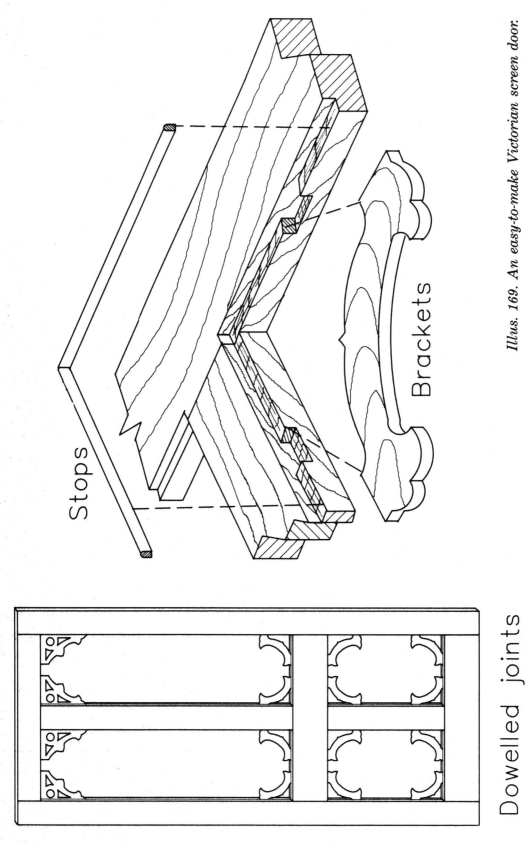

Stops

Brackets

Dowelled joints

Illus. 169. An easy-to-make Victorian screen door.

lightness (Illus. 169). The stock is milled down from a thickness of 1½ inches to 1 inch. Mortise-and-tenon joints at the corners are necessary to give strength to such a light door, especially since screen doors often take the brunt of the weather, and are slammed a lot because of the springs that people put on them. The corner brackets, cut from ¼-inch marine plywood, and glued and nailed into slots, will also help strengthen the door, as well as support the screen somewhat.

Begin by cutting the frame pieces to size, leaving enough extra length on the rails for the tenons (unless you choose to make spline-tenon joints). The vertical mullions do not have to be tenoned. Dowels or a short spline-tenon joint will serve here. Glue up the frame and allow it to dry before cutting the rabbets for the screen.

When the assembled frame has dried, use a rabbeting bit with a ball-bearing guide to cut a ⅜-inch deep by ¼ inch wide rabbet around each of the "panels" on what will be the inside of the door. The corners will have to be squared out with a sharp chisel (Illus. 170). Go slowly with the routing to avoid chipping out the material.

Now, the corner brackets can be marked out on the ¼-inch material and cut out carefully with a scroll saw. Leave ¼-inch tabs on the ends of the brackets to provide attachment to the door. Take each bracket and from the corner of the frame measure a set distance out to where the mortise will start that the tab will fit into. Position the tabs for each bracket on the door, and mark around it; then use the router with the same rabbet cutter, but set the tab mortises ¼ inch deeper. You will have to square out the mortises by hand with a sharp chisel (Illus. 171), but the router will help get the depth right.

Glue and nail the tabs in place (use a good weatherproof glue), and paint or finish the entire door before applying the screen. First staple the screen in place, and then apply wooden stops to cover the edges of the screens.

Illus. 170. The corners of router-cut rabbets must be marked and squared out by hand with a sharp chisel.

Illus. 171. Use a sharp chisel to square out the mortises that hold the corner brackets.

Illus. 172. Corner bracket.

Door with Applied Moulding, Raised Panel, and Glass

This simple Victorian door will work nicely as either an entryway door, a kitchen door,

or a back door (Illus. 175). The panel in this door is constructed by applying a ½-inch-thick piece of redwood to ½-inch exterior plywood (inside and out). A narrow applied moulding is glued and nailed around the appliqué to give the impression of a fancy raised panel.

Once the stock has been prepared and the joints have been cut, the door can be laid out on the assembly table (minus the panel and glass) and carefully clamped together. Check each rail for squareness, and position the lock rail so that the top edge of it is 39 inches above the bottom of the door. When everything is right, make some indexing marks across the joints where each piece meets another, and label each piece to help keep them straight when it comes to final assembly. For now, leave the door dry-clamped together with the rails in their exact positions so that the panel slots can be routed.

The slots can be cut for the lower panel with a slotting cutter like the one shown in Illus. 173. Two cutters can sometimes be stacked on one arbor to achieve a ½-inch cut, or two passes with a single ¼-inch cut-

Illus. 173. Use a two-wing slotting cutter to cut the slots for the panel.

Illus. 174. Square out the ends of the slot cuts by chopping straight in with a sharp chisel.

ter can be made. If the two passes are made, one from each side of the door, the slot will be exactly centered, though this is not necessary.

When you have cut the slots all the way around, disassemble the door and square out the ends of the cuts on the stiles by chopping straight in with a sharp chisel (Illus. 174). The ends of the rails may need a little attention, too.

When the slots have been cut, measure the hole for the panel, and be sure to cut the panel at least $1/16$ inch smaller in both directions than the size of the hole (from bottom of slot to bottom of slot). Now set your marking gauge for two inches, and mark the positions for the corners of the appliqués on both sides of the panel. Use these marks to determine the size of the

appliqués, and cut them out. Plane them to thickness if necessary. If you plan to do any routed or carved design in the appliqués, its probably best to do it before gluing them to the panel.

Finally, coat the insides of the appliqués with a fairly thick but even coat of urea resin or epoxy glue, and clamp them in place, doing both sides at once. Be sure to remove any squeezed-out glue before it sets. An alternative construction for a large panel is the three-layer lamination shown in Illus. 177.

Once the glue has set, the mouldings can be nailed and glued in place on the lower panels. Be sure to completely sand and coat all the panels with an oil or sealer before assembling the door. It is especially important to seal the edges and end grain. You may want to dry-assemble the door at this point to be sure the panel will fit in the slots. Hand-plane if necessary to achieve a fit, but leave it as tight as possible.

A ONE—PANEL, ONE—LIGHT APPLIED MOULDING DOOR

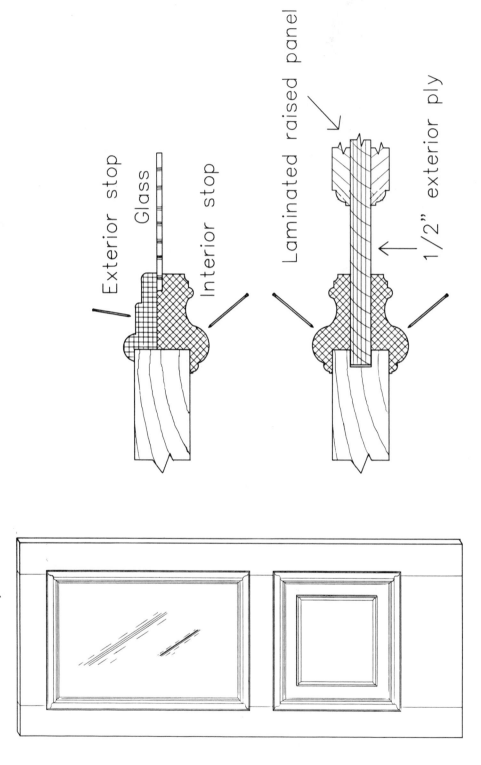

Exterior stop

Glass

Interior stop

Laminated raised panel

1/2" exterior ply

Illus. 175. A simple Victorian door made with a laminated plywood panel and bolection mouldings.

LOW—AND—HIGH PROFILE MOULDINGS

Illus. 176. Cross sections of the mouldings used on the door.

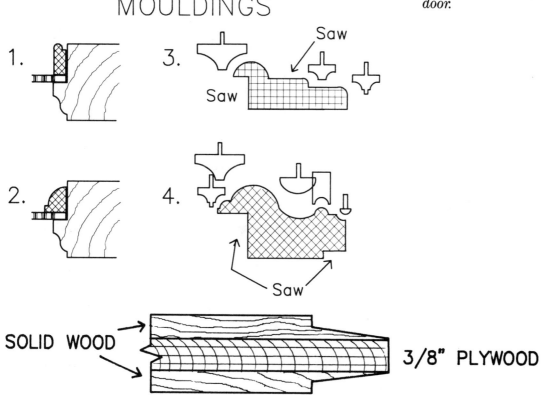

1.

2.

3. Saw

Saw

4. Saw

SOLID WOOD → 3/8" PLYWOOD

Illus. 177. To make the raised panel in this door glue ½-inch-thick solid wood pieces to both sides of a piece of ½-inch exterior plywood. Rout the edges of the appliqués before applying them.

When you have achieved a satisfactory dry fit, you are ready for the final glue-up. Apply a thin, even coat of glue to both sides of all the joints and assemble as described on page 126. Once again, clean up any squeezed-out glue, and allow the glue to cure thoroughly.

Completely flatten and smooth the framework with the hand plane and sander before applying any of the mouldings. Mouldings come in many sizes and patterns, and can generally be applied in one of two ways. The simplest moulding technique is to use a low-profile moulding that fits in along the inner edge of the framework, and comes up approximately flush with the face of the framework. The best results are obtained with this method if the back edge of the moulding is rounded or recessed. This will help hide any irregularities or cracks between the moulding and the framework. The corners are mitred and you can easily mark them by cutting one end, holding the piece in place, and marking the other end with a sharp knife. Small nails should be driven through the moulding at an angle and into the framework to hold it in place (Illus. 178). No glue is necessary.

A more high-profile moulding like the one used for this door can be obtained by rabbeting the back of the moulding to fit over the corner of the framework. This is called a bolection moulding. It is a much better weather sealer, and has a deeper profile, but is tricky to install because the rabbet must be exactly the right depth (you'll have trouble if you had to do a lot of hand planing in places to flatten your framework).

The mitre cuts are difficult to mark because they must be gauged off the rabbet on the back of the moulding. To make the mitre cut, start by mitring one end of the stock (Illus. 179–181). Now lay the moulding

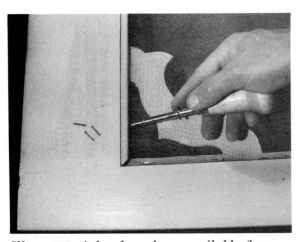

Illus. 178. A brad pusher—available from most hardware dealers—can be used to nail in low-profile mouldings in soft woods.

in place and mark where the rabbet meets the stile. Remember, your marks must be on the inside edge of the rabbet, not on the outer edge of the moulding that will lap over the frame of the door.

Now, flip the moulding over and lay it on the strip that has been tacked on the cutoff table, to hold the flat side of it parallel to the face of the table. Cut the mitre direct-

ly through the mark. Careful attention in setting up the saw and the support strip is necessary to get good results.

To form the rabbet that holds the glass in the upper part of this door, glue a bolection-type moulding to the interior side of the door after the framework has been permanently assembled. Another moulding, or stop as it is called when it holds glass in place, should then be nailed in on the exterior side to hold the glass in place. This stop should not be glued, so that it can be removed in case the glass is broken. You may want to make your own mouldings on the router table, or purchase them precut. Profiles of the mouldings used for this door are shown in Illus. 176.

Alternative Methods of Cutting It is possible to cut all the slots in the pieces for the lower panels with a dado cutter on the table saw. The rails present no problem, but the cuts on the stiles would have to be stopped where the bottom of the lock rail comes in. The best plan, if you want to do it this way, is just to make the cut run between the mortises in the kick and lock rails; however, stop cuts on the table saw are tricky, so be careful.

You can eliminate cutting slots for the panels altogether by carefully gluing and nailing the bolection-type moulding to the edges of the framework after the frame has been assembled in the same manner as the glass (Illus. 182). First do one side and give it time to dry; then insert the panels and attach the moulding to the other side. Here, the outside moulding can also be glued in, but care must be taken that excessive amounts of glue are not used, to avoid gluing the panels to the moulding. With this

Illus. 179–181. To apply bolection-type mouldings, mitre one end, as shown here; then lay it in place and mark the other end on the place where the back of the rabbet meets the stile (Illus. 180). Tack a stick of scrap of the right height to the cutoff saw table to support the moulding so that the flat side of it is parallel to the table (Illus. 181).

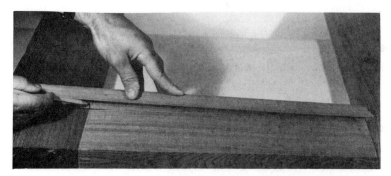

Illus. 180.

Illus. 181.

BOLECTION MOULDED PANEL

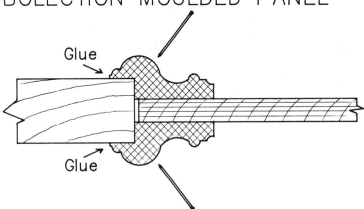

Glue

Glue

Illus. 182. Cutting panel slots in the framework can be eliminated altogether with bolection-type moulding.

method, you can even seat the panels in a bedding of a flexible caulk, to improve the watertightness of the construction. Still, with this type of construction there is a much greater chance of the panels warping and breaking the moulding loose; so it should only be used on interior doors or doors that are well protected from the weather.

Two-Panel Door with Routed Moulding and Tongue-and-Groove Panels

This is another door (Illus. 183) that is best not used in exposed places because of the largeness of the panels and the fact that the tongue-and-groove boards can shrink, opening up cracks between them, in dry parts of the year. Still, this would make an excellent closet or interior door. For a very lightweight door, you might want to plane the framework down to 1⅜ or 1¼ inch and use ⅜-inch tongue-and-groove panelling that is available from many building-supply dealers. You can also make your own T&G stock to any thickness you want and from any wood you want on either the router table or table saw.

After you have prepared all the stock and made all the corner joints, assemble the framework and clamp the pieces in the exact positions that they will occupy in the finished door. Now, choose a router bit to make the decorative bead around the inside edges of the framework. A quarter-round ogee or even a cove or chamfering bit will work nicely (Illus. 184). The critical factor here is the depth of its cut. You will need a space between your beads (on each edge) that will be wide enough for a slot for your panel stock plus at least ⅛ inch on either side for the guide bearing of the slotting cutter to ride on. If you are working with 1⅜-inch frame material and ⅝-inch panel material, you won't have room for a quarter-round and bead on both sides. The most you could do would be an ⅛-inch cove or chamfer.

For a closet or cabinet door, you might consider doing the decorative bead on only one side, but for an entry or passage door, the best solution would be thicker frame stock and thinner panel stock.

It is always best to use router bits with ball-bearing guides if you have them, but if you are using a pin-type guide, a coat of wax or silicone on the pin, light pressure (make several light passes), and constant, fairly rapid movement of the router along the wood will help prevent difficult-to-remove burned spots. Be especially careful not to linger in the corners. Here the cutter is in contact with more wood, and will also tend to burn. Burned marks on the decorative bead itself are especially hard to remove (use coarse sandpaper or a very sharp chisel or scraper), and are mainly caused by dull bits or too slow a feed rate.

If you do have a few burn marks from the guide pin, wait until after you cut the slot to remove them. Once again, the slot is best cut with a slotting cutter in the router, but can also be done with the dado cutter on the table saw. On this door, you could cut the slots all the way through on the stiles if you leave haunches or stub tenons to fill them.

Make sure you chop the corners of the

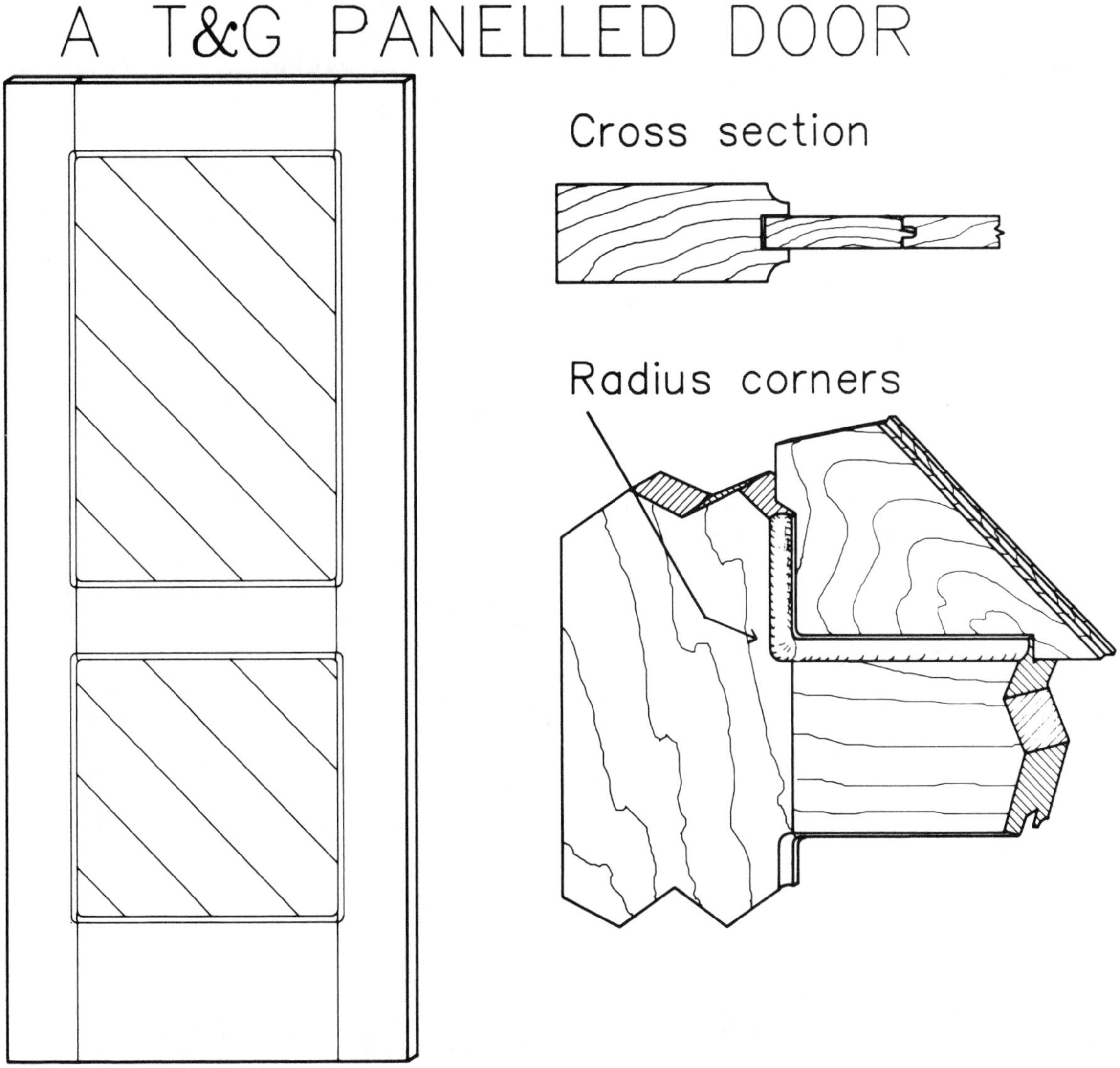

A T&G PANELLED DOOR

Cross section

Radius corners

Illus. 183. A tongue-and-groove panelled door works well in sheltered or interior applications.

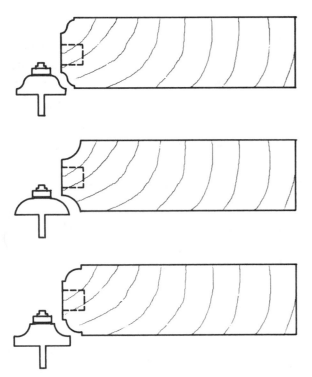

Illus. 184. Several different bead patterns will work, but enough edge must be left for the router-bit guide pin or bearing to ride on, and for the slot.

Illus. 185. Be sure the rails are held firmly square while you are cutting and fitting the panelling. Take the measurement off the previous piece and use it to cut the short side of the next piece.

slots square; then put all the rails in their places on one of the stiles, and either stand it up on edge or lay it flat on the assembly bench, whichever you are more comfortable with. Check the rails to make sure they are square and in their proper positions (Illus. 185). You may want to clamp a straightedge along the ends of the rails where the other stile will go to guide you in cutting the lengths of the panel pieces, and to help keep the rails in the proper positions.

Begin cutting pieces of your tongue-and-groove panelling and fitting them into place. Measure the outside edge of each piece before you put it in place, and use that measurement to cut the next piece. As always, be careful not to get the panel pieces too tight against the bottom of the grooves.

When all the panel pieces are cut and in place, put the other stile on to complete the dry assembly; then lay the door flat on the workbench, and disassemble it carefully so that you won't lose track of the order of the panel pieces. The panel pieces should be completely sanded and sealed before the final assembly of the door. Be sure to soak several coats of oil or other sealer into the end grain of these pieces, and don't forget to do the tongues and grooves. Sanding the edges of the pieces slightly round to soften them will improve the look of the panels.

Cross-Buck Dutch Door with Rabbeted Panels and Glass

Careful layout and precise cutting are the keys to success with this door. The layout is complicated, but the technique is really quite simple (Illus. 186). The thin visual line between the frame members and the raised panels creates a very clean, stylish look.

134

A CROSS—BUCK DUTCH DOOR

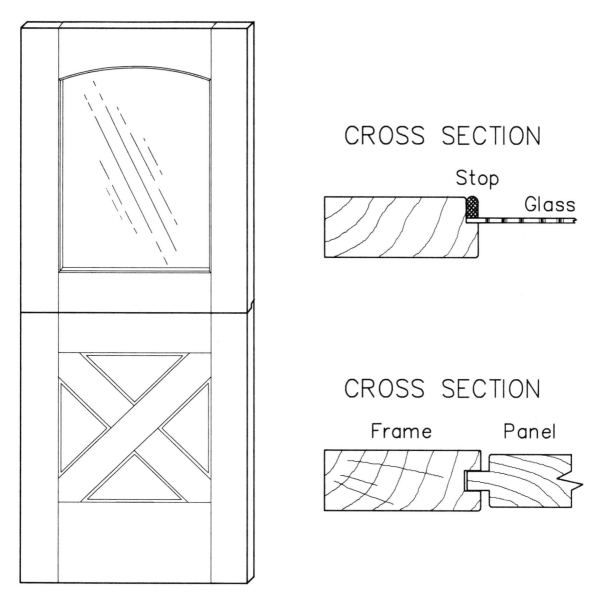

CROSS SECTION

Stop

Glass

CROSS SECTION

Frame   Panel

Illus. 186. This arched-topped cross-buck door is really quite simple to make.

Dutch doors are great for kitchens, solariums, shops, etc. For a door 80 inches tall, the lower half should be about 39 inches tall, while the upper half will start out at 41½ inches. The extra ½ inch is for the overlapping rabbet between the two sections. This type of door must open out, because the high part of the rabbet on the bottom piece must be on the inside to prevent water from running inward if it drips down the door.

Start by making the two sets of stiles and

rails. Cut the top rail on this door from 7½-inch-wide stock, so that the narrowest part of it will be the same width as the stiles. Narrow the two center or lock rails by 1 inch to lighten up that part of the door. The cross bucks should also be 1 inch narrower than the width of the stiles. All of this can be varied, depending on the width of the door you are making and your own sense of proportion, but make sure that the inside of the lower section of the door is a perfect square to avoid cutting a lot of odd angles for the cross bucks.

Make your corner joints now, before proceeding. After you cut the arc in the top rail, you won't have a straightedge to cut from.

On a 25-inch rail, a radius of 50 inches will give you the 1½-inch-high arch shown in Illus. 188. To mark this, drive a small nail through a thin piece of wood exactly 50 inches from one end. Now lay the rail out on

Illus. 187. When laying out a Dutch door, be sure to allow an extra ½ inch in height for the overlap where the upper and lower sections meet.

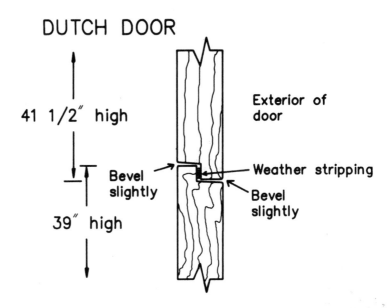

DUTCH DOOR

41 1/2" high

39" high

Bevel slightly

Exterior of door

Weather stripping

Bevel slightly

Illus. 188. A scrap of wood and a small nail can be used to mark the radius for the arched top.

the assembly table, draw two lines out parallel to the ends of the rail, and poke the nail into the bench top exactly halfway between them at the proper distance from the bottom of the rail. Hold a pencil against the end of the stick, and pivot it around the nail to draw the arc. Cut the line as carefully as possible with the band saw or jigsaw, and save the scrap—you will use it to make the stop for the glass. Don't bother trying to smooth the cut edge of the rail yet. It will be much easier after you make a preliminary rabbet and bead cut.

Now dry-assemble the upper part of the door, and use a rabbet cutter to make a rabbet about $\frac{5}{16}$ inch to $\frac{3}{8}$ inch wide and $\frac{5}{8}$ inch deep in which you will set the glass. Remember, the rabbet for glazing is always on the exterior face of the door so that any water running down the face of the door will be forced outward instead of inward, as it would be if it were reversed (Illus. 189). When this is done, flip the door over and use a bead cutter to make a decorative bead around the inside edge of the frame.

Now's the time to clean up that ragged edge where you band-sawed the arc in the upper rail. Instead of the ragged part being $1\frac{1}{2}$ inch wide, it is now only about $\frac{1}{4}$ inch wide. The router cut will be a little bumpy, but after you carefully sand and smooth out the $\frac{1}{4}$-inch edge and go back

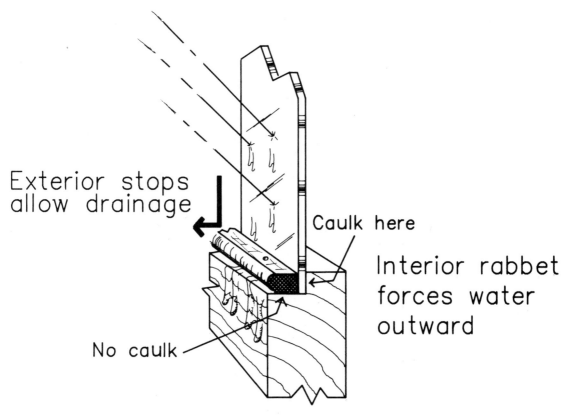

Exterior stops
allow drainage

Caulk here

Interior rabbet
forces water
outward

No caulk

Illus. 189. Doors and windows should always be installed so that the rabbet on the inside forces running water back to the outside. Caulk the bottom of the rabbet before applying glass, but don't caulk the stops.

over the router cut, it will look very clean. Both the rabbet and the bead could be done after the upper part of the door had been glued up, but if you do them before gluing the door together you can easily redo any parts if they don't come out right (Illus. 190).

It is best not to install the glass until the door is completely trimmed to size and finished, but when you are ready to install it, bed it in a bead of a flexible caulk like butyl caulk or acrylic caulk to help prevent leaks from wind-driven rain. The stops are made from strips of the same type of wood as the door. They should be exactly the same width as the rabbet, and should come up just flush with the face of the framework. A simple quarter-round or quarter-round-and-bead cut with a small router bit on the outer edge of the stop will give it a smart look and hide any cracks between it and the framework. The curved upper stop will have to be carefully cut out on the band saw and sanded smooth by hand. The arc is just gentle enough here so that you can cut this piece from solid wood. If you saved the scrap from the top rail, you already have one of the cuts made.

The angle of the mitre on the ends of the arched piece and the upright pieces that meet it won't be exactly 45 degrees, but it is essential that the angles on the two

Illus. 190. Cutting the router bead and rabbet before sanding the arched edge smooth will greatly reduce the width of the surface that must be worked. A second light pass with both router cutters after smoothing and fairing the edge completes the task.

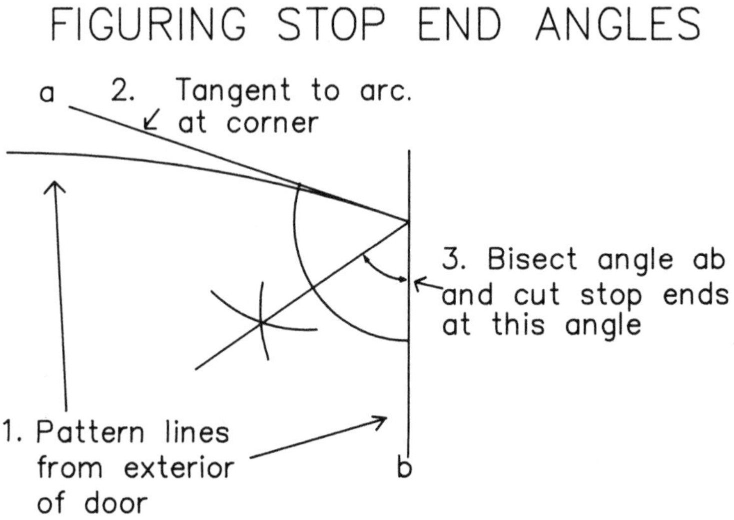

Illus. 191. To figure out the angle at which to cut the ends of the curved stop and the ones that meet it, first draw a pattern from the exterior side of the door; then mark a line tangent to the arch where it meets the stile, bisect angle AB, and set your cutoff saw at that angle.

FIGURING STOP END ANGLES

a

2. Tangent to arc. at corner

3. Bisect angle ab and cut stop ends at this angle

1. Pattern lines from exterior of door

b

meeting pieces be exactly the same or the meeting surfaces won't be the same size (Illus. 191). Use a compass to divide the angle; then use a bevel gauge to transfer that angle to your chop saw. Make both cuts for one end only first, and hold the pieces in place to check the angle.

To complete the lower section, clamp the stiles and rails together, and use a slotting cutter to cut a centered slot ¼ inch wide and deep all the way around the inside of the frame. Now, lay one of the pieces for the cross bucks under the frame, and line it up so that the corners of the frame are perfectly centered on it. Use a sharp pencil or knife to mark where it will be cut. These cuts must be very exact. There is no margin of error here. Splines will be used to hold these pieces in place, so you needn't worry about a tenon on the ends of them. A chop saw may give you the best accuracy for making these double 45-degree cuts.

When the first piece is cut, put it in position in the frame, and repeat the procedure for marking the cuts for the other cross buck. The other cross buck is actually two pieces that will be splined into the first one. Once again, accuracy is essential.

When all three cross-buck pieces fit perfectly, remove them from the frame, and rout the slot all the way around all of them, including the ends. Be sure the distance from the faces of the pieces to the slots is exactly the same as on the other frame pieces. You can do this either by clamping the pieces in the vise or to the table, or by carefully resetting the router bit in a table-mounted router.

Splines can now be made and carefully glued into the ends of these pieces to hold them in the slots in the framework. Be

Illus. 192. To mark the end cuts for the cross bucks, draw a center line near each end of the rough piece and align it with the corners where the rails meet the stiles.

careful not to leave any excess glue on the ends of the pieces that will prevent the joints from fitting tightly later in the final assembly (Illus. 193).

When the splines are dry, assemble the lower part of the door again, and lay it on top of the stock that will be used to make the panels. For this door, the panel stock should be ⅛ inch thinner than the frame stock. Carefully mark the inside edges of the frame holes on the panel stock; then remove the frame from the panel stock, and draw another series of lines ⁷⁄₁₆ inch outside of the first ones. Cut the outside of these lines to cut out your panels.

Now set the dado on the table saw to cut

Illus. 193. Make sure that all excess glue is cleaned off the splines.

⅝ inch wide and deep enough so that a ½-inch stub tenon will be left around the edges of the panels to fit in the slots. Clamp a piece of wood to the saw fence or make a clamp-on fence, since the dado cutter will be cutting right up to it. Make as many test cuts on a scrap piece as you need to be sure you've got it just right; then make the rabbet cut all the way around both sides of the panel pieces. Afterward, clean this cut up with a sharp rabbet plane or by sanding, and sand the sharp edge on the panel to a nice soft roundness. The inside edges of the frame members should also be sanded round. Dry-fit the door, and make adjustments with hand planes until the fit is right. Don't forget to sand and seal the panels before final assembly.

Once both parts of the door have been glued together and planed down, you can go back with the table saw or router and cut the rabbet on the meeting edge. A surface-mounted barrel bolt is generally used to keep the two sections together.

Multi-Light, Three-Panel Door

Doors with multiple panes of glass divided by mullions and muntins can be constructed with the same techniques that are used to make window sash (Illus. 194). Because the muntins and mullions are so narrow and delicate in this type of construction, it is impossible to use dowel or spline joints to secure them to the rest of the door. Cope-and-stick sash, made with matched router or shaper cutters, has an interlocking cope cut on the ends of each that will hold the pieces in place, even without a mortise-and-tenon joint. But for this routed door, small mortises and tenons where each muntin or mullion meets a stile or rail will be essential. Where the muntins and mullions cross in the center, a half-lap joint is employed. The three raised panels, two vertical and one horizontal, in the lower part of the door, are made from solid wood. This is a common Victorian pattern that works well when glass is used only in the upper third of a door, and which can be made easily without shapers.

To build this door, prepare the stiles and rails, and dry-assemble them without the upper muntins or mullions in place. Now, measure along the inside edges of the lock and top rails to find the exact middle of each of them. On the stiles, find the center of the space between the inside edges of the lock and top rails, and mark these two points with a square line across the inside edge of the frame pieces. Draw another square line ¼ inch to each side of these center lines, and use your marking gauge to mark lines parallel to the face of the piece ½ inch and 1 inch from the face. The square thus formed will be the edges of the mortises you will cut to accept the tenons on the ends of the muntins. These tenons will be ½ inch square and ½ inch deep. Most of the waste from the mortise holes can be bored out with a brad-point drill bit; then the holes can be squared out with a ½-inch or smaller chisel.

The muntin and mullion stock can now be ripped to 1-inch widths and cut to length 1 inch longer than the distances between the stiles and rails. The tenons can be sawn on the table saw in the same manner as a larger tenon. Remember to position them the same distance as the mortises from the face of the door that you marked the mortise holes from.

A THREE—PANEL, FOUR—LIGHT DOOR

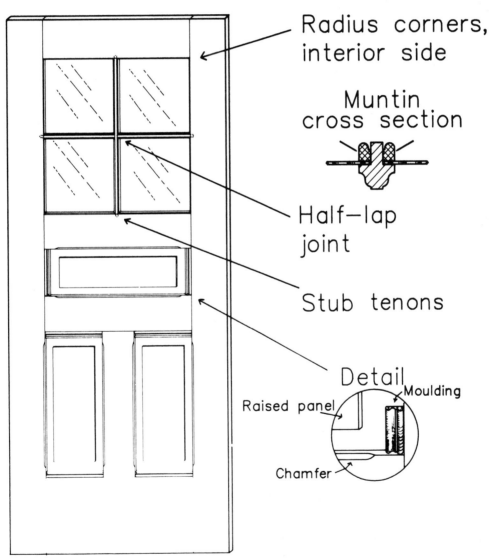

Illus. 194. This three-panel door combines chamfered frame edges and short pieces of moulding.

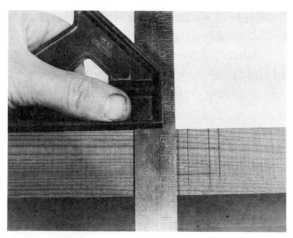

Illus. 195. Markings for the stub tenons that hold the muntins in place.

Illus. 196. A half-lap joint is employed where the muntin and mullion cross.

Check each muntin and mullion individually to be sure it fits well in the frame, and mark the outside edge of each one where it meets the stile or rail to which it is attached. Then, with the muntin in place, lay the mullion on top with the ends on the marks you just made, and mark the intersecting points on both the muntin and mullion pieces, one on top and the other on the bottom. Repeated cuts on either the table saw or the radial arm saw can be used to remove the waste from the notches for the half-lap joint where the two pieces meet (Illus. 196). Cut from the top on one piece, and the bottom on the other, to a depth that is exactly ½ the total thickness of the stock. A sharp chisel or file can be used to clean out the bottom of the joint, and light planing along the edge will help ease a joint that is too tight.

Now the entire framework can be dry-assembled, and the rabbets for the glass and the decorative bead can be routed around each light in the upper part of the door. Square out the corners of the glass rabbets with a sharp chisel. The slots for the panel in the lower part of the door can also be routed at this time with a ½-inch cutter or a pair of ¼-inch cutters stacked on one arbor. Now put a chamfering bit in your router and set it so that it cuts approximately ¼ inch deep. Mark the frame members 1 inch to 1½ inch from the ends on the long sides of the panel holes all around (depending on the width of the moulding you will be using at the ends of the panel) and start and stop the chamfer cuts of these points. Don't forget to square-out the corners of the slot cuts for the panels. Once the raised panels have been cut, sanded, and finished, assemble the door. After the glue has dried and you have planed and sanded the frame, the final step is to cut and apply the mouldings in the short ends of all the panels.

Fabric-Panel Closet Doors

These doors are quite simple in their construction techniques but are visually very exciting (Illus. 197). Because they are bifolding closet doors, there is no need to make the inside look the same as the outside. Dowels will work fine for the structural joints on this lightweight interior door.

The middle or lock rail is cut down from an eight-inch-wide piece on the band saw. Use a marking gauge to draw a straight line parallel to one edge where you are going to cut; then use a compass to draw the curve where the line sweeps down to meet the existing edge (Illus. 198). Repeat the procedure on the other side of the board, so that the two small curves seem to be about the same distance apart as the width of the board (after the two pieces are cut out of it).

Cut these lines carefully on the band saw,

Illus. 197. Striking effects are achieved with fabric panels in this simple closet door.

and use rasps, drum sanders, orbital sanders, or belt sanders to smooth the edge. In this case, it won't do as much good to wait until after the rabbet is cut to smooth it. As you sand, round the corners where the curves sweep into the old edges. Now use this first piece to mark the lines for the remaining pieces if you are making more than one door.

Now assemble the doors with the front sides up, and mark across the ends of the rails and stiles for the dowel holes. Drill these with a dowelling jig, horizontal boring machine, or drill press, and reassemble the door with ½-inch stub dowels in the holes to help index the pieces while you do the routing.

Make the stopped chamfers on the outside of the door by marking the frame pieces 1 inch from each corner. Drop the bit in at the the first mark, and cut smoothly and evenly until you come to the end mark. Pull the bit away from the work here, and go to the next mark, always working in the same direction so that you are resisting the pull of the bit as you advance the router along the work. This detail has a nice visual effect, and is a good way to avoid the rounded corners that are caused by routing the decorative beads on rectilinear doors and windows. This same treatment (stopping the cut near the corners) can be used with cove and quarter-round cutters as well.

First cut the rabbets that will hold the panels with the router to a depth of about ⅝ inch; then remove the center rail and use the table saw to "square-out" the rabbet so that a curved panel and stop will not be necessary (Illus. 199). Two cuts with a blade will accomplish this.

MARKING THE RAILS

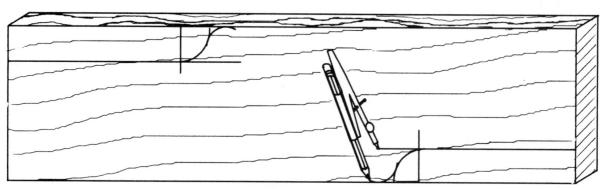

Illus. 198. A marking gauge and compass are used to draw the cloud-lift patterns.

Illus. 199. To simplify the panels, square out the rabbet on the lock rails with the table saw.

Now, glue the doors together and plane, sand, and finish them with varnish or oil before inserting the panels. You can glue the fabric for the panels with a spray adhesive or a light coat of white glue to ¼-inch Masonite or plywood. Trim the fabric carefully around the edges. You can also use wallpaper in the same manner. Now, just insert the panels cut, and nail in stops in the same manner you would do for a piece of glass.

Multi-Panel, Multi-Light Door

This complex door employs many of the techniques discussed in previous doors, plus a few new ones (Illus. 200). Its complexity gives it a beautiful ambiance that is bound to make even the most jaded passerby pause and take note.

The door consists basically of one upper panel with a large oval light cut in it, and four smaller lights at its corners. Two upright mullions are edge-glued to the panel, and 12 small sidelights are formed, six on either side of the panel, by short muntins. The lower part of the door has three cross rails, and four flat panels that are divided in the middle by two different types of upright mullions. The lower panels are all flat, which solves the problem of raising an irregularly shaped panel, but the upper two of them have appliqués glued in, not to their centers but to their edges, to give the appearance of different layers. Inlays of contrasting woods are also used as highlights to add interest.

This door begins, like many doors, with two stiles and four main rails. The stiles and rails on this door are made from white oak a full 2 inches thick. The stiles are perfectly straight, and present no special problems. The rails all have the offset, "cloud-lift" curves cut in them.

This motif has its origins in the Orient, where it signifies clouds and mist, and was popularized in this country by Greene and Greene, the great architects and builders of craftsman-style homes who worked mainly in Southern California during the early part of this century. It is possible to make templates to guide a router for cutting these curves (see door with template-cut curved raised panels, pages 149–155, for discussion of template-cutting), but because each set of curves is positioned differently, and this is a one-of-a-kind door, it is probably not worth the effort in this case. Instead, the builder of this door simply marked out the curves with the marking gauge and compass as described in the building of the fabric-panel closet doors discussed on pages 142–144, cut them out on the band saw, and then planed, scraped, and sanded the edges to a fine finish.

The central panel in the upper part of the door is 1¾-inch-thick oak. Here, it is advisable to use a template and a long cutter with a guide bearing in the router to trim the work to its final shape. It would be nearly impossible to cut this large a panel accurately with either a jigsaw or a band saw. Making a template, on the other hand, allows you to make these difficult cuts on a piece of ¼-inch plywood, clean them up carefully by hand, and then transfer the lines, very exactly, to the workpiece.

First cut out the template to the proper width and height, plus 1½ inch in both directions. Then mark a vertical line through the center of the panel template and measure out about 12 inches from the center of this line towards the top and bottom. Drive a small nail at each of these two points. Then tie in a loop a piece of string about twice the length of the oval from top to bottom, lay it around the nails, and use it to guide the pencil in drawing the ellipse. Mark out the four corner lights with a compass pivoted from each corner. Cut these out carefully with either a band or jigsaw, and use rasps, sandpaper, or whatever works best for you to clean and "fair out" the edges to perfection. Finally, screw four ¾-inch × 1½-inch pieces of wood to the edges of the template so that the inside edges of these pieces will be exactly on the lines that will be the edges of the final panel. These pieces will position the template on the panel, and provide solid attachment to the panel for the template (Illus. 201).

The panel itself should be edge-glued and cut to the proper outside dimensions. The edges should be carefully planed or jointed so that they are perfectly smooth and straight. Now, position the template on the panel, and draw the lines for the lights. Use a jigsaw or band saw to cut as close to these lines as you can without actually cutting on them. The router is great for trimming, but on a piece this thick, it will "chatter" if you try to remove more than about ⅛ inch at a time. As with previous doors, you can use the decorative bead and rabbet cutters with their guide bearings to remove part of the rough edge in a preliminary cut, before using the straight cutter and template to make the final trim.

To make the final trim, place the template on the work, and screw through the edge pieces into the edges of the panel to secure the template. Now, make sure that the guide bearing is riding fully on the template. You can use a spacer between the template and the panel if necessary, but you shouldn't need it in this case if you did the

A MULTI–PANEL MULTI–LIGHT DOOR

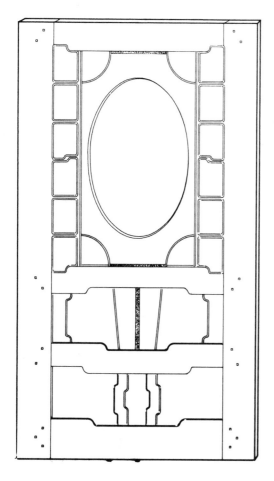

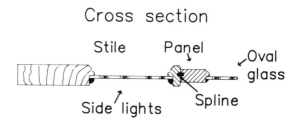

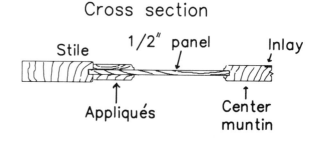

Illus. 200. A very complex frame-and-panel door.

146

TEMPLATE FOR UPPER PANEL

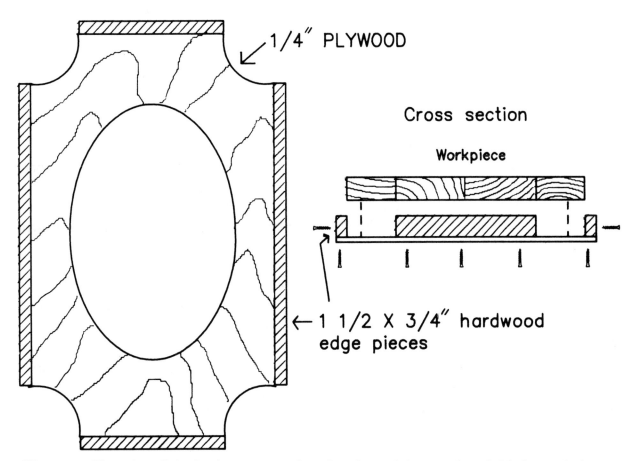

1/4″ PLYWOOD

Cross section

Workpiece

← 1 1/2 X 3/4″ hardwood edge pieces

Illus. 201. The 1½ × ¾-inch pieces screwed to the edges of the template hold the workpiece securely in place. Drive screws through them and into the edges of the workpiece where the holes won't show.

preliminary bead and rabbet cuts. When everything looks secure (the vibration of cutting can cause movement if the template is not very secure), make the final trim. If done properly, this technique should produce a perfectly smooth edge that hardly needs sanding.

When the panel is completely finished, the sidelight assemblies can be cut out. Start by making the upright mullions from 1-inch-wide stock. They each have a ½-inch stub tenon on either end; so make them ex-

actly 1 inch longer than the panel. The panel will be joined with a spline, top and bottom to the rails, and edge-glued to the mullions.

To make the short horizontal muntins, start with two pieces 7 inches wide, and 1 inch longer than the width of the lights. First, cut a ½-inch-long stub tenon on both ends of each piece; then rip out eight 1-inch-wide pieces and two 2-inch-wide pieces from this stock. This method ensures that the length from shoulder to shoulder on the mullions will be exactly the same throughout. Now, go back and carefully reset the saw for the shoulder cut, and cut a ¼-inch-deep side shoulder for each tenon, so that the remaining tenons will be ½ inch × ½ inch and ½ inch deep.

Before gluing the upright mullions to the panel, rout a ½-inch-deep slot in each end of the panel, and a corresponding one along the edge of the rails that will hold the panel. Also mark the positions for the mortises to receive the stub tenons on the ends of the upright mullions, and bore these out with a ½-inch-diameter brad-point drill. Square the mortises out with a chisel.

Clamp the top and lock rails to the panel with the mullions in place, and check to be sure that everything is right. You may also want to clamp the stiles in place to be sure that the rails are not offset in one direction or the other. If everything works right, take it apart and apply glue between the panel edges and the upright mullions. Reassemble the whole upper part of the door to be sure that everything is held in the proper place; then clamp the mullions tightly to the panel and allow the glue to set.

While the door is assembled like this, you can use a framing square or large T-square to mark the positions for the mortises that will hold the stub tenons on the ends of the short horizontal muntins. After the glue has set, the door can be taken apart again, and these holes can be bored and squared out with a chisel.

Now, reassemble the door with the lower three rails in place, and use the slotting cutter in the router to cut the slots that will hold the panels and the splines for the upright mullions in the lower part of the door. Now is also the time to rout the

decorative beads and rabbets around the edges of the upper lights, and around the edges of the rails and stiles where the panels will be. Use a small quarter-round around the panels, and plane the upright mullions ½ inch thinner, so that they fit tightly below the level of the quarter-round. The same will be done with the appliqués when they are added later.

Before breaking the door down completely again, cut and insert the upright mullions between the lower rails, and lay the panel stock under the assembly so that the lines for the shape of each panel can be drawn on it. You will have to draw a new set of lines $^{7}/_{16}$ inch outside of these lines to get the final shape of the panel. Remember to either square out the corners of the slots or round the corners of the panels.

Once again, break the door down, and reassemble it with the panels and upright mullions in place. If you want to do any inlay work, do it before the final assembly. Note that inlays can sometimes be used to cover mistakes or errors made when cutting pieces to length.

When everything is ready for the final assembly, get someone to help you. This door is far too complex to try to assemble by yourself. The little "cloud-lift" pieces at the outside edges of the middle panels can be cut and applied after the rest of the door is assembled. Once again, this type of appliqué can sometimes be used to cover an error.

Make the moulding for the oval light with the sandwich method used for the door described on pages 126–132. To avoid squaring out the corners of the smaller lights and having to fit mouldings to these tight curves, make leather or lead stops which are flexible enough to be bent into position and tacked into place (Illus. 202). For extra strength and stability, glue the glass into the holes with clear silicone caulk. Note that the tenons on this door are pegged through the face. Square out the upper part of the peg hole after inserting the peg and glue in a square piece of a contrasting-color wood to cover the peg (Illus. 203).

Aside from the sheer complexity of this door, it is of interest because it presents solutions to several design and construction problems. In review, these solutions are as follows: One, curving frame members can easily be used with flat panels. Two, appliqués can be applied to look like either frame

Illus. 203. A round tenon peg with a square inlay.

Illus. 202. Leather stops are glued in place on this door, but lead would be a better flexible stop material in a door that is exposed to weathering.

members or the raised parts of panels. (Illus. 204). Three, one way you can avoid the rounded corner caused by routing the edges of frame members around panels is to make pieces of different thicknesses that meet at right angles, so that you can continue the router cut through the pieces without causing a gap between them. And fourth, you can use flexible materials for stops in tightly curved window panes (Illus. 202).

Door with Template-Cut Curved Raised Panels

By using templates and straight-cutting router bits with different-sized guide bearings, it is possible to make a raised panel that follows the curve of the frame members that surround it (Illus. 205). It is also possible to perfectly edge-join two

149

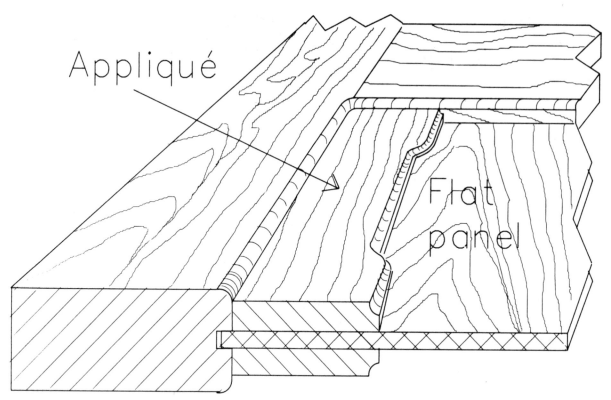

Appliqué

Flat panel

Illus. 204. Appliqués can be applied to look like frame members.

boards that have totally arbitrary curves along their edges. This technique will open up a whole new realm of possibilities for the door and window maker. It can be applied to windows as well as doors, and can also be used to make curving corner joints that match each other perfectly.

The door shown in Illus. 205 has two large panels made from alternating pieces of curly redwood and straight-grained Douglas fir; these pieces are tapered and joined so that they convey the idea of rays of sunlight emanating from the round window in the upper panel. The darker outer framework is made from black walnut wood. The panel stock can be cut out on the table saw with a tapering jig, or marked and cut freehand on the band saw. In either

case, the edges of each piece must be carefully straightened on the joiner. The upper panel is the most complicated, and must be glued up in stages, using clamping from more than one direction at once (Illus. 206).

Once the upper panel is completely glued up, it can be roughly cut to size, and the lines can be extended out to find the tapers for the lower panel. Be sure to include the width of the lock rail in your calculation of the angles for the tapers. To get the exact angles, totally complete the upper panel and the framework before cutting the pieces for the lower panel.

Note that once again, as with the door described on pages 144–149, the stiles have completely straight inner edges. The curvature is all in the rails and the following raised edge of the panels. With the techniques used to make this door, it would be quite possible to cut curves on the inner edges of the stiles, but leaving them straight simplifies matters some and gives a visual sense of continuity to the door.

The rails all start as straight boards with tenons cut on their ends to fit in the mortises that have been worked into the stiles. Now, make two templates, one for the middle rail and one for both the top and bottom rails. The templates should be made

FOLLOWING CURVES ON A RAISED PANEL DOOR

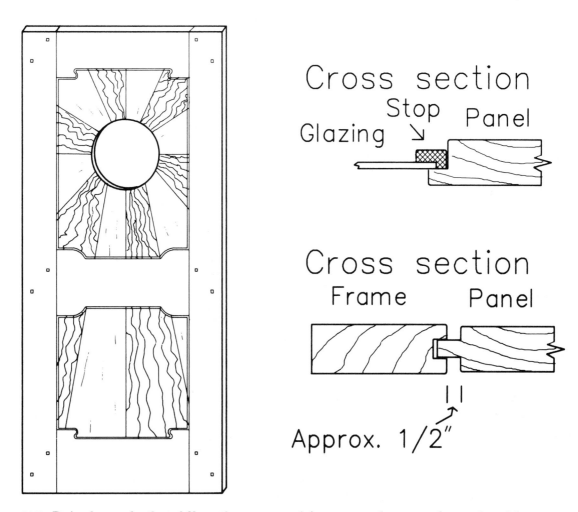

Cross section

Glazing   Stop   Panel

Cross section

Frame   Panel

Approx. 1/2"

Illus. 205. Raised panels that follow the curves of frame members can be made with router cutters and templates.

ASSEMBLING PANEL FROM TAPERED PIECES

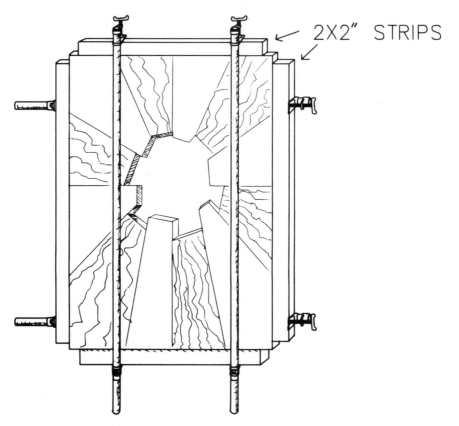

2X2" STRIPS

Illus. 206. Trim the outer edges of the upper panel carefully, and clamp from both directions at once. Cut and trim the window hole later with the router.

from ¼ inch or thicker plywood with as many laminations as possible, and no voids. Particle board or Masonite can be used, but it is more likely to get soft along the edge and lose its crisp edge.

The template pieces should be an inch or two longer than the rails, and can be attached through half-inch spacer pieces to either the ends of the rails or the tenons, any place where the screw holes won't show in the finished piece. First, mark the lines to be cut on the rail, and cut as close as possible to them with the band saw or jigsaw. Now, attach the template securely

to the workpiece, and it is ready to be trimmed with the router.

You will use a couple of different router bits and bearings in the construction of this door. For this cut, you will need a 2-inch long, ½-inch straight cutter, with a ½-inch-o.d. (outside diameter) bearing (Illus. 207). You can place the bearing on either end of the cutter for this trimmer bit; just make sure that it rides firmly on the edge of the template and that the cutters are not cutting any of the template.

When you reach the part of the curve where the bit is cutting against the grain

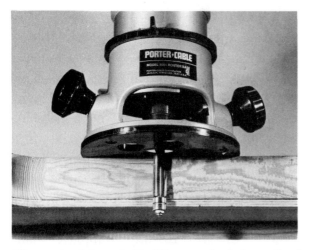

Illus. 207 (above left). Use a 2-inch-long flush-cutting bit to trim thick stock to a template shape. Illus. 208 (above right). A flush cutter with an inboard bearing is necessary for cutting panel shapes to follow the framework.

of the wood and is in danger of breaking it out, take the bit away from the work, move ahead of the curve, and very carefully cut backwards through the curve. The bit will try to pull itself in the direction of the cut, but if you brace yourself carefully and go slowly, you can make this part of the cut this way without danger of breakout.

Once the rails have been trimmed to shape, assemble the framework and position the panel stock under it, so that the first set of lines can be drawn to guide you in cutting out the panels. When you have traced all the way around the insides of the frame on the panels, remove the frame and draw the second set of lines, $7/16$ inch outside of the first set. Cut these lines to cut the panels to their final size.

Now make a template from the templates used to cut the rails; this template will fit over the panels and guide you in cutting the curves that follow the curves on the rails. One simple way to accomplish this is to assemble the framework and lay it over a piece of template stock that has been ripped to the exact width of the panels. The straight lines on the edges of the panels are very important, because they will help you to keep the template straight and square. Be sure that the template stock is perfectly aligned under the frame by marking $7/16$ inches in from each edge, top and bottom, and then simply drawing a line with a very sharp pencil guided along the rail, so that the line is $1/8$ inch from the rail at all points along the curve. Mark both ends , but don't worry about the straight sides; they will be cut afterwards with either a dado or a router bit and fence.

Now cut and shape the template exactly to the line. Position the template on one side of the panel using the lines that were traced from the framework as guides. Screws can be screwed into the edges of the panel, where the side rabbets will later be cut, to hold the template in place. Now it is a simple matter to cut the curves on the ends of the panel using a straight cutter with an inboard bearing, like the one shown in Illus. 208. Figure the depth you will need

153

from the thickness of the panel stock and the width of the panel groove, and, if necessary, space the template up from the panel so that the cutter cuts to the right depth with the bearing riding solidly on the template.

Before removing the template from the first side of the panel, make some indexing marks at the corners to help you get the end-to-end alignment right when you move the template to the other side. Be careful not to flip the template over when you move it to the other side of the board. The side of the template facing away from the panel on the first cut will now be towards the panel on the second side.

Use the indexing marks you made to align the panel, and repeat the process on the second side. After both ends have been cut, the straight sides can be cut to the same depth with the dado or a router and fence guide. Now, all the hard edges on both the panel and the framework can be light-

ly rounded over by sanding, and the door is ready for final fitting and assembly.

You can get more precise following curves with this method if you make a second template from the first, and use it as an intermediate template for making a matching template (Illus. 209). Align the first template on top of the stock for the intermediate template, with the piece that will actually be used for the intermediate template on the off side. When making the cut for the intermediate template, make sure that the bearing rides solidly on the first template at all times. Any deviation will cause a defect in the intermediate template.

The intermediate template will match the curves of the first, but only when the two templates are held apart the width of the router bit. To get a template that exactly matches the first one, you must use the intermediate template and a router cutter with a bearing that is 1 inch wider in its

MAKING MATCHING TEMPLATES

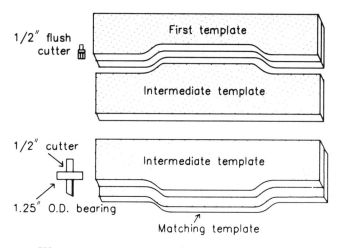

TEMPLATE CUTTING MATCHING RAILS AND PANELS

Illus. 209. Intermediate templates and cutters with various-sized bearings can be used to make precise following curves or edge joints with curved edges.

o.d. (outside diameter) than the cutter. The bearing will follow the intermediate template, and the cutter will cut the final matching template $\frac{1}{2}$ inch away from the intermediate template so that the curves match perfectly. By using a bearing that is $\frac{7}{8}$ inch wider than the cutter, you could get matching lines that are $\frac{1}{16}$ inch apart.

Bearings for this type of work can be bought in many sizes for both the inside bore and the outside diameter. The bearing should have an inside diameter exactly the same as the shank of the router bit you are using, and can be dropped onto the bit from the shank end before it is put in the router collet. The sizes of bearings are in thousandths of an inch. A .500-inch i.d. (inside diameter) bearing will fit very snugly on most $\frac{1}{2}$-inch shank router bits, sometimes so snugly that heat must be applied to the bearing to expand it, or cold (a couple of hours in the freezer) applied to the router bit to shrink it enough to slip the bearing on. These techniques can be used to cut curving joints where the rails and stiles meet, or to join contrasting woods along curved lines for panels.

7
Production Door Making

Here I describe techniques that will be of interest to small woodshop owners, home-builders, or anyone who needs to build several doors of the same or similar type at one time. The idea here is not mass production, but the production of doors, usually by the order, to fulfil the needs of a few customers at a time. When working in this manner, there is still plenty of room and need for careful design consultation and the production of a unique product. Organization becomes critical here, and the correct use of the proper tool can make the difference between a successful job and a lot of ruined material.

Several types of tools and machinery are important for this type of work, none of which are beyond the means of most serious woodworkers. Spindle shapers, mortising machines, and tenoners are the major "special" tools that would likely be found in a production door-and-window shop. A 12-inch jointer and a 12-inch or larger planer would also be considered necessities by most production door-and-window makers, and many would consider large table or stroke sanders equally as important, although hand planing and orbital sanding are nearly as fast.

Certainly, the most important and versatile tool in the production shop is the spindle shaper. The shaper is like a large router in an inverted position, as it would be on a router table, except that instead of having a collet that accepts the arbor of a cutting bit, the spindle shaper has a spindle on which are stacked two or three wing-cutting bits that are hollow-bored in the middle. You can stack spacers and bearings on the spindle, so that the shaper can cut the complete profile of a frame member, including both beads and the central slot or a bead and a rabbet, in one pass (Illus. 210). Cutters commonly come in matching sets for cope-and-stick joinery so that the ends of the rails, muntins and mullions can be undercut to match the bead cut and slot of the stile, forming an interlocking joint that appears to be mitred in the corners. This joint is stronger than a straight butt joint because it is intricate; it is also cleaner looking than the rounded corners caused by routed beads, and much quicker to make.

Most production shops have at least two shapers set up for each type of cut, so that both the stick or bead cut and the matching cope or end cut can be made without having to break down and reset the cutters on the shapers. A third shaper, with a larger table and a more powerful motor, is often used solely for cutting the profiles for raised panels. Power-feed units, auxiliary tables so that two sets of bits can be stacked on one shaper for making both cope and stick cuts, and many other options are available for shapers.

In recent years, the trend in shapers has been toward smaller, less powerful machines. Many types of cutters are now becoming available for ½-inch spindles that were once available only for larger shapers with 1-inch or larger spindles.

Generally, a well-constructed ½-inch spindle shaper can handle the forces generated in cope-and-stick cutting, as long as the feed is slow and steady and the rotation speed of the cutters is high enough. A ½-inch spindle is light enough to flex slightly, causing "chatter" and rough, inaccurate cutting if it is not driven by a powerful enough motor and a heavy, steel-drive pulley. Chattering can also cause the spindle bearings to fail rapidly. The drive pulley must also be carefully balanced to prevent unnecessary vibration (Illus. 211).

If you plan to invest in one or more ½-inch shapers, make sure that the drive components are of the heaviest quality and are in good condition if you plan to do production-type work with them. Panel-cutting makes even heavier demands on the machinery, but it can also be accomplished with ½-inch shapers if care is taken. See pages 54–57 for more information on shapers and their cutters.

The doors described in this chapter illustrate a variety of techniques, including organizational techniques for large production runs and different possibilities for a more unique and exciting usage of shapers in door making.

Wood for Production Doors

The doors described in previous chapters are custom-made and could be made with various types of woods, depending on availability, design, and the willingness of the craftsperson to struggle with a difficult though beautiful wood like some mahoganies or western walnut. For the production-oriented worker, these concerns become even more amplified by the increased amount of lumber that will have to be bought, cut, shaped, and finished.

The cost of the lumber is generally a rather small part of the cost equation, amounting to less than a third of the overall cost of the product. A 3-foot-wide door made entirely of 1½-inch-thick lumber will use about 45 board feet of wood. If that wood costs $2 per board foot, the lumber cost will be $90 for the door. If a cheaper grade of lumber can be gotten at $1.50 per board foot, the savings will be $22.50 for the door, but how much more time and effort will it take to cut around and plane out defects in the cheaper lumber? How much more lumber will be lost to the scrap heap if the cheaper grade is used?

Usually, it is not worth it to try to save money by buying cheaper lumber for production work. The workability and stability of your lumber become more important as the size of the production run increases, and the increased time and waste caused by using lower-grade lumber adds up.

The workability of a wood depends on the character of its grain and its relative hard-

VARIOUS SHAPER CUTTER SETS
FOR DOORS AND WINDOWS

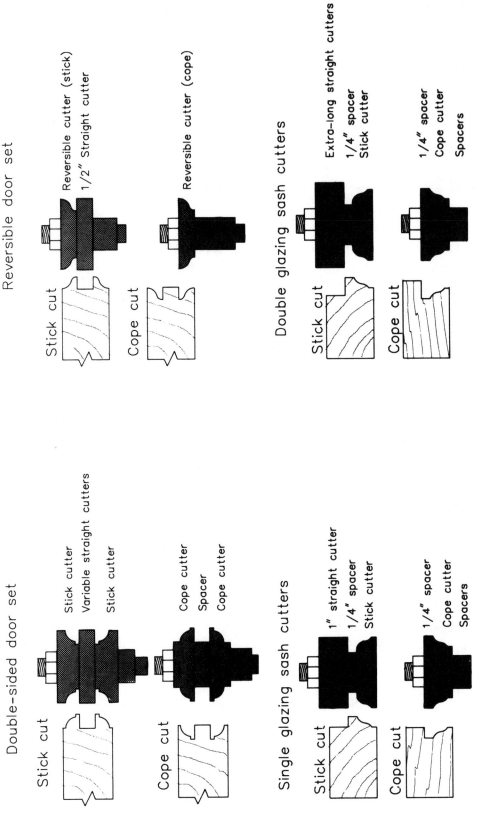

Reversible door set

Reversible cutter (stick)
1/2" Straight cutter

Stick cut

Reversible cutter (cope)

Cope cut

Double-sided door set

Stick cutter
Variable straight cutters
Stick cutter

Stick cut

Cope cutter
Spacer
Cope cutter

Cope cut

Double glazing sash cutters

Extra-long straight cutters
1/4" spacer
Stick cutter

Stick cut

1/4" spacer
Cope cutter
Spacers

Cope cut

Single glazing sash cutters

1" straight cutter
1/4" spacer
Stick cutter

Stick cut

1/4" spacer
Cope cutter
Spacers

Cope cut

Illus. 210. By stacking several cutters and/or spacers on a shaper spindle, you can cut the complete profile of a frame member in one or two passes.

158

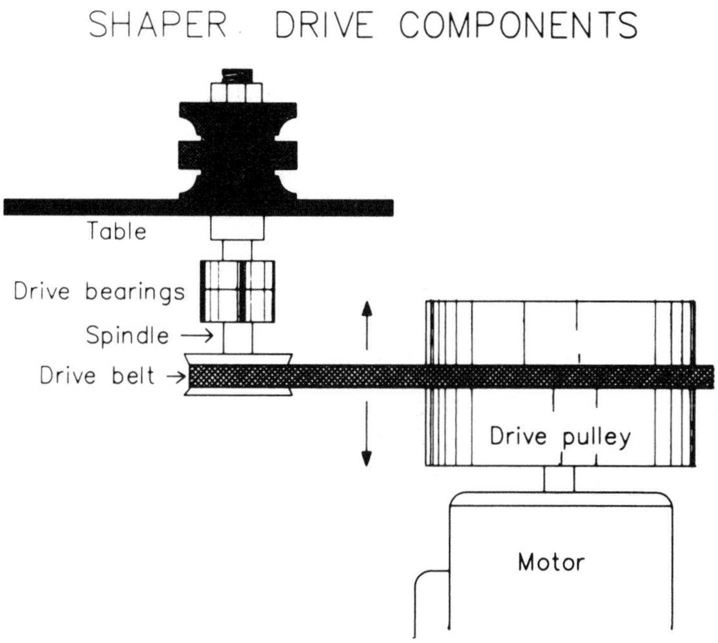

SHAPER DRIVE COMPONENTS

Table

Drive bearings

Spindle →

Drive belt →

Drive pulley

Motor

Illus. 211. Drive pulleys for shapers are flat (not V-grooved) and several inches wide so that the drive belt can move up and down when the spindle is moved. For best results, this pulley should be heavy and well-balanced.

ness or toughness. The hours spent in smoothing, scraping and sanding a difficult wood like Honduras mahogany can add up to a considerable expense in labor costs, and since the production shop often works on the basis of a bid, that cost may have to be borne by the shop if it is not forseen and included in the bid. Softer woods like pine and redwood will be damaged easier by marring and scraping once the finished product is hung, but will be much faster and easier to work with. If doors are to be painted, less desirable species of lumber such as hem-fir or pine can be considered, and the use of fir plywood for panels becomes completely acceptable.

Rot resistance is also an important factor in the selection of lumber for doors, but not nearly as important as it is with windows. A wood like alder that rots very quickly should not be used in an exterior setting, but is perfectly acceptable for interior doors.

The stability of the wood, on the other hand, is a key factor in the choice of lumber for all kinds of doors. Because of the larger expanses of wood needed to build a door, warping and shrinking are much harder to control here than in windows. Trees that grow straight, tall trunks and few large side limbs tend to be the most stable because the side stresses that they must resist are few. Trees like oaks and walnuts that have massive side limbs can sometimes have a lot of tension bound up in the structure of the grain that will release rapidly if the board is ripped, or more slowly over time, causing serious warpage problems.

The way lumber is cut from a log also affects the tendency of a board to crack, warp, and peel (Illus. 212). Three standard cutting methods are used by most saw mills. Flitch- or plain-sawing is the cheapest and most efficient way to cut a board, but produces a large proportion of lumber that is flat-grained, meaning that the wide side of the

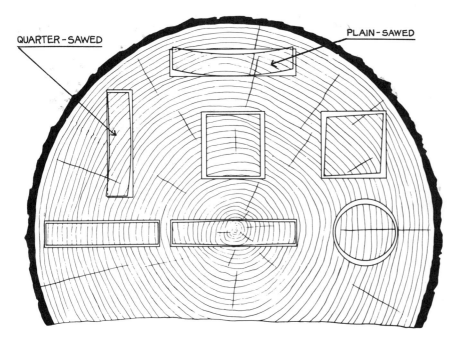

QUARTER-SAWED

PLAIN-SAWED

Illus. 212. Warpage (as shown), peeling grain, and hard-to-finish wood can cause major problems for production door makers. Know your lumber and use only the best to avoid these problems. Drawing from Gluing and Clamping, *by Patrick Spielman (Sterling Publishing Co., Two Park Avenue, New York, New York 10016).*

board runs tangentially to the growth rings of the tree. This type of board is most subject to warping and peeling, and should be rejected for all exterior usage. Kiln-dried, flat-grained wood is sometimes acceptable for interior use as long as the boards are not wider than approximately 6 inches, and there is no sign of the grain peeling.

There is a better method of sawing a log. If this method is used on hardwood, it is called quarter-sawing. If it used on softwood, it is called straight-grain or edge-grain sawing. For this method, a log is first cut into quarters or cants. These cants are then cut so that the growth rings on the ends of the boards run nearly straight across the boards. This type of lumber and rift-sawn lumber, in which the growth rings run from 30- to 60-degree angles to the surface of the board, are the most stable types to use, and should always be chosen for frame pieces of exterior doors. Rift-sawn lumber is the most ideal type for door and window makers because it generally has

straight, vertical grain, and has less tendency than quarter-sawn wood to split and crack.

Another important factor in determining the stability of lumber is its dryness and the method by which it has been dried. Generally speaking, for production work, only kiln-dried lumber should be considered. Air-dried lumber, if carefully checked in numerous places with a moisture metre, may be acceptable for windows, but should not be trusted for doors. Even the best air-dried lumber has a tendency to expand and shrink a lot.

Kiln-dried lumber should also be tested with a moisture meter before use to be sure it has not been stored in a place where it has reabsorbed too much moisture. For interior work, the moisture content of your materials should not be over 10 percent, while it may be acceptable to use wood with a moisture content of up to 15 percent for a door that is going to be hung on the exterior of a building.

160

Organizing Your Production Run

A standard, four-panel door consists of over a dozen separate pieces, and multi-light French-style doors can have many more. If you are making a series of doors of varying sizes and designs, or even a production run of several of the same door, you will need a good organizational system to keep track of all these pieces (Illus. 213).

During the design stage, a picture of the door or doors to be built is nearly always drawn. Use this drawing to generate a complete list of all the pieces you will need for each door you will be making during your production run. You can refer to this list as you are purchasing the lumber for the job, but generally you have to rely on a lot of guesswork at this stage because there are often hidden defects and surprises in your rough boards that won't become apparent until you begin to rip and plane them. For this reason, you should always purchase at least 25% more lumber than you think you will need.

The process of converting the raw lumber into the proper-sized stiles, rails, mullions, and panels is the same as that described for custom door making (pages 122–123), except that more care must be taken not to duplicate or skip pieces. It may be helpful to begin by making all the stiles first, since the straightest lumber is essential here; then begin cutting rails and mullions for each door, and stack them with stiles for that door, so that all the pieces for each door are kept together (Illus. 214). You do not have to cut panel pieces until after the frameworks have been completely finished.

As soon as you have cut all the pieces for a door, lay the pieces out on the workbench and label them with a number to identify the door, and a letter or two to identify the piece and where it goes. Keep the pieces for each door in their own separate pile as

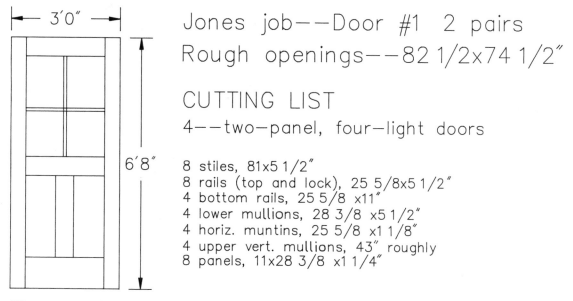

Jones job——Door #1   2 pairs
Rough openings——82 1/2x74 1/2"

CUTTING LIST
4——two-panel, four-light doors

8 stiles, 81x5 1/2"
8 rails (top and lock), 25 5/8x5 1/2"
4 bottom rails, 25 5/8 x11"
4 lower mullions, 28 3/8 x5 1/2"
4 horiz. muntins, 25 5/8 x1 1/8"
4 upper vert. mullions, 43" roughly
8 panels, 11x28 3/8 x1 1/4"

3'0"

6'8"

Illus. 213. A drawing and a cutting list will help keep you organized, especially when you are making several doors.

Illus. 214. To avoid confusion, mark and stack the pieces for each door together.

you work on them, and be sure to number and name each piece so that you can easily tell which door it belongs to and where it goes in that door. Write the name and number on one side of the door only, and always on the same location in relation to the bottom of the door, so that each door can easily be reassembled in the proper sequence just by looking at the markings. A flat cart on wheels or a dolly will be very helpful in moving the piles of pieces for each door around the shop to the various places where they will be worked on.

Shaper Use in Door Production

The use of spindle shapers in door and window production makes it possible to work in a more efficient, assembly-line-like manner. The tedium of carefully dry-assembling the door and making multiple passes with the router is eliminated, as well as all the hand work of squaring out the corners, applying mouldings, etc. Instead, the pieces can be taken separately to the shaper for the cope and stick cuts, which will allow them to fit cleanly together with a stronger joint that looks like a perfect mitre in the corners (Illus. 215). Panels can be raised with various profiles on the shaper much more cleanly and quickly than on the table saw or by hand, and large, high-profile mouldings can also be made with one or more shaper cutters. It is also possible to use a shaper with a guide bearing to cut curved pieces and to follow templates much as you would with a router.

All this and more is possible with shapers, but be forewarned: Shapers are among the more dangerous tools in the workshop. The cutters rotate at speeds of up to 10,000 RPM, and motors of up to five horsepower are used. Use extreme care and follow proper safety procedures, especially when shaping small pieces like the ones that are needed for multi-light doors and windows.

If you don't already own a shaper, see pages 54–57 for advice on purchasing one or more machines. Cutters are also a major expense, and should be considered carefully before buying. A large variety of carbide-

Illus. 215 A and B. The cope-and-stick joint appears to be a perfect mitre in the corners, and is a stronger glue joint than a simple butt joint.

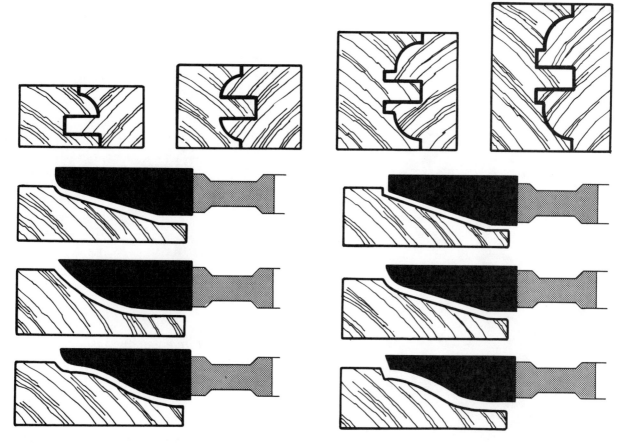

Illus. 216. A variety of panel-raising cutters and cope-and-stick carbide cutters is available, even for smaller spindle shapers.

tipped cutters is available even for the smaller ½-inch machines these days, including cope-and-stick cutters and many types of panel cutters (Illus. 216). If you are considering investing in a carbide cope-and-stick set, make sure that it will handle a variety of door thicknesses ranging from 1⅜ to 1¾ inches, and that you can use it with various straight cutters and spacer collars both for slotted doors, to hold panels, and for rabbeted doors, to hold glass. If you are ordering by mail, make sure that you have the option of returning the merchandise if the cutters are poorly matched or if the sharpness and workmanship are not of high enough quality.

Grinding Your Own Cutters

High-speed steel cutters are much cheaper to purchase, and are available from companies such as Greenley and Delta. Even though steel cutters won't stay sharp nearly as long as carbide cutters, you can easily sharpen them yourself and regrind them if they don't match perfectly. You can lightly sharpen them without changing the profile by grinding only the flat side of the cutters on either a small carbide grinding wheel or a 1-inch belt sander like the one shown in Illus. 217.

Reshaping the profile of the cutter may be necessary from time to time, and can be done by grinding the bevelled side of the

Illus. 218. More extensive resharpening and reshaping can be done on a fine carbide wheel.

cutters on a fine carbide grinding wheel that has a slightly rounded edge for getting into tight corners and curved areas. The grinding wheel should be run at a slow speed, not over 1,750 RPM. High-speed grinders are unsafe for this type of work, and can also quickly ruin your cutter profiles.

Illus. 217. Grinding the flat sides of high-speed steel cutters will help sharpen them without changing their profiles noticeably.

Keep in mind that you can only grind away the cutters; you can't add to them. Also remember that the cutters are the negative to the positive finished piece. By grinding away the cutters, you add to the profile of the workpiece.

When grinding matched pairs of cutters, make a pair of test cuts first; then grind only in the areas where the test pieces don't quite come together (Illus. 219). Hold the bit on the top and bottom only, to avoid getting your fingers between the cutting edge and the tool rest or grinding wheel, and use a sweeping motion on the curved parts of the cutter.

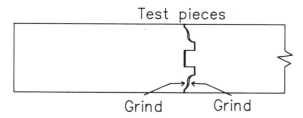

Test pieces

Grind   Grind

Illus. 219. To improve the match of cope-and-stick cutters, make a pair of test cuts, and then grind only in the areas where the pieces don't quite come together.

Grinding is usually used only to make the curved parts of the cuts fit each other better. By grinding back your straight cutters, you can sometimes improve the relationship between the bead cut and the slot cut, but this can usually also be accomplished by moving the fence in or out on the cope cut.

High-speed steel blanks that lock into a head that fits on the shaper spindle can be purchased and ground to fit your own special needs (Illus. 220). These are especially good for making high-profile bolection mouldings. These loose-knife cut-terheads have a reputation for being unsafe, but recent OSHA (Occupational Safety and Health Act) regulations have forced modifications of the design to make them safer. When grinding these knives, it is important to get them balanced and cutting smoothly. Grind one knife to shape; then use it as a pattern to carefully mark out and grind the others.

Cope-and-Stick Cutters

Getting a cope-and-stick profile to match nicely depends on the straight cutters that cut out the slot, as well as the beading cutters. Door cutters are usually stacked on the spindle in the following order: a beading cutter on the bottom, and then one or more straight cutters to cut the slot for the panels or the rabbet for the glass, and sometimes another beading cutter on the top. The top cutter is optional, as the same result can be achieved flipping the workpiece over, end for end, and repeating the cut. Some types of cutters, such as reversible cutter sets, where the same cutter cuts both the cope bead and the stick bead, are stacked the opposite way for the stick cut, with the single bead cutter on top (Illus. 222).

The cope, or end cut, for panel doors, on the other hand, does not use straight cutters. Spacing collars are stacked in place of the straight cutters, and bead cutters that are the negative of the stick cutters undercut the ends of the rails or mullions so that the bead can fit into them. This cut leaves a stub tenon of a variable depth that will fit into the slot cut by the stick cutters. The cope cut, therefore, depends on the placement of the guide fence for the relationship between the bead and the stub tenon.

165

Illus. 220. Cutterheads that hold removable knives that can be ground to your own specifications are available for most shapers.

VARYING CUTTER—DEPTH RELATIONSHIPS

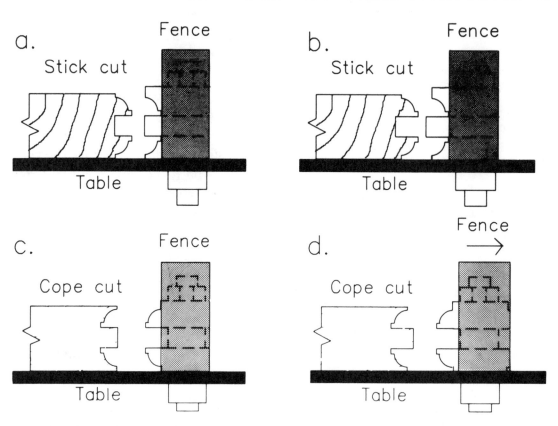

Illus. 221. As shown in a and b, the depth of the groove on the stick cut can't be varied by moving the fence. A longer straight cutter is used in b to cut a deeper groove. One can see in c and d, however, that when you move the fence back a longer stub tenon will result.

Illus. 222. Some cutters, such as this reversible set, use the same bit for both cope and stick beading. The bit cuts near the bottom of the workpiece for the cope, and at the top edge (as shown) for the stick. To complete the cut, flip the workpiece end for end and run it through a second time.

Shaper Fences

Standard shaper fences usually consist of two "tables" that are independently adjustable, much like the in-feed and out-feed tables of a jointer. Since many shapers are equipped with a special switch that will reverse the rotation of the cutters, either table of the fence can be either in-feed or out-feed, depending on the direction of the cut. Different cutting directions can be useful for template cutting, difficult grain, reversible cutters, or other special needs.

This type of fence (two independent tables) is useful for some types of moulding cutting, but can also cause problems when one is setting up for cope-and-stick cutting or panel cutting. Here, it is more important that the fence be absolutely straight, and square to the table of the shaper.

You can modify a two-table fence to work better for stick cutting or panel cutting by attaching a wide, carefully jointed board, with holes cut out for the cutters, to the existing fence mechanism. This will help keep the in-feed and out-feed sides better aligned. You will almost never be removing the entire edge from the workpiece when stick-cutting; so there will be no need to off-set the two parts of the fence.

For cope cutting you will want to make another special fence like the one shown in Illus. 223. With this fence you can greatly improve the accuracy of your cope, especially on small pieces. This fence has a thin piece of wood let into the face on the fence at the right height so that the stub tenon of the workpiece is constantly in contact with it as it passes the cutters. This prevents the workpiece from accidentally

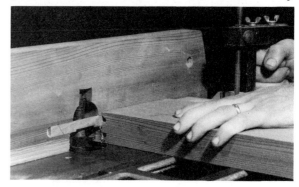

Illus. 223. By making yourself a special fence for cope cutting, like this one, you can greatly improve the accuracy of your cuts. The thin strip of wood let into the face of the fence supports the end of the workpiece at all times so that it can't drop too deeply into the cutters.

falling too far into the cutters as it passes the cutout where the cutters project through the fence. A mitre guide or special holding jig (Illus. 228) for small pieces helps keep the workpiece square as it is fed past the cutters, and a backer block is necessary when cutting across the grain to prevent chipout as the cutter comes through the back of the workpiece.

Preparing Stock for a Cope-and-Stick Door

Remember the following when preparing your stock for a cope-and-stick door:

1. The cope-and-stick joint interlocks in such a way that you will have to add a certain amount to the length of your rails to compensate for the undercut on the ends of the rails. So, if you are making a 3-foot-wide door, and your stiles are $5\frac{1}{2}$ inches wide, leaving 25 inches between them, you will have to add twice the depth of the cope cut to get the actual length to which you should cut the rails. If the cope cut is $\frac{7}{16}$ inch deep, the rails should be cut to $25\frac{7}{8}$ inches.

2. If you are going to use a true mortise-and-tenon joint, a special type of cope-cutting bit, with an auxiliary table and fence, will be necessary (Illus. 224). Because the tenon will be projecting out from the ends of the rails, and will usually take up the same width as the stub tenon that is formed between the cope cuts, use a cope-cutting bit that is hollow inside to accept a lock nut. This lock nut shouldn't project above the top of the bit, and the bit must fit on the very top of the spindle. This allows the tenon to pass over the bit. The end of the tenon rides against a fence that

Illus. 224. If you are using a true mortise-and-tenon joint, a special cope-cutting setup will be necessary. A nut that fits down inside the cutter holds the cutter on the spindle, allowing the cutter to cut right up to the tenon as it passes over it.

is offset the proper amount. Often, a raised auxiliary table must be clamped to the shaper to raise the work high enough for this kind of cutting with the bit on the very top of the spindle.

A simpler solution to this problem is to use the spline-tenon method described on pages 120 and 121 for your stile and rail joints. With this method, the mortises are all cut before the shaper work is done, and a normal setup of the cope cutters can be used for all rail and mullion ends.

Cope-and-Stick Cut with One Shaper

Begin making your cope-and-stick run by making a sample of the stick cut on a scrap piece that's exactly the same thickness as the stock you will be using. The depth of the cut will depend on the design of the cutters you are using, but should usually be just enough to cut the full profile of the bead. If you cut any deeper, you will be removing wood from the edge of the piece, and will have to offset the out-feed fence to support the work as it leaves the cutters. When the depth is just right, the full profile of the bead will be cut, but no width will be removed from the edge of the board.

Once you have a good sample of your stick cut, you can break down the machine and set up the cope cutters and cope fence. Use another scrap to get a cut that matches the stick cut so that the joint closes perfectly, and you are ready to begin making the cope cut on your workpieces.

It is usually best to make the cope cut first, using a square backer piece to prevent breakout as the cutter comes through the end of the piece (Illus. 225), but, if necessary, you can make a backer with the cope cut on it to back a piece that already has the stick cut on it. Also, if you have lots of muntins or mullions of the same length, you can cut them to length as wide pieces and put the cope cut on the ends first before ripping them and shaping the stick cut on each (Illus. 226). Make sure you don't miss any. If you have muntins for multiple lights, make some extra pieces in case you miscut any when making the stick cut.

Illus. 225. It is usually best to make the cope cut first, using a piece of scrap stock to back the work and prevent chip-out as the cutters go through it.

Illus. 226 A and B. Muntin ends should be coped before the stock is ripped to final thickness to both ensure safety and uniform length in multiple muntins.

When all the cope cuts have been made, break down the setup again, and put the stick cutters and the stick-cutting fence in place. Make test cuts on scrap pieces until they match your cope cuts perfectly. Be sure to use some type of protective cover over the top of the cutters when making the stick cuts. This cut removes more wood, and often the cutters project up past the top of the workpiece. A piece of 2 by material clamped to the fence just above the work will help keep the workpieces flat against the table, and will help keep your fingers out of harm's way (Illus. 227).

For the stick cuts on the stiles, it will be very helpful to set up an auxiliary roller for both in-feed and out-feed, if possible. It is critical that the stiles be fed smoothly and flatly all the way along their length, and it's

a real struggle to do so without something to support their length at the beginning and end of the cut. Be especially careful not to drop the beginning or the end of the stile into the hole in the fence as you go by it. Keep the workpieces tight against the in-feed as you start the cut, and transfer your pressure to the out-feed fence as you near the end of the cut. If you do end up cutting too deep on a stile or rail, you can usually take it to the jointer and remove $\frac{1}{16}$ or $\frac{1}{8}$ inch, and then make the cut again; however with thinner pieces, such as the muntins between panes of glass, this will be impossible. That's why it's a good idea to cut a few extra pieces.

When stick-cutting muntins and other small pieces, you can make a special push stick or holding jig that will steady the

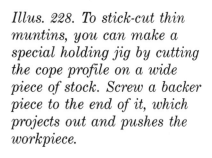

Illus. 227. When stick-cutting with a fence, be sure and clamp a cover piece to the fence, both to hold the stock flat on the fence and to keep fingers away from exposed cutters.

Illus. 228. To stick-cut thin muntins, you can make a special holding jig by cutting the cope profile on a wide piece of stock. Screw a backer piece to the end of it, which projects out and pushes the workpiece.

170

pieces and keep your fingers away from the cutters (Illus. 228). Take a piece of scrap 6 inches wide by 12 inches long, and make the cope cut along one edge. Round the corners on the other edge, and plane the coped side down so that it's just a little thinner than the workpieces and won't bind on the cover piece you clamped to the fence. Now, screw a backer piece to the back end of the piece so that it projects out about ¼ inch. The workpieces can now be pushed past the cutters with this block. The first edge of the workpiece is relatively easy to keep straight because it still has a wide bottom edge on the table, but for the second cut there would be more chance of it tipping one way or the other if it were not for the coped edge on your pusher, which will interlock with the already cut edge and keep the piece straight.

Cope-and-Stick Cut with Two Shapers

If you have two shapers, one with the cope cutters and one set up with the stick cutters, the cutting procedure is basically the same, except that you can go back to either machine at any time and remake a piece or a cut. This is especially helpful when doing multi-light doors or windows, as it can be very difficult to accurately figure the lengths of the upright mullions without first making the stick cuts on the rails and horizontal mullions. Even a small error here can become a large one when it is repeated several times.

If only two shapers are being used, be sure to make all the frame pieces and dry-assemble the entire framework before taking the bits off the stick-cutting machine to set up for panel shaping. Usually, the same fence that is used for stick cutting can be used for making the panels.

Panel Cutting

Flat panels of a uniform thickness are the first prerequisite for successful panel cutting. It will be impossible to get a uniformly thick edge on a twisted or bowed panel, though small inconsistencies can be planed or sanded out by hand.

Panels can be made in either of two ways on the shaper (Illus. 229). Either lay the board flat on the table and use a large diameter, low-profile cutter, or stand up the board perpendicular to the table and guide it along a high fence. This type of panel cutter has a high-profile and a much smaller diameter, which is better for smaller, less powerful shapers, but cannot be used to follow the edge of a curved or irregular-shaped panel, like the low-profile panel cutter can. With the high-profile cutter, it is also much easier to make the mistake of dropping the end of the panel into the cutter hole, and for this reason you may find it necessary to make a special high fence for panel cutting that allows you more control of the workpiece.

Always make the cuts across the end grain of the panels before doing the edges. This way, any wood that is chipped out at the ends of the cross-grain cuts will be removed by the edge-grain cuts.

Because panel cutting removes a lot of wood, and puts a considerable strain on the shaper and cutters, it is best with smaller machines to start with a partial cut, and allow yourself two passes all around to complete the panel raising. This will also decrease the risk of chipping out large hunks of wood where the grain is contrary

SHAPER-RAISED PANELS

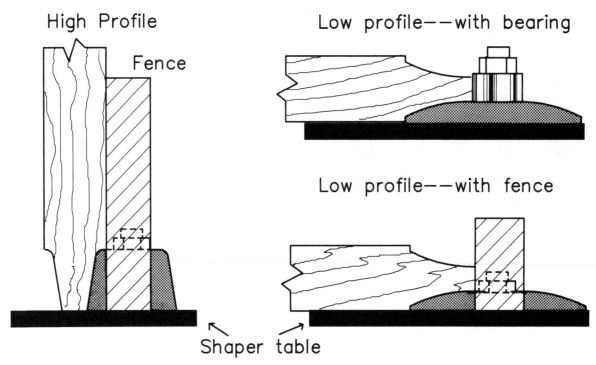

Illus. 229. Panels can be shaped either in a vertical position against a tall fence or flat on the table with a fence or bearing to guide them.

to the rotation of the bits, and generally makes for a smoother cut and less need of finish sanding.

Even the sharpest cutters will leave a surface that needs a little finish sanding, especially where you have cut across the end grain. The low-profile cutters, when they are sharp, will cut almost perfectly on the sides of the panels. The high-profile cutters leave a scalloped machine mark like that left by a planer or jointer that should be sanded out.

Shaper-Made Doors

Four-Panel Door

This door, though not the simplest one to make, is a very popular interior-passage door (Illus. 230). An order for 20 or 30 four-panel doors for the interior of a home or building is not uncommon.

The proportions of this door are determined by the position of the lock rail, usually centered on 36 inches from the floor, the height of the kick rail (about 11 inches), and the width of the door itself. A 3-foot-wide door with 5½-inch stiles and a 5-inch center mullion will need panels 11 inches wide, which is about the widest that a solid wood panel should be built. For slightly narrower doors, the stiles and mullions can be left a little wider, but should be reduced proportionately for doors under 30 inches wide.

To build this door, prepare your stock and cut the rails to the exact length you will need. Leave the two pieces for the center

A PRODUCTION FOUR-PANEL DOOR

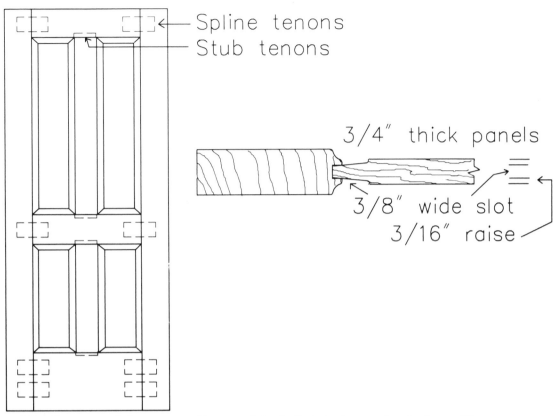

Spline tenons
Stub tenons
3/4" thick panels
3/8" wide slot
3/16" raise

Illus. 230. Four-panel doors are often used in both interior and exterior settings.

mullions long until after the cope and stick have been cut on all the other pieces. Assemble the stiles and rails, with the lock rail at the correct distance from the bottom of the door; then measure the length for the mullions from the bottoms of the grooves in the rails. Cut them to length and make the cope-and-stick cut on them. No mortise-and-tenon or dowel joint is necessary where the mullions meet the rails; the cope-and-stick joint itself will be strong enough.

Mark the center of each rail, and also the center of the ends of the mullions. Line these marks up as you dry-assemble the door, and check with a long straightedge to be sure that the center mullion is perfectly straight and centered.

Now, cut the panels to size and shape them to fit the groove in the frame. Use a scrap piece or one of the rails to check the thickness of the panel edges, and sand or plane the panels where necessary. Be sure to finish the panels entirely before assembling the door.

Refer to the description of the assembly of the old-fashioned frame-and-panel door in Chapter 5 (pages 98–111) for more information on assembly techniques for this door.

Two-Panel, Four-Light Door

Two different shaper profiles are needed for the upper and lower parts of this door (Illus. 231). The bottom part takes a panel slot that's about $7/16$ inches deep, and the upper part needs a sash profile that cuts a rabbet that is only $1/4$ inch deep; this is in order to keep the mullions as narrow and light-looking as possible. This can be accomplished by using different straight cutters for the upper and lower parts of the door or by going back over the lower slots with a router slotting cutter to deepen the slots.

Begin the door by preparing the stiles and rails. When you are ready to cut the rails to length, add $1/2$ inch to the length of all of them to compensate for the undercut of the cope cuts on the rail ends ($1/4$ inch on each end). It is generally easier to make the horizontal muntins run continuous from stile to stile, and break the vertical mullions

to fit between them. Make the muntin just slightly longer than the rails so that it won't fit loosely when the door is put together.

Lay the stiles and rails out on the worktable, and decide first what the distance between the lock rail and the kick rail is going to be. The lock rail of most doors, as already mentioned, is centered 36 inches from the floor, but this makes for a long, out-of-proportion upper window; so the lock rail is often higher when the upper part of the door is glazed. Once you have determined the height of the kick rail, make the lower vertical mulllion, but lay the pieces out once more to determine the lengths of the upper vertical mullions. A small error in length here can become a

A TWO–PANEL, FOUR–LIGHT DOOR

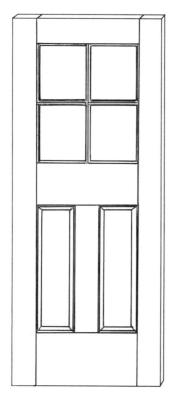

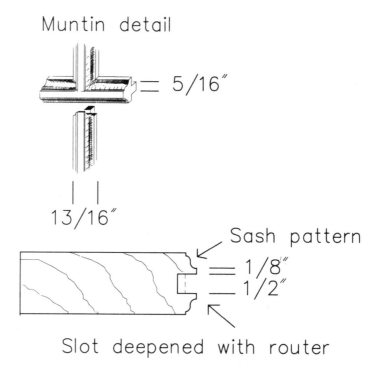

Muntin detail

= 5/16″

13/16″

Sash pattern

= 1/8″
= 1/2″

Slot deepened with router

Illus. 231. A two-panel, four-light door—simple, but tricky.

large one when it reoccurs in two or more mullions.

Extra-long straight cutters (the same type used for cutting sash for double-glazed windows) are available, and can be used to cut the parts for the lower part of the door. The rails and the vertical mullion can be cut right through, but you will have to stop the cut on the stiles at the bottom of the lock rails, and change to the shorter straight cutter for the upper parts. The other approach is to cut the whole door with the short cutter, and go back with a router and slot cutter with the door dry-assembled to deepen the rabbet.

Depending on your cutting method, you may also want to use a flush trim bit to remove the bead from one side of the upper part of the door after it is dry-assembled. This will turn a panel-slot cut into a glass-rabbet cut quite easily.

When everything fits nicely, cut and finish the panels and assemble the door. When making multi-light doors with the shaper, it is not necessary to cut mortises and tenons to hold muntins and mullions, because the interlocking nature of the cope-and-stick joint will hold them in place. Glue should be applied to the ends of the mullions, though, to seal the end grain as well as to help hold them in place.

During your last dry assembly, give yourself some marks on the stiles and rails and horizontal muntins so that you will know where to place the mullions when the door is glued together and where to check the squareness of the mullions after the door has been clamped together. If you have to move a muntin or mullion that is tightly held in place, make a small block with the cope cut on the end, and fit it to the piece; then tap it with a hammer or mallet (Illus. 232). This will prevent the piece from splitting from uneven pressure.

Illus. 232. Use a tapping block, with the cope cut on one end, to move tightly held muntins without splitting them.

There is a simpler approach to this type of door. You can simply use the door-slot cutter for the entire door, and dry-assemble the door; then, with a flush trim bit, remove the bead from one side of the lights in the upper part of the door. The mullions will look slightly heavier because of their extra width, but considerable time that would have been spent changing shaper setups and chopping the bead cut square will be saved.

24-Light, Bevelled-Glass Door

The techniques used for this door will apply to just about any French-style door (Illus. 233). For this one, you will use 6- × 9-inch bevelled glass panes, available from stained glass suppliers; so the size of the glass is predetermined, and the rest of the door must be made to fit it. A 3-foot-wide door of this type will have 24 lights, while a

Illus. 233. This complex-looking door is really quite simple to make.

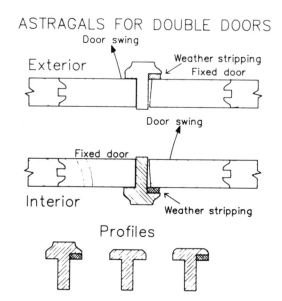

Illus. 234. An astragal or T moulding is usually applied to either the opening or fixed door when doors are hung in pairs.

30-inch-wide door can be made with only 18 lights. Note that an especially wide kick rail is used. Another row of glass panes would reduce the kick rail to under 9 inches in width, which seems too narrow; so we must use a kick rail 18 inches in width.

French doors that do not use glass of a predetermined size can be made to any proportions you like, but generally the lines tend to look right if the panes are taller than they are wide. Eight-light or ten-light French doors with a single run of vertical mullions are typical. Often, French doors are hung in pairs, which means leaving enough space in the jamb for an astragal (usually ½ inch) to help seal the closure between the doors (Illus. 234). French doors,

like this 24-light door, also work well if they are wide and have fixed sidelights.

To build this door, begin by joining up enough frame stock to get an 18-inch-wide kick rail. The stiles and the top rail should be 5¾ inches wide to start. A set of sash-cutting bits of the kind used in window making is used for making all the cope-and-stick cuts. The rabbet for the glass is about ¼ inch deep on the set used here. You want the minimum rabbet depth in this case so that as much of the glass bevels as possible can be exposed. Make the space for each pane about ⅛ inch bigger all-around than the size of the glass. This will also help show more bevel.

When the glue is dry on the kick rail, cut the rails to length at 27 inches, and cut enough pieces of stock to get all the horizontal muntins to a length of 27¹⁄₃₂ inches. Now cut enough pieces of frame stock to 9¼ inches to get all 18 upright mullions. Use a positive stop on your cross-cutting jig on the table or radial arm saw to ensure that all these pieces are exactly the same length (Illus. 235). Any fluctuation in the lengths of the upright pieces on this door will make things extremely difficult for you.

At this point, you can take all your frame stock to the shapers and cut the cope cuts on all the pieces. Be sure to make a cope-cutting fence like the one described earlier in this chapter (page 167) for cutting the narrow mullion and muntin ends.

Once the cope has been cut on the ends of the mullions, you can take them back to the table saw and rip them all to their $^{13}/_{16}$-inch width. Now, return to the shaper with the stick cutters and run the stick cut on all the pieces. Be sure to use the pusher block described earlier in this chapter (page 175) for pushing the small mullions and muntins past the stick cutters.

I find it best to set the stick cutter to cut just a little deep. After the pieces have been

shaped, take them to the jointer and joint the flat part of the edge down far enough so that the fit is just right. This way, the jointer will remove any small chipouts and saw kerfs that are left showing on this part of the stick cut, and a much cleaner job will result.

Before attempting to assemble this door, take all the horizontal muntins and the two rails and line them up next to each other so that their ends are even (Illus. 236). Now, divide their lengths into quarters and, using a square, make marks across the top of them that will be the center lines of the vertical mullions. Now it is easy to lay the pieces out between the stiles, and to assemble them working from one end to the other.

After a dry assembly, during which you should check to be sure that all your panes are of equal width, you are ready to glue the door together. Once again, the ends of all the mullions and muntins should be sealed lightly with glue. Don't put any more glue on them than necessary, as it will be

Illus. 235. Use a positive stop when cutting many muntins to the same length. Note that the stop is clamped up off the surface of the jig, so that sawdust buildup won't affect the cutting length.

Illus. 236. Line up all the horizontal muntins and rails and mark the centers of the vertical mullions on them before assembly.

difficult to clean the squeeze-out from the corners. If you do have glue that has to be cleaned out of hard-to-get to places, use a small, stiff-bristled brush with water to remove it (Illus. 237).

When the door is completely clamped together, use a long straightedge, or a straight piece of board to line up the upright mullions precisely. If you have trouble getting the upright mullions tight, ease off the side-to-side clamps, and apply two long clamps from end to end, near the ends of the rails. When the mullions are tight, retighten the side-to-side clamps and remove the long ones.

This door should be completely finished before the glass is installed. Apply a couple of coats of finish before cutting the stops for the glass; then cut the stops and put them in place. Now, they too can be coated with finish, and later removed one pane at a time so that you can install the glass. Wooden stops like the ones described in the previous chapter should be made to hold the panes in place. Since all the upright mullions are exactly the same length, these stops can be cut by putting a mark or a stop on your chop-saw fence or other cutting device. The size of the horizontal panes may vary a little, but you can start cutting an average-size pane and then make it a little

Illus. 237. A stiff bristle brush will get squeezed-out glue out of corners and hard-to-reach places.

smaller or bigger as the need arises. Use small brass #18 escutcheon pins ¾ inch long, to hold the stops in if the door is varnished or oiled, or use galvinized nails of the same size if it is painted. The glass panes should be bedded in a flexible caulk such as clear silicone or butyl caulk.

Window Making

8
Designing Windows

"Of the making of windows there is no end."
—*Handbook of Doormaking, Windowmaking, and Staircasing*

And, we might add with a modern perspective, the ways of making windows are always changing. Windows have come a long way from the crude "wind openings" in the castles and keeps of our European ancestors to the high-tech, energy-efficient, and infinitely variable mechanisms available today. Over the centuries, many different techniques of shaping, joining, and hanging jamb and sash have developed to accommodate the needs of both the craftsmen and the customers of the time.

In this chapter, I'll explore design factors that pertain to windows. I'll begin with a historical overview and a discussion of standard window terms used in most parts of the country today, and then present some different types of windows. Also included is information on the solar and thermal properties of windows and the different materials that can be used in building them, drawings and descriptions of framing details for various sizes and types of windows, and a section on window dressings and trimming methods. The following chapters will cover specific techniques and methods of construction.

Historical Overview

Wooden sash and jamb construction was first developed in 17th-century Europe, where skilled and specialized sash jointers worked out the basic configurations of casement frames and sliding sash. At that time, large windows were often divided into two or more sections called "squares of sash." One section could be opened either by pivoting on a hinge (in which case it was called casement) or by sliding in a track. The sliding windows were called sash, from the French work *châssis*. Each window frame was divided into smaller lights or panes by a lattice work of mullions and muntins.

The glass used during the 17th century was very thin and fragile, and as many as 12 panes per sash were common because the panes could not be made very large. Pegged mortise-and-tenon joints that held together even in the absence of reliable glues were sawn, bored, and chopped by hand. Rabbets and decorative beads called "ovolos" were worked with hand moulding planes. The corners of the decorative bead

180

where cross members met were first mitred with a careful 45-degree slice of the craftsman's chisel; then the ends of the joining pieces were undercut (following the line of the mitred cut) with a coping saw or gouge to form the interlocking joint known as the cope-and-stick.

Today, the parts of most manufactured wooden sash windows are shaped on power-feed spindle shapers and assembled in large factories, but several methods of construction are also possible using power and hand tools that are readily available to the home craftsman and the small-scale professional woodworker.

Windows are really a luxury item, and an expensive one at that when you consider all the costs involved in making them, installing them, trimming around them, and, of course, the heat that is lost through them (Illus. 238). But, for most of us they are a necessity as well. They bring the beauty and fresh air of the outdoors into our homes.

Windows themselves are things of beauty too, their structure and decorative trim harmoniously unifying the inner and outer realms, a thought that may inspire anyone who has an artistic or creative bent to consider building one himself. You don't have to be a high-tech woodworker to do it; you just need a little information and the inclination to be creative.

Illus. 238. Windows are an expensive luxury, but worth it because of the beauty and light that they bring into our homes.

Terms

The word *jamb* is commonly used to refer to the rectangular construction that lines the rough opening and holds the sash, if there is one, or the glass and stops, if there is not. More specifically, the jambs are the side pieces of this construction. The top piece of the jamb is known as the *head*, while the *sill*, always at the base of the jamb, is usually set at a slope of 15 degrees or more to direct rainwater off the window.

The word *sash* refers to the usually moveable frame that holds the glass and mounts in the jamb by various means. The word sash can be used generally to refer to all types of windows or, more specifical-

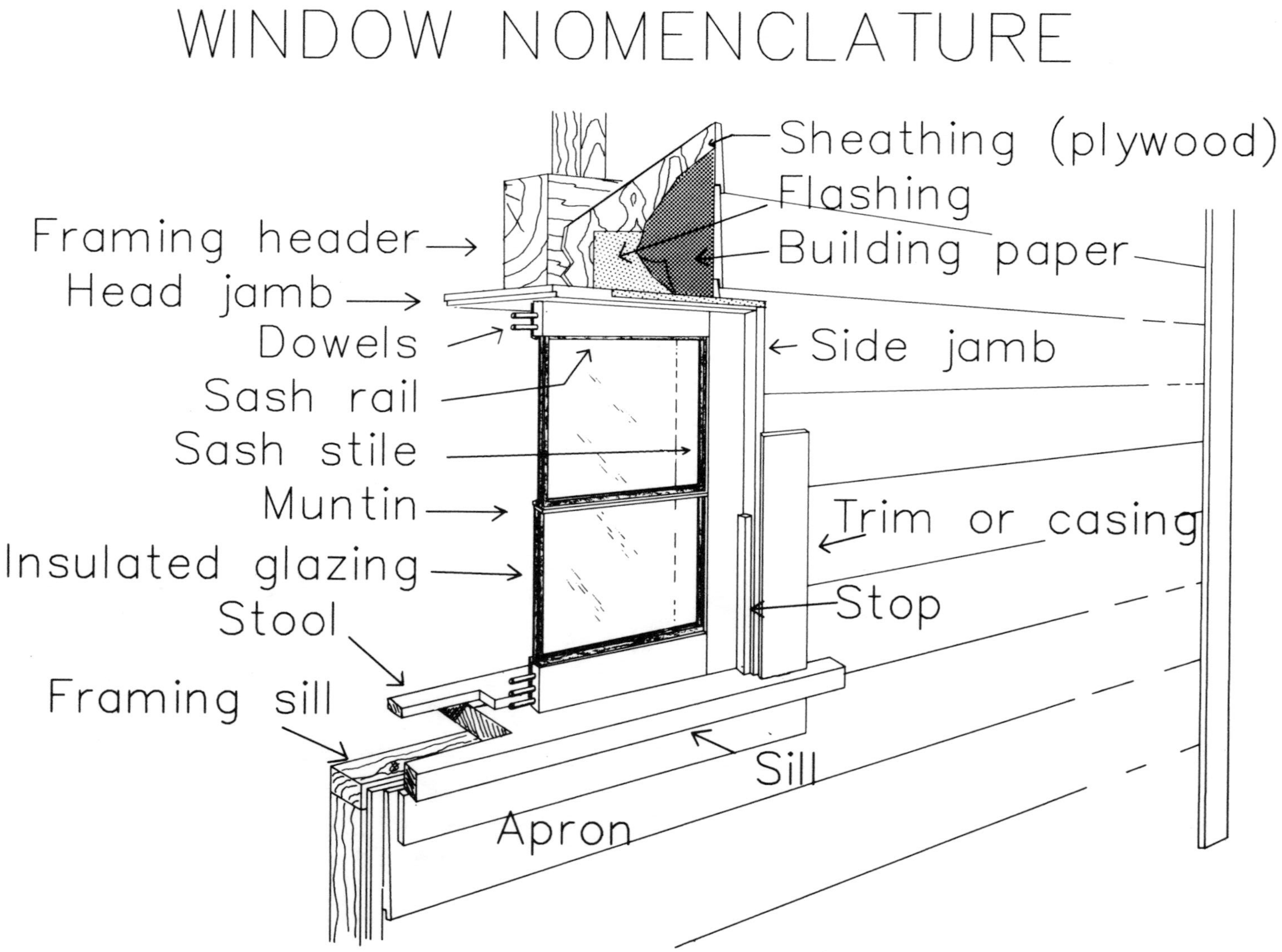

WINDOW NOMENCLATURE

Sheathing (plywood)
Flashing
Building paper
Side jamb
Trim or casing
Stop

Framing header
Head jamb
Dowels
Sash rail
Sash stile
Muntin
Insulated glazing
Stool
Framing sill

Sill
Apron

Illus. 239. Common window terminology.

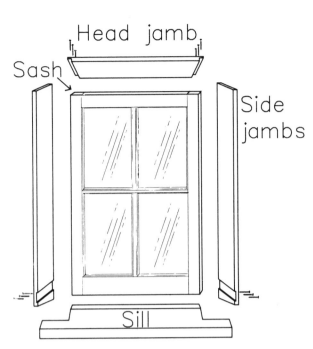

Illus. 240. An exploded view of the sash and jamb. Rabbet the head jamb to hold the side jambs, and make a slot cut at 15 degrees in the side jambs to hold the sill.

ly, for just double-hung windows. The word *casement* is used when referring to the frame that holds the glass in hinged windows. The outer frame of the sash is made up of horizontal rails and vertical stiles. *Vertical mullions* and *horizontal muntins* form the lattice that divides the glass into smaller panes.

Stops for either fixed or operable windows can be made from strips of wood, sometimes with a decorative edge on the inside, or by cutting a rabbet in a jamb made from 1½-inch stock. The word stop also refers to smaller strips of wood that are used to hold the glass in the sash. Glazing putty can also be used instead of wooden stops to hold the glass in and seal it to prevent leakage. *Interior* and *exterior casings*, and the *stool* and *apron*, are trim

pieces that cover the gap between the siding and the jamb.

Opening windows can be catagorized, according to the way they open, into two main categories. *Hinged windows*, the first category, are called *casements* if they open to one side (double casements are two casements mounted in one jamb, opening on both sides), *awnings* if they hinge at the top, and *hopper* or *transom* windows if they hinge at the bottom (Illus. 241).

The most common form of wooden sliding window is the *double-hung*, in which the two sashes slide up and down (Illus. 242 and 243). The *parting bead*, usually set in a groove in the jamb, separates and holds in place the two moving sashes that ride in tracks formed by the blind stop on the outside, the parting bead itself, and the finish stop on the inside. The *meeting rails*, which run from edge to edge, unlike most window rails, are bevelled in such a way that they come together to form a weathertight closure when the sash fastener is closed.

Until recently, counterweights called *sash weights* were hidden behind the casing of this type of window to counterbalance the sash so that it would open almost effortlessly (unless the wood swelled from moisture or was painted where it shouldn't have been). Most modern double-hung windows are counterbalanced by springs, which can be purchased separately, and are mounted in the center of the jamb. Spring-loaded metal tracks that mount in the jambs are also available for modern double-hung windows. These provide a good air-tight seal, and have built-in counterbalance springs.

Windows that appear to be double-hung, but actually hinge at the bottom, like an inward-opening transom window, are also

HINGED OPENING WINDOWS

Transom window

Awning window

Double casement window

Fixed sash

Operable sash

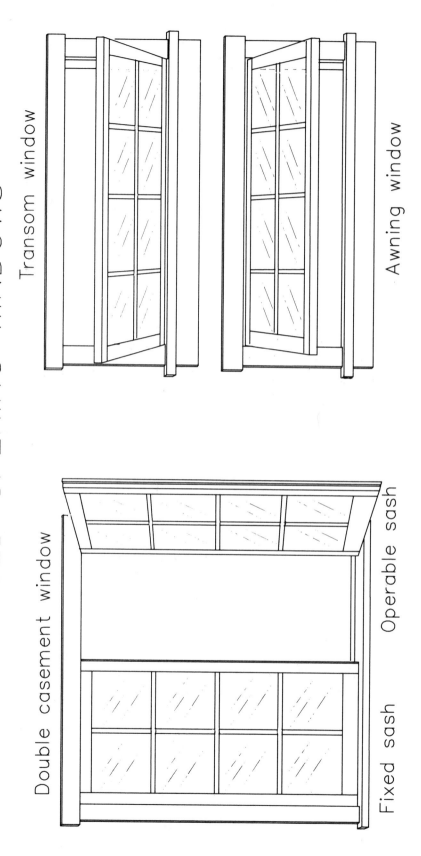

Illus. 241. Casement windows can be mounted one, two, or even three to a jamb, and are hinged on the side. The words transom and hopper refer to windows that hinge at the bottom; awning windows hinge at the top.

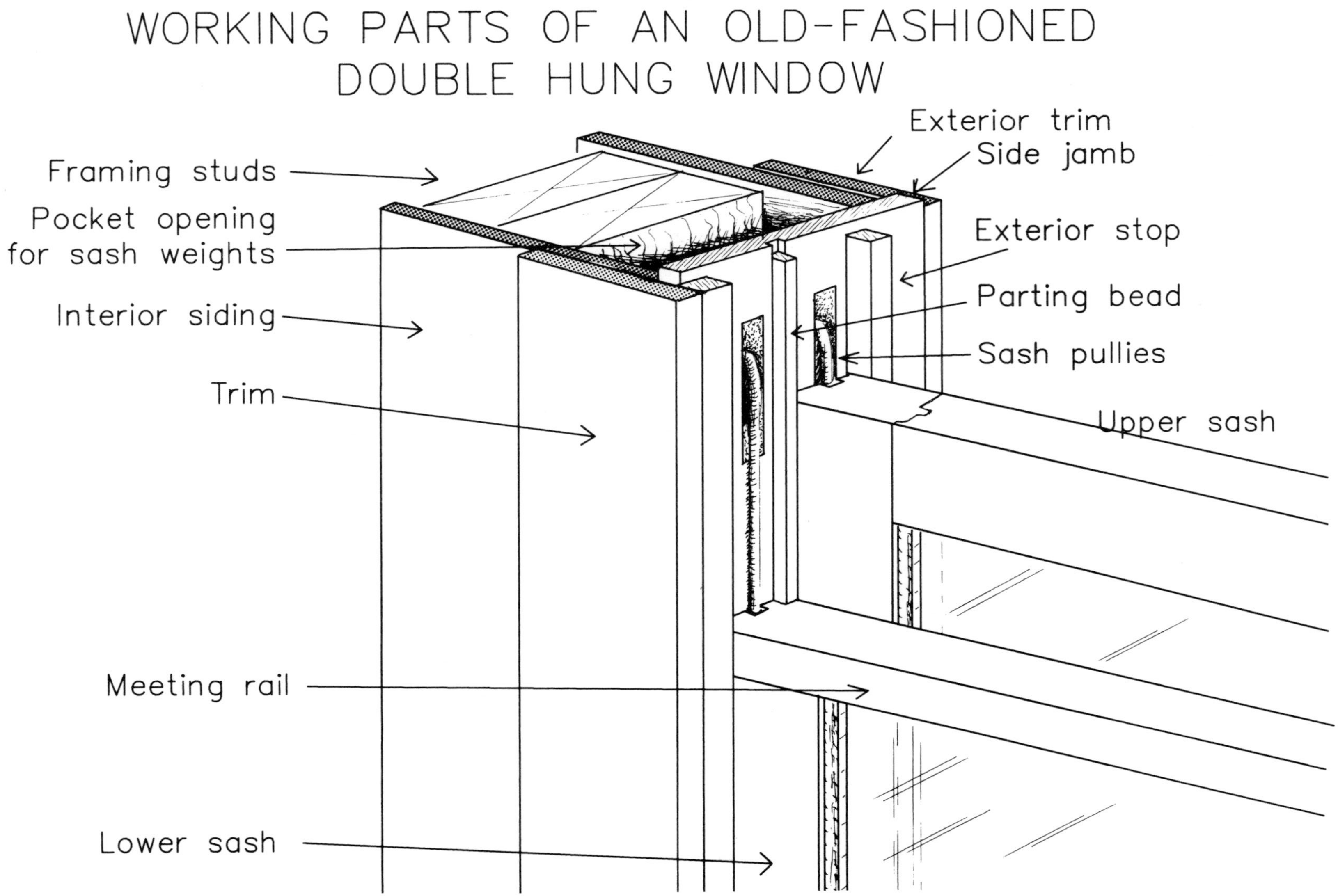

WORKING PARTS OF AN OLD-FASHIONED
DOUBLE HUNG WINDOW

Exterior trim
Side jamb
Exterior stop
Parting bead
Sash pullies
Upper sash

Framing studs
Pocket opening for sash weights
Interior siding
Trim
Meeting rail
Lower sash

Illus. 242 and 243 (next page). Double-hung sashes slide up and down in their jambs. It can be seen from the cross section that the meeting rails overlap when closed to form a weathertight seal.

DOUBLE-HUNG WINDOW CROSS SECTION

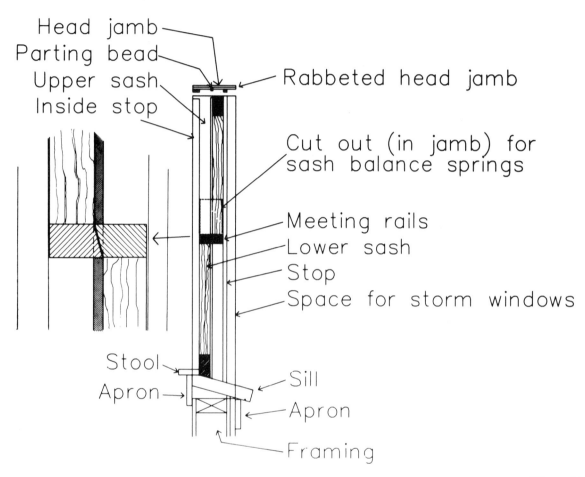

Head jamb
Parting bead
Upper sash
Inside stop

Rabbeted head jamb

Cut out (in jamb) for sash balance springs

Meeting rails
Lower sash
Stop
Space for storm windows

Stool
Apron

Sill
Apron
Framing

Illus. 243.

becoming more popular today (Illus. 244). They work easily, and allow for the placement of outside screens or storm windows.

Storm windows are generally hung outside of the permanent windows in the wintertime to improve the thermal efficiency of a building, and can be replaced in the summer by screens. If storm windows and screens are to be used, the jambs must be built to accommodate them.

Energy Efficiency and Windows

Unless careful consideration is given to the placement and construction of windows in a building they can easily become the biggest energy drain in the structure. Glass is a poor insulating material to begin with. In colder climates, where the National

A HINGED DOUBLE—HUNG WINDOW

Illus. 244. Inward-hinged windows that look double-hung have dependable hinges, and you can put screens or storm windows up on the outside.

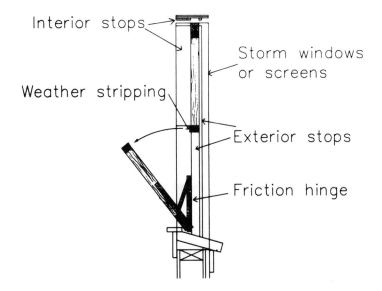

Interior stops

Storm windows or screens

Weather stripping

Exterior stops

Friction hinge

Bureau of Standards recommends wall insulation of R19 or better (R representing resistance to heat loss), and a roof insulation of R30, a double-glazed window with an exterior storm window (3 layers of glass) still only has an R factor of 2.67. If only two layers of glass are used, the R factor goes down to less than 2. So, even a perfectly airtight window loses heat more than five times as fast as well-insulated wall space. If there are any air leaks around that window, it could become a major heating expense. A few slightly drafty windows can account for 20% to 50% of the yearly expenditure for heating your home.

But windows can help your house gain heat as well. A single sheet of glass transmits only about 84% of the heat energy that is radiated to it by the sun, but the energy that does pass through it is effectively trapped inside the structure. This can be either a blessing or a nuisance, depending upon the climate and the time of year. In the summer, radiant heat gain can put an extra strain on your air-conditioning system, once again driving up the cost of keeping your home comfortable. In the winter, on the other hand, radiant heat gain is desirable and, depending on the climate, can be counted on to contribute as much as 50% of your heating needs if your home is properly designed to take advantage of it. In other words, properly designed, well-built, and properly placed windows can be made to pay their own way in areas where there is plenty of winter sun. In areas that receive too little winter sun, the emphasis should be on minimizing heat loss through smaller, better insulated, and tighter windows.

SOLAR GAIN

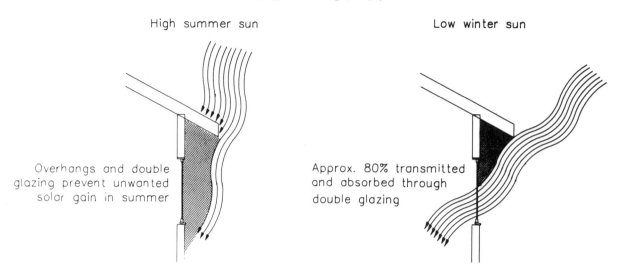

High summer sun

Low winter sun

Overhangs and double glazing prevent unwanted solar gain in summer

Approx. 80% transmitted and absorbed through double glazing

Illus. 245. Solar heat gain can be either a blessing or a nuisance. Overhanging roofs or awnings and double glazing can help moderate its effects in the summer and make it work for you in the winter.

Design Tips for Solar Efficiency

The choices you make in the size and placement of your windows should vary according to the climate where you live, but a few general rules will apply to most climates found in the mid-latitudes. Generally, one should take as much advantage of radiant heat gain in the winter as possible by maximizing the amount of glazing on walls facing south, and minimizing glazing on walls that receive little or no solar radiation. Solariums, rock beds, and other forms of thermal storage can be used to trap and store solar heat in your home.

Since the angle of the sun is lower in the winter than in the summer, overhanging roofs can often be made to work like awnings, shading the windows in the summer and allowing maximum insolation (solar gain) in the winter. Though double-glazing increases the R factor only slightly, it has the added advantage of nearly eliminating radiant heat gain in the summer, when the sun is high, while still allowing some radiant heat gain from the lower winter sun. Special insulating draperies or insulating shutters on the inside of your windows can greatly improve your home's resistance to heat loss at night or on cloudy days. The most important factor in preventing heat loss around windows is making them as airtight as possible. Therefore, weather-stripping and storm windows are extremely important in cold winter climates (Illus. 246).

Thermopane or Insulated Glass

Thermopane or insulated glass is made by gluing two pieces of glass together with a

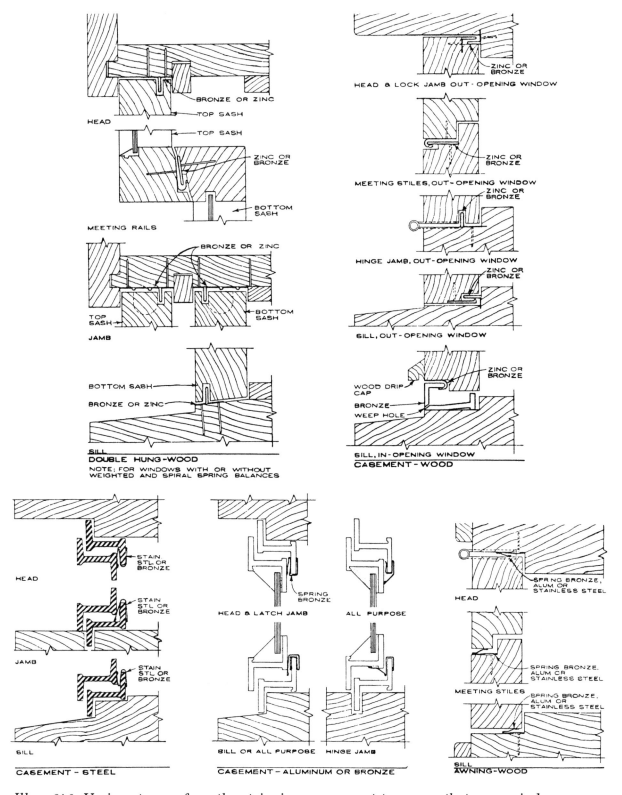

Illus. 246. Various types of weatherstripping are a must to ensure that your windows are airtight when closed.

189

INSULATED GLAZING

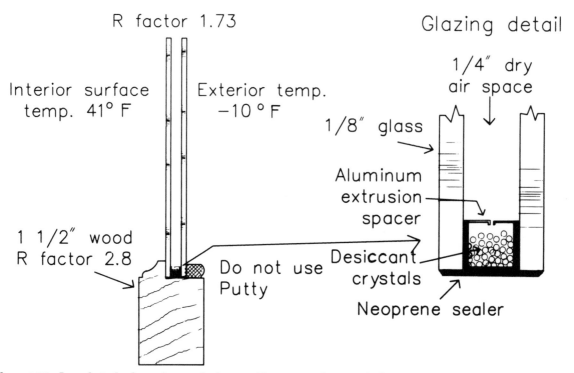

R factor 1.73

Glazing detail

Interior surface
temp. 41° F

Exterior temp.
−10 ° F

1/4″ dry
air space

1/8″ glass

Aluminum
extrusion
spacer

1 1/2″ wood
R factor 2.8

Do not use
Putty

Desiccant
crystals

Neoprene sealer

Illus. 247. Insulated glass is made by sealing two sheets of glass together with a neoprene seal. A dry air space is created between them, nearly doubling the R factor of the glazed areas, and helping to prevent heat gain in the summer.

neoprene sealer and an aluminum spacer between them (Illus. 247). The aluminum spacer contains pellets of a highly absorptive chemical that quickly locks up all the moisture that is trapped between the sheets of glass. This dry air space between the two sheets of glass boosts the insulating value of the glass from about R1 to R1.73, nearly doubling the R value of your window area. Thermopane glass also will not collect moisture condensation or frost on the inside when outside temperatures fall below freezing. When the outside temperature falls to −10 degrees Farenheit, the inside temperature of a single-glazing win-

dow in a typical house heated to 68 degrees will be about 15 degrees. Under the same conditions, the inside temperature of Thermopane glass will be 41 degrees. As mentioned before, Thermopane glass will also help keep your home cooler in the summer by reflecting much of the higher-angle solar radiation that would be transmitted by single glazing.

But Thermopane glazing does have its drawbacks. It costs nearly three times as much per square foot as single-strength glass, and the neoprene glue and spacer take up about 3/8 inch of space around the edge, which must be covered by the window sash and stop, both for appearance's sake and to prevent the breakdown of the neoprene glue caused by exposure to the sun. This means that multi-paned windows with very thin, delicate mullions and muntins of the type that can be found in old-fashioned windows are not possible with Thermopane glass. Where a mullion as narrow as ¾ inch is not uncommon with single glazing, the narrowest mullion possible with Thermopane is about 1⅜ inch.

Special router or shaper cutters must be used when making Thermopane sash to cut the rabbet extra deep (about 9/16 inch) (Illus. 248). Do not use putty with Thermopane glass to hold the panes of glass in the sash, because a chemical reaction between the putty and the neoprene will quickly destroy the neoprene seal, causing the glass to become permanently fogged.

New Advances

New technologies have recently been developed for coating glass with extremely thin layers of special metals and metal oxides to lower the emissivity of the glazing in the

Illus. 248. Use special extra-long straight cutters when shaping sash for insulated glass. The rabbet must be at least ½ inch deep to cover the spacer and sealant around the edge of the glass. Shown at left are single-glazed sash and cutters, at right double-glazed sash and cutters. At far right is a safer way to cut this deep rabbet. First cut a slot, and then use a table saw to form a rabbet.

infrared area of the spectrum without greatly affecting its transparency to visible light. Normal glass absorbs and reemits about 84% of the heat energy that strikes it, but various types of low-emissivity glass reflect up to 95% of that radiant heat. This will both improve the insulating value of your windows in the wintertime and lower your cooling bills in the summer by preventing unwanted heat gain.

Many variations of coatings and coating technologies exist already, and improvements are being made all the time. Some scientists predict that coated glass will become the norm in new construction and remodelling in the next few years. Coatings also are available that increase the emissivity of the glazing rather than lower it, thus improving the thermal gain of south-facing glazing in greenhouses and heat traps. The prices of these new coated glasses vary greatly, but they are generally 10% to 50% more expensive than comparable uncoated glazing.

Modern, high-tech windows are decidedly worth the extra money and trouble for buildings in colder climates and homes that burn expensive fuels for heat. And, believe it or not, wood is still by far the best insulating material that you can buy for framing your glazing. An inch-and-a-half of solid wood has an R factor of about 2.8, much better than either metal or plastic sash.

The more windows you have, and the more heating and cooling your climate demands, the more you will save in yearly energy bills by building wooden sash windows and investing in the best glazing materials for your particular situation. Assuming a yearly heating bill of $1,000 for a home with single-glazed aluminum windows, and figuring (conservatively) that 33% of that expenditure is being lost through the windows, a doubling of window efficiency will save $330 per year in heating costs. If storm windows or insulated draperies are added, the yearly saving approaches $500. From these figures, it can be seen that even a complete retrofit (tearing out the old windows and putting in new ones) will pay for itself in fuel savings within just a few years.

Aesthetic Design Factors

Of course, efficiency is not the only criteria by which windows will be judged. The beauty and appropriateness of the windows to the style of the building is also of great importance. Doors and windows are two of the key elements in establishing a harmonious decorative style in your home.

Over the years, particular patterns of home construction have developed based partly on function (adaptation to regional climactic conditions) and partly on the aesthetic principles of the day. Economics also plays its part in this equation, of course, but even the cheapest of homes aspire to some style. A quick review of some of the home-building styles that have been popular in your area may help you in designing your windows to best suit the style of your building.

Let's explore some general aesthetic and functional considerations in designing windows. In most cases, the heads of your windows should be at the same height as the heads of your doors, about 80 inches above the floor. Windows in a kitchen area above counters (usually 36 inches high) should start no lower than 42 inches above the floor. Tempered glass should be used whenever glazing extends lower than 14 inches from the floor or whenever large panes of glass such as picture windows are used.

Cross-ventilation is one of the important things to consider when planning the placement of openable windows. A gentle breeze blowing through living areas or bedrooms is certainly the cheapest and most natural way to stay cool and comfortable. When planning a new home or the installation of retrofitted windows, you should consider the prevailing direction of winds in your area during the warm seasons. Place windows so that cool air will be drawn in near floor level, and hot, stale air will be vented near the upper part of the room. Bathrooms especially should have good ventilation, more for dryness and freshness than for a cooling effect. You may also want to use opaque glass in bathroom windows.

Of course, light is an important consideration. The placement of windows in a building can greatly affect the quality and amount of natural light that will be available in the various rooms of the home. Because the track of the sun is across the southern part of the sky for the United States most of the year, it should be kept in mind that southern windows will admit strong, sometimes glaring light during the middle part of the day, while northern windows will admit subdued soft lighting. Strong southern lighting can have a bleaching effect on draperies, carpets, and woodwork; so it may be best to avoid skylights on the south side of a building unless shades can be drawn to moderate the light at times.

A breakfast nook should most certainly be on the east side of a home, while the golden light of afternoon will best be viewed from the westernmost rooms. View windows should be carefully planned to enhance nature's handiwork. An expansive view will demand wide, horizontal windows, while tall vertical windows may have a striking effect in forested areas or where the view is more vertical. Combinations of horizontal and vertical windows can also result in an amazing effect.

Exciting Window Nooks

Bay windows, window boxes, window seats, and solariums are wonderful ways to use windows to create visually interesting exteriors and cozy, yet functional nooks and corners in larger interior spaces (Illus. 249–252).

A bay window can be constructed in several ways; some can be more easily incorporated into an existing wall than others (Illus. 253 and 254). A bay window is usually a three-, four-, or five-sided nook jutting out from a larger room. It will have windows on at least three sides, so that someone standing in it will have a full 180-degree view of the outside. The corners of the nook are often, though not always, angled at 45 degrees to the other walls to soften them and give them the traditional bay-window look. A Victorian bay will usually have angled corners, where a more Gothic or modern approach would be to avoid the angled corners.

When laying out the rough framing of a bay, it is important that you tie the floor securely into the rest of the structure, either with common joists or with joists that are supported on a rim ledger and their own foundation. It is also important that where the 45-degree walls meet the regular walls, the angles on the ends are equal; otherwise, the ends of the walls will be of different widths.

The roof joists for a bay should all radiate from a single point, though that point may be an imaginary one somewhere inside the building. With these factors taken into consideration, a bay can easily be added on to an existing structure, or incorporated into a new one with otherwise conventional building techniques.

A partial bay does not extend completely from floor to ceiling, but begins at the bottom of the windows, and may be nothing more than a series of windows set at slight angles to each other so that the structure bows out more or less fully from the wall. This type of structure must generally be supported by brackets on the exterior of the building, or by the side walls, if there are any. A window seat is created on the inside of the bay because the structure does not extend to the floor. This is really just a more complex form of a window box.

Nearly any window can be turned into a window box if you tear out the existing window and trim and frame a small box or bubble that projects out from the wall (Illus. 255). The important thing here is making sure that the roof of the structure is properly "flashed" where it meets the existing wall, to prevent leaks. Also, the base of the structure must be properly supported with brackets or other diagonal bracing. The interior of your window box will be like a miniature greenhouse or terrarium, adding a touch of vitality and beauty to your structure.

Illus. 249–252 (above and below). Bay windows, dormers, window boxes, window seats, and solariums all create interesting and comfortable areas that accent the beauty of windows. Photos at top right and below show bay windows.

Illus. 251.

Illus. 252.

194

A BAY WINDOW FLOOR PLAN

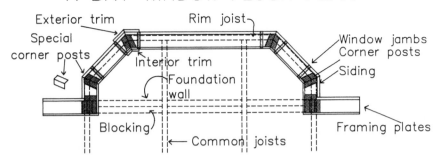

Illus. 253. This five-sided bay window has two narrow windows and one wide picture window. Special corner posts must be made for the angled walls, and the structure is supported by extended common joists.

ROOF FRAMING FOR A BAY WINDOW

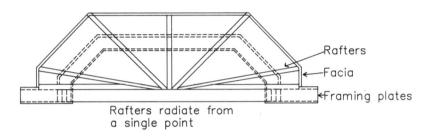

Rafters radiate from a single point

Illus. 254. The roof rafters on a bay window should radiate from a single point, even if it is an imaginary one inside the main structure.

Illus. 255. Nearly any window can be made into a small window box.

A window seat can be built in under nearly any window, but is most often found in bays or other small nooks where it does not project into the room. A built-in window seat can be constructed with a hinged top or front, so that it can provide storage space as well as a comfortable place to sit and contemplate the natural world from the comfort of the indoors. A larger window seat can also be a great place for a guest bed or a built-in couch-type structure.

A solarium is usually a separate room on the south side of a building with a maximum amount of glazing that captures the sun's warmth during the day (Illus. 256). This heat is then transmitted into the house by either ducting or by simple convection through windows or doors; the solarium can be closed off from the rest of the house during the cool parts of the day to prevent heat loss.

Solariums can be great entryways and

wonderful greenhouses, though the functions of solar collection and optimum plant growing aren't always in perfect harmony. Large, fixed glass panels predominate in the construction of a solarium, and either glass or specially designed fibreglass sheeting can be used for the roof. If you intend to do a lot of gardening in your solarium, be sure to look into materials that will shield your plants from ultraviolet rays.

Illus. 256. A solarium can be a wonderful addition to your home that will increase your solar gain and beautify your home.

Skylights

A skylight is a window that is also part of your roof. Installation of skylights, whether in an existing structure or a new one, should not be attempted without a thorough understanding of roofing principles and an appreciation of the intensity of the weathering forces at work on your roof. A poorly installed skylight will leak for sure, no matter how much caulk and roof-patching tar is applied to it, but one that is done properly can bring light and beauty into dark parts of your home.

The skylight design shown in Illus. 258 works like the hatch cover on a boat. The curb is built into the roof, just like the jamb in a window, except that here it must extend several inches above the layer of shingles that sheds the water from your roof. Four inches above the top of the shingles is usually about right; you don't want the curb sticking out so far that it looks funny, but it should be out far enough so that it won't be flooded when a sudden downpour hits.

The interior treatment of the curb depends on the type of ceiling. In an area of open-beamed ceilings, you can simply extend it in to the inside of the panelling and end it flush, or let it protrude an inch or so. It can be trimmed out like a window or, if the panelling fits tightly, left untrimmed. If the skylight goes in an area with a drop ceiling, you will want to create a light well by panelling or installing sheetrock (plasterboard) between the ceiling and the curb.

Once the curb is in place in the hole in the roof, you can apply the metal flashing that will deflect the water. Top and bottom saddle pieces are usually made to fit by a sheet-metal shop. These pieces are soldered together and wrap around the corners of the curb. It is especially important that the top saddle not be nailed, and that the flat part of it extend back up the roof far enough so that water won't be able to run back up under it. This will depend somewhat on the pitch of the roof, but usually it is sufficient if the top saddle extends the length of a shingle. For wide skylights, a ridge called a cricket is built into the upper part of the flashing to help shed the water and prevent it from puddling along the upper edge of the curb.

The sides of the curb are usually done with step flashing that is worked in under each layer of shingles as they are laid in. This is also critical, since water can run sideways and back under the shingles if a single long piece is used.

With the curb and flashing in place, and the shingling completed, the skylight is ready to be covered with the sash frame, which acts as a hatch cover. The frame should be made with very sturdy corner joints, and a groove instead of a rabbet to hold the glass. Note in Illus. 257 that the glass runs out over the bottom edge of the frame. This is very important. Many people make the mistake of enclosing the bottom edge of the glass with the frame, but this will obstruct the free drainage of water off the glass and divert it into the house. The glass must drain freely at the lower edge. Use a metal L-bracket or a wooden clip to support the glass and prevent it from slipping out of the groove.

Caulk the groove with a clear silicon caulk before sliding the glass into place, and apply the metal flashing shown in Illus. 258 to help protect the wooden sash frame from weathering. Weathering is very intense on a roof, especially if it is facing south, and this flashing will help prevent the rapid destruction of the sash frame.

Illus. 257. The wood of this skylight is as weathered as the shingles, but it doesn't leak because it is properly designed to shed water. Note that no wood covers the bottom edge of the glass.

197

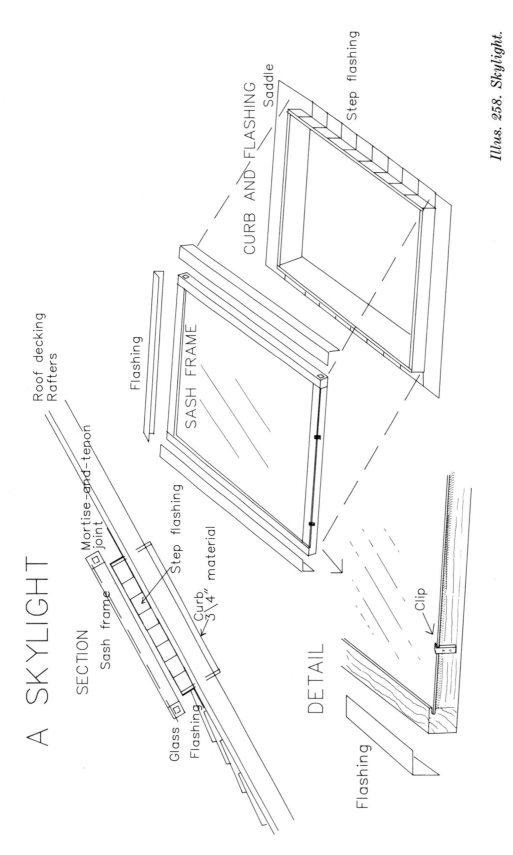

A SKYLIGHT

SECTION

Roof decking
Rafters

Mortise-and-tenon
joint

Sash frame

Step flashing

Curb
3\4" material

Glass
Flashing

Flashing

SASH FRAME

CURB AND FLASHING

Saddle

Step flashing

DETAIL

Clip

Flashing

Illus. 258. Skylight.

9
Basic Window-Making Techniques

In this chapter, I will review some construction methods that worked for our ancestors, and which will still work today for the patient, self-sufficient craftsman. I will also outline more modern methods for amateur and professional small-shop woodcrafters, and discuss various ways of building jambs and joining the sash that can be used for most windows. Later chapters will cover various specific tools, techniques, and types of windows.

Planning and Organization for the Small Shop

One of the most critical parts of window making is organization. Even the simplest window has many parts, and if you are building more than one window you are going to have lots of parts to keep track of. Making lists and marking parts to keep track of them as you work are essential to avoid costly and frustrating errors.

In a factory, the same-sized window is made over and over again, and the customer buys what he knows he needs.

The custom window-maker, on the other hand, is building windows especially to fill a one-time need. If your completed window somehow ends up being too big for its rough opening, it may be a long time before you have a call for that size and type of window again. It cannot be stressed too much that the custom window maker should double-check and triple-check his measurements, and above all stay organized.

One method of organization handed down to us from the old-time sash jointers is the story stick. As with doors, the important vertical marking points of the window are marked out along one side of a stick of wood, and the horizontal marks are made on the other side with enough notation to keep things straight. The story stick is then laid or clamped next to the rails and stiles after they are cut out, and the marks are transferred from the stick to the workpiece. Several windows can be marked out quickly and accurately by using a square to transfer the marks. This method works well if you are doing a lot of identical windows, but if you find yourself with 20 windows of varying sizes and shapes, it won't help much in keeping things straight.

If you are building your own windows or doing a set of custom windows for someone else, you will probably have a list of rough openings of specific sizes and shapes, and some kind of description of the windows that will fill them. Often, architects will develop a window schedule detailing all the windows required for a particular structure. Whether you are given such a list or not, it is a good idea to give each one of these windows a number and a name such as "East Bedroom #1," so that you can communicate easily with the owner or builder as questions and changes arise. Write the name or number of the window on the sill of the rough opening or on the builder's plans, and in your own notebook. By copying and using the window scheduling form shown in Illus. 259 for all your jobs, you will avoid lost time and confusion when sizing up a job.

Below the name of each window in your notebook, draw a picture of the configuration of the intended window showing how the lights will be divided by muntins, whether or not the window will open, how it will be hinged (or hung, in the case of a double-hung window), and any other important details of its construction. If at all possible, check the rough openings yourself for size and squareness, and note these measurements with the picture. This is especially important for remodels or retrofits, since settling can cause rough openings to fall out of square. If the building is being framed by someone else while you work on the windows, be sure to keep in touch with him as the work progresses. Window sizes often change when plans are translated into reality.

Once you have this "master list," you can begin making cutting lists. These will list the size and number of each piece you will need as you progress through the construction of your windows. Your first cutting list will actually be your buying list.

As you prepare for each new operation, make an accurate list of the number and sizes of the pieces you are going to cut. Give the pieces identifying marks as you make them, such as BR #1 for bottom rail, window #1, and check them off your list to avoid duplication. Keep them in neat piles, with all the pieces for each window together.

Build the jambs first whenever possible (Illus. 260). The spacing between the jamb and the framing is not critical (it should be between $\frac{1}{4}$ inch to $\frac{1}{2}$ inch all around), but the fit of the sash in the jamb must be precise. It is easier to build the sash to fit an existing jamb than the other way around.

WINDOW SCHEDULING FORM

Picture

Job
name _____
Window
number _____
Rough   Horiz.   Vert.
opening _____   _____
Wall thickness _____
Glazing _____
Hinge side _____
Hinge type _____
Cutting lists:

Illus. 259. Organization is very important to the custom window builder. Use a notebook or this form to list the pertinent information for every window you are building.

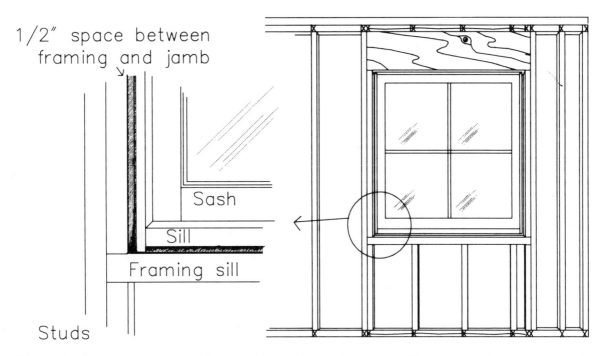

1/2" space between framing and jamb

Sash

Sill

Framing sill

Studs

Illus. 260. Build your jambs first. A ¼ to ½-inch clearance all around between the rough opening and the jamb is standard. Once you've built the jambs, you can use them to get the finer tolerances between the jamb and the sash exactly right.

Buying Materials

Start by making a complete list of all the pieces of both ¾- and 1½-inch stock you will need. The lengths don't have to be precise at this point. You can use the rough-opening dimensions, which will ensure that the lengths will be a little longer than needed. From this list, you can make a good estimation of the running footage of ¾- and 1½-inch lumber of specific widths that you will need. Buy about 20% extra lumber to account for wasted ends and defects.

Good-quality, kiln-dried lumber is essential for window building. Only the smallest, tightest knots should be used. It is best to use only lumber with the growth rings oriented so that they are within 30 degrees perpendicular to the interior and exterior surfaces. Reject any boards where the grain is flat or parallel to the surface, as these will tend to warp or peel (Illus. 261).

Sometimes you can save considerable money in purchasing your lumber by buying shop-grade or defective pieces and cutting around the knots and other defects. You may also be able to cut your materials cost by buying a complete unit (usually around 1,200 board feet) of lumber from the mill or from a bulk-lumber dealer. If you have a large band saw and a planer, you can even resaw your ¾-inch boards from rough

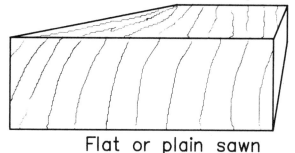

Rift sawn or vertical grain

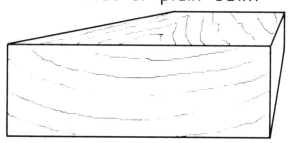

Flat or plain sawn

Illus. 261. Sash should be built only with vertical-grained wood. Rift-sawn wood is preferred.

2-inch stock, but generally the money you save by buying cheaper materials will be offset by increased labor costs and rejects.

Many different types of wood have been used over the centuries for the construction of windows. A soft, workable, stable wood with good rot resistance should be used. At one time, English oak was used extensively, but avoid the common red oak. It is very unstable and rots quickly. White oak, on the other hand, is excellent to use. Pine is used by most manufacturers today, but many varieties of pine also rot rather quickly. Yellow and sugar pine seem to have the best rot resistance. Redwood and cedar are also excellent window materials, as are various types of mahogany.

Building the Jambs

Windows are usually made and installed as units, with the sash mounted in the jamb and completely finished before being put in place in the wall (Illus. 262). It is much more difficult to install a sash in a jamb that is already mounted in the wall, or to work on a window in place, and this should always be avoided.

Illus. 262. Whenever possible, install the sash, complete with glass and stops, in the jamb before putting the jamb into the wall.

Figure the outside dimensions of the jamb from the rough-opening size. Simply subtract ¼ inch in both directions and make your jamb no larger than that. If you are replacing windows in an old house that may have settled and gotten out of square, be sure to leave enough space between the jamb and the framing to square up the window. Once you have built the jambs for your windows, you can use them as a very precise rule for determining the lengths of the stiles and rails of the sash.

In earlier times, it was common to mould the edges of the jambs and join the jamb pieces with mortise-and-tenon joints, similar to the way sash is joined. Today, this is rarely done. Most decorative work is done with either the stops or the trim, and the jamb serves merely as a frame that holds the sash and covers the wall framing. Slots in the side jambs hold the sill in place, and the head jambs are rabbeted to accept the ends of the side jambs. The frame formed by the jambs, head, and sill is simply nailed together and wedged in place, and then nailed into the rough openings.

The width of your jambs will be determined by the thickness of the wall where the window is located. The jamb for a window in a wall consisting of 2 × 4 framing, ½-inch plywood sheathing, ¾-inch siding, and ½-inch Sheetrock on the inside will be made from lumber ripped to 5⅜ inches wide. Note that an extra ⅛ inch is added to allow for imperfections in the materials and construction, a layer of building paper, etc. It is okay to plane a little off the inside of the jamb once it is installed, but no good at all to have a crack between the jamb and the trim caused by too narrow a jamb.

The width of your jambs will be determined by the thickness of the wall where the window is located. The jamb for a window in a wall consisting of 2 × 4 framing, ½-inch plywod sheathing, ¾-inch siding, and ½-inch Sheetrock on the inside will be made from lumber ripped to 5⅜ inch wide. Note that an extra ⅛ inch is added to allow for imperfections in the materials and construction, a layer of building paper, etc. It is okay to plane a little off the inside of the jamb once it is installed, but no good at all

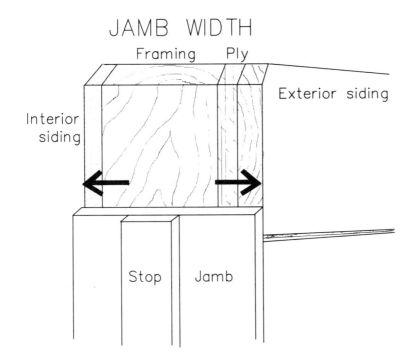

JAMB WIDTH

Illus. 263. The jamb must span the distance from the inside surface of the interior siding to the outside surface of the exterior siding.

to have a crack between the jamb and the trim caused by too narrow a jamb.

Try to buy your lumber in dimensions that will be easy to handle and will result in the least amount of waste. If you need 5⅜-inch-wide jambs and can only get 1 × 8's, perhaps you can use the leftover ripping for your stops.

Depending on the length of the boards when you buy them, you may want to begin by rough-cutting them to pieces just a little longer than the finished pieces you will need, for ease of handling. Rip everything to its finished width; then make the final crosscuts so that your side jambs are 1 inch shorter than the vertical rough-opening measurement. The head should be a ½ inch

shorter than the horizontal measurement of the rough opening.

Once the pieces are cut, you can cut the slots in the side jambs that will hold the sill (Illus. 264). The two side-jamb pieces must be mirror images of each other. If you make all the angled slots in one direction, you will have all left- or all right-side pieces.

The slots can be made with repeated cuts of a radial arm or hand saw, or with a router. If you are using a router, you can do the head rabbet either on a router table or by using a fence or a guide board clamped to the workpiece. You may want to make a jig like the one shown in Illus. 265 to do the sill slots. The ¾-inch cleat can be screwed or clamped to the outside edge

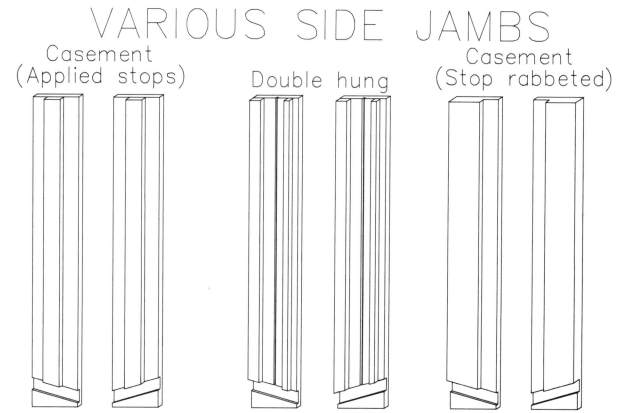

Illus. 264. Various types of side jambs. Always be sure that your side jambs are mirror images of each other.

Illus. 265. This reversible jig can be used with two passes of a straight-cutting router bit to make the sill slot.

Illus. 266A and B. Mark out the ears or returns with a T square and bevel gauge, and then cut them either with a hand saw or a band saw.

of the jamb piece to hold the jig in position. The bottom edge of the sill slot should start about ¼ inch up from the bottom, outside corner of the jamb piece.

Use 1½-inch stock for sills in woodframe walls. The sill stock should be ripped to about 1 inch wider than the jambs. There is some room for variation here, but the sill stock must be wide enough to project outward about 2 inches past the edge of the jamb, and inward far enough to form a ledge to nail the stool to. The sill can now be crosscut to the inside dimension of the jamb plus the depth of the slots, plus the width of the casing on both sides, plus one inch.

Next, mark out the "ears" or returns by making square lines across the sill that are as far apart as the bottoms of the slots on the insides of the side jambs, and equal distance from the ends of the sill (Illus. 266). You may want to clamp the side-jamb pieces to the head to check the inside measurement. Use your marking gauge or sliding T-square to mark a line 2 inches in, parallel to the outside edge of the sill from the ends of the sill to the crosscut lines you just marked. Now, use your bevel gauge to mark a 15-degree bevel on the ends of the sill where the 2-inch line ends.

The most practical way to cut these lines is with a good, sharp hand saw. A band saw can also be used, but the table will have to be reset several times for the angle cuts on different ends. Jigs can be made to hold the pieces at the right angles if you are doing a lot of sills at once. Do not cut these pieces with a table saw.

To make these cuts by hand, hold the work in a vise and first rip, and then crosscut, being very careful to make your crosscuts square to the surface and straight. Once the ears are cut, you can use the table saw to rip a small drip kerf about ¼ inch in from the outside edge on the bottom. You can also bevel off the back upper edge of the sill with the table saw at a 15-degree angle to provide a flat ledge for the stool to be nailed to. Be sure to figure out this cut so that it will start just inside the inner edge of the sash.

An alternate method is to cut a bird's-mouth out of the stool to fit over the sill, but the first method is quite a bit quicker and easier. In the alternate method, as shown in Illus. 267, the sill is not set in a slot. It is simply nailed or screwed in place between the jambs, but should be well caulked and supported from underneath if this method is used.

When you are finished cutting the slots, you can nail the jambs together. Six or 7d galvanized nails will usually be fine, although you may need to predrill the holes to avoid splitting the headpiece. It is also a good idea to apply caulk or glue such as

Illus. 267. An alternate way of installing the sill. First cover the ends of the sill where they will meet the jambs with construction adhesive, and then nail or screw through the side jambs into the ends of the sill.

ALTERNATE STOOL INSTALLATION

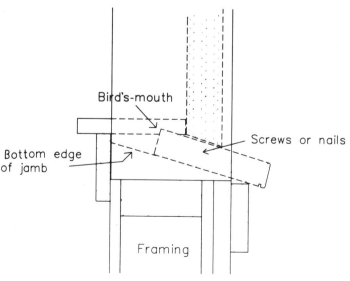

F-26 construction adhesive to the ends of the sill where they fit into the slot. This will help prevent water from working its way through this joint and into the wall, and will also help protect the end grain from rot. The jambs can now be set aside, and work can be started on the sash. Stops can more easily be applied to the jambs later when the sashes are being put in place.

Window Joinery

Whatever method you use to shape the parts of your sash, it will be held together mainly by the joints between the stiles and rails at the four corners. Although the mortise-and-tenon joint has traditionally been used here, ½-inch-wooden dowels are now used by some window-makers to hold these joints together (Illus. 268).

If it is made of the same type of wood as the sash, and carefully glued, a dowel will

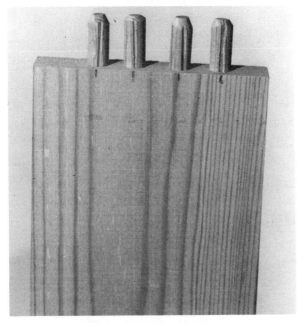

Illus. 268. One-half-inch wooden dowels are now used by many sash makers to hold the stiles and rails together.

hold up well if it has the added strength of the interlocking cope-and-stick joint. Butt-jointed windows (any window made without a shaper) have very little inherent strength in the corner joints, and should always be reinforced with some type of mortise-and-tenon joint.

Dowels with cope-and-stick joints are adequate on fixed sash, but should be considered only marginally acceptable for openable sash. In any case, use a good weatherproof glue, and completely coat all surfaces of both sides of the joint. The development in the last 50 years of good, long-lasting, weatherproof glues has done a lot to lessen the need for time-consuming joinery here, but the gluing surface of dowels is still minimal compared to that of a mortise-and-tenon joint. Most of the area where the dowel contacts the stile is end grain, and end-grain glue joints are notoriously weak.

Even so, dowelling is the simplest and least expensive way to fasten these joints, and is used by many window makers today. You can use a dowelling jig like the one shown in Illus. 269 (there are many varieties on the market, some of which are not designed for this type of joinery), and an electric hand drill to get good, accurate results.

One problem with dowelling jigs is that they are quite slow and cumbersome to use if you are doing a lot of dowelling. The production-oriented window maker will eventually want to invest in a horizontal boring machine to speed up this process. Boring machines with both single- and multiple-bit capabilities are available. Some use compressed air to hold the work and advance the bits. Less expensive models

Illus. 269A and B. A dowelling jig and electric hand drill will give accurate results, though they are a bit slow for production work.

use a hand-operated cam to hold the work securely, and a foot pedal to advance the bit.

As stated earlier, it is best to use dowels made of the same type of wood as you are using for the construction of your sash. Ready-made dowels (usually made of birch), with grooves to let the glue run and improve the holding power, can be purchased in various sizes and lengths. You can make your own dowels by ripping pieces of the wood you are using to ½ × ½-inch sticks, and then using a ¼-inch-radius round-over bit in a table-mounted router to round the corners of these sticks (Illus. 270). The rough dowels are then driven through a sizing hole of the right size, and can be driven through a groover to groove them. Finally, the dowels should be cut to the right length (a chop saw or radial arm saw is good for this), and the ends bevelled slightly with either a pencil sharpener or on a sanding wheel. It sounds like a lot of work, but you

can make up a batch in a couple of hours that will get you through several jobs.

Another problem with dowels is that they don't allow for any small up or down movement of the rails along the stiles as the joint goes together. If your dowel placement is not very accurate, a rail may be forced out of its proper position, and the vertical mullions will not fit tightly against the rails. If you are more interested in doing it the right way rather than the quick way, use the good, old mortise-and-tenon joint or the newer spline-tenon joint. Besides being much stronger, the mortise-and-tenon joint will give you better control of the positions of the rails as you assemble the sash.

If you want to cut a mortise-and-tenon joint by hand, the way our ancestors did, you'll need a sharp 20-point or finer back saw, a sharp half-inch chisel (preferably a mortising chisel), a mallet, a good square, and a marking gauge. Mark out the lines for the tenons all the way around the pieces

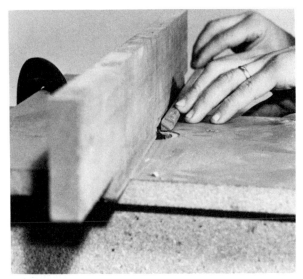

Illus. 270A and B. You can make your own dowels by ripping sticks to ½ × ½ inch (above left), then rounding the four corners off with a router (on a table) and driving them through a sizer (above right).

before you start cutting. The tenon, usually on the ends of the rails (except with double-hung windows, where it's on the top ends of the stiles of the lower sash), should extend all the way through the stile. Here's where the story stick comes in handy. Using it will assure you that all the marks are in their right places and that everything will come out square in the end. If you don't use a story stick, lay all the stiles and all the rails of the same size side by side, and mark across them all at once to make sure they are identical.

Begin by crosscutting the shoulders for the tenons. Since sash is almost always made of soft wood, you can use a sharp knife to score the shoulder line very accurately on both sides, and then use your chisel to gouge a shallow groove on the tenon side of the line in which to start your saw. For the joint to close tightly, it is essential that you get the shoulders to line up perfectly.

Once you have cut the shoulder to its proper depth on both sides, you can either saw or chisel the waste away from the cheeks of the tenon. Leave the tenons a little thick; if anything, they can always be pared or planed down later.

Use the marking gauge to mark the edges of your mortise. First, find the center of the edge of the stile by adjusting your marking gauge until it makes one line from either side. Then, make a mark ¼ inch to one side. Put one edge of a ½-inch chisel just inside the line, and tap it to make a mark where the mortise will go. Now, set the marking gauge to the other edge of the chisel mark, and mark the other side of the mortise.

You can use a brace and bit or hand drill to prebore the mortises. Mark the position of each mortise on both edges of the piece, and bore into the center from the outsides of each mortise. This will avoid large chipouts caused by boring all the way through from one edge, and will also give you much more accurate results.

Once the holes have been bored all the way along each mortise from both sides, you can easily clean them out and square out the ends with the chisel. Be especially careful not to break out the end of the stiles when cleaning out these joints, as they are quite delicate on windows.

When the mortise is good and clean, plane or pare a little bevel around the end of the tenon to ease its entry into the mortise, and begin testing the fit. Plane or pare the cheeks of the tenon where necessary until the fit is right. It should be a nice friction fit that goes together without forcing.

Sash joints were traditionally held with pegs, the holes for which were bored first through the stile, and then offset slightly on the tenon so as to draw the joint tightly together. This method held well, even without reliable glues.

Tenons can be cut more quickly and accurately today with a table saw and the cutting jigs shown in previous chapters. A router, drill press, or boring machine can also be used to cut the mortises in the same manner as the ones made for doors. Routing mortises for sash with a hand-held router and a fence attachment, as shown in previous chapters on door making, is difficult because the pieces are smaller and the mortises must be closer to the ends of the stiles. If you want to cut mortises in this manner, build a jig like the one shown in Illus. 160 to hold the work and support the router. A horizontal mortising machine, with a sliding table and a stationary router-cutter, will work much better for work of this scale, and will produce a superior joint. This mortiser, which utilizes a standard accessory table for a well-known table saw, can be made for about $300.

Because of the narrowness of window stiles and rails, yet another variation on the spline-tenon is possible (Illus. 271). Deep slots can be cut with the table saw through both the stile and the rail, and the splines inserted. These splines will show from the edges, but will be very strong because of their width and the cross-bonding effect achieved by gluing.

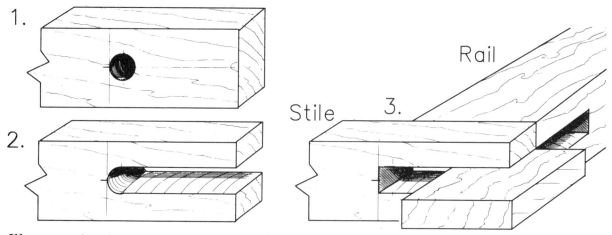

Illus. 271. Another type of spline-tenon, which can be cut with a drill and table saw, works well for sash.

210

10
Making Sash

Window sash, like doors, can be made entirely by hand or with various combinations of power tools. In this chapter, I will give several examples of sash-construction methods ranging from early hand methods to modern shaper techniques. Many of the techniques are very similar to those described in the chapters on door making, and certainly the accomplished door-maker will find sash making easier, though perhaps a more delicate technique. Still, it is not easy to make a wooden window that will work properly for years, resist rot, look beautiful from inside and out, and be energy efficient. It's a skill that takes patience, concentration, and organization, but you will always be well rewarded.

The earliest sash jointers most likely got their stock from either a water-powered mill or a group of craftsmen who cut boards with pit saws from recently fallen English oak or European pine logs. Rough lumber of the right sizes and lengths was stickered and stacked in either a drying shed or the rafters of the shop for drying. Many months later, when the wood had dried out and warped as much as it was going to, it would be taken into the workshop and laboriously

sawn, planed, chiselled, and pegged together to make a wonderfully complex frame (the word sash comes from the French work *chassis*), in which were mounted wavy, imperfect, and very delicate panes of glass.

The earliest sash, from 17th-century France, was characterized by a quarter-round ovolo and bead on the interior side of the sash, and a profile that is quite heavy compared to today's light and airy multipaned windows (Illus. 272). Often as much as an inch of wood separated the panes of glass, making the mullions and muntins as much as 2 inches wide. The rails were tenoned into the stiles, and the upright mullions were tenoned into the rails. Cross-muntins were cut through and tenoned into the upright mullions.

During this period, a sharpened in-canal gouge (bevelled on the concave side) of the proper size was commonly used to undercut the ends of the rails, mullions, and muntins. Later, Victorian sash became lighter, with a bead that was deeper than it was wide. Other innovations, such as quicker methods of cutting the cope, and counterbalanced, sliding double-hung sash, came

VARIOUS MUNTIN PROFILES

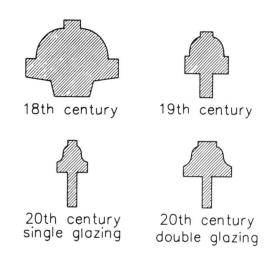

18th century

19th century

20th century
single glazing

20th century
double glazing

Illus. 272. The sectional profiles of window muntins as they have developed through the years.

into use as sash making became more refined and mechanized.

The basic configuration and joinery concepts developed by these early craftsmen are still in use today. Though we have come up with some labor-saving improvements in the tools and techniques used to cut and shape the wood, the basic forms are as valid as ever. What is needed is a frame with a little step or rabbet (this word comes from the earlier English word, rebate) all the way around the inside edge to hold the glass, and a decorative bead or ovolo to ease the severity of the inner edge of the frame. These cuts can be easily made with hand moulding planes, routers, or spindle shapers.

The main difficulty is how to join the corners where the rail, muntin, and mullion ends meet the moulded edge of stiles, rails, or each other. If you were to take a couple of moulded pieces of sash stock and con-

sider this problem (ignoring for the moment the need for a structural joint like the mortise-and-tenon or spline to reinforce the joint), you will realize that there are two simple solutions that immediately come to mind. One is to remove the moulding from the stile in the area where the end of the rail meets the stile; the other is to under-cut the end of the rail so that it laps over the moulded part of the stile (Illus. 273). Both methods have been used over the years, and many contemporary books illustrate very careful techniques for executing the first method. The second method, however, is by far the best and strongest.

These early methods of cutting and joining sash by hand, are not as difficult as it might seem, and are still valuable today for the patient craftsperson who doesn't want to invest in expensive shaping machinery.

Making Hand-made Sash with Mortise-and-Tenon Joints

The old-time sash-makers began their work by setting out all the important measurements for the sash they were about to make on a story stick like the one described on page 101. If you are making sash with mortise-and-tenon joints, instead of dowelled or splined joints, you will have to mark the places for the cuts on the stiles on one side of your story stick, the place for the cuts on the rails on the other side, the places for both the vertical mullions and horizontal muntins on the other two corners.

Mark the places for the stiles first, beginning with the bottom end of the piece; then

212

TWO BASIC WAYS OF JOINING SASH MOULDING

1. Mitred butt joint

2. Cope and stick

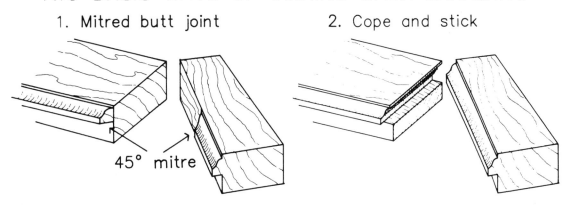

45° mitre

Illus. 273. Two basic approaches to joining moulded rails and stiles; 2 is by far the stronger.

mark the places for the beginning and end of the bottom mortise, the inside edges of the rails, and the beginning and end of the top mortise. Make your mortise at least an inch shorter than the width of the rail it meets, and not too near the bottom of the sash were it may be exposed by trimming.

Now go back and figure the positions of the cross-muntins by subtracting the widths of all the cross-muntins mortises from the total distance between the inside edges of the top and bottom rails, and dividing the remainder by the number of lights from top to bottom (Illus. 274). This will give you the size of each light.

Start at the bottom and measure off a light, a mortise, a light, etc., until you are done. If the last one comes out the same size as the others, your arithmetic was correct. If not, divide the remainder by the number of lights, and reposition your lines.

For the rails, you will have to mark the end of the piece and the shoulder of the tenon on both ends; then go back and repeat the procedure for finding the placement of the mullion mortises. The markings

for the upright mullions will have end points and tenon shoulders on each end, and mortise marks that correspond to the mortises on the stiles. The vertical mullions can be set out as continuous pieces like the cross muntins, and then sawn through in the middle after they have been moulded.

Once the setting out has been done on the story stick, transfer the marks to the workpieces, and use a single- or double-toothed marking gauge to mark the sides of the mortises and the cheeks of the tenons. Now, bore and chop the mortises through to the middle from both edges of the stiles. Saw the tenon shoulders before actually moulding the edges with the bead and rabbet cuts.

In the old days, the muntins for casement sash were often tenoned through the stiles, which greatly strengthened the entire sash. A short stub tenon was left on the muntin ends, which could be no longer than half the thickness of the space between the lights, and which simply served to help lock the piece in place (Illus. 275). In modern sash, both these tenons are often omitted.

Once the moulding is complete, cut or split the waste away from the tenons. By waiting until after the moulding is complete to do this, you will help protect the shoulders of the joints from marring (Illus. 276). Cut the mitres after the tenons and, finally, undercut the rail ends with the coping saw or gouge.

Illus. 274. To get your muntins and mullions positioned so that all the lights are of equal size, measure from bottom of rabbet to bottom of rabbet, subtract the total width of thin parts of muntins, and divide by the number of lights.

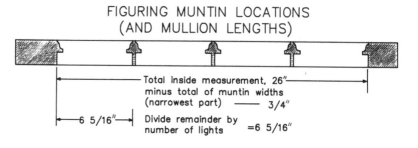

FIGURING MUNTIN LOCATIONS
(AND MULLION LENGTHS)

Total inside measurement, 26″ minus total of muntin widths (narrowest part) —— 3/4″

6 5/16″

Divide remainder by number of lights = 6 5/16″

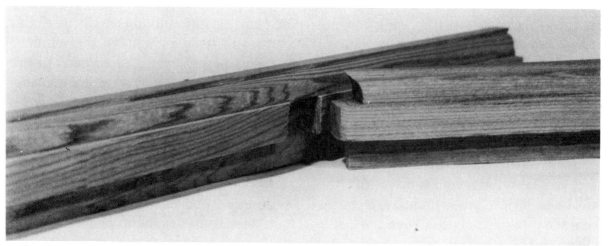

Illus. 275. Until recently, a stub tenon was left on the ends of muntins to lock them in place.

Illus. 276. Waiting until after the mouldings have been cut to remove the waste from the tenons will help protect the shoulders from accidental marring.

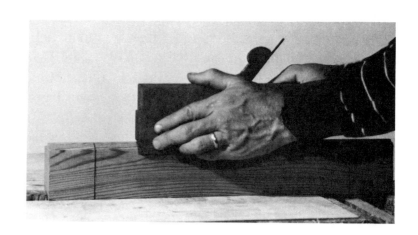

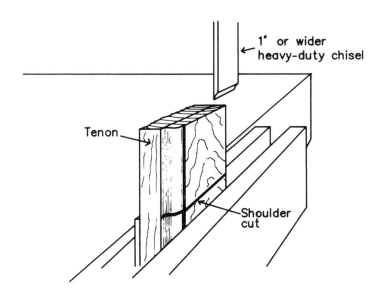

Illus. 277. Splitting the waste away from the tenons with a chisel.

1″ or wider heavy-duty chisel

Tenon

Shoulder cut

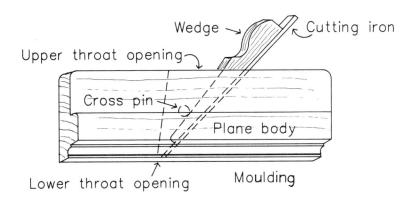

Wedge — Cutting iron

Upper throat opening

Cross pin

Plane body

Lower throat opening

Moulding

Illus. 278. The only metal part of this 19th century sash-moulding plane is the cutting iron, which was ground to the opposite profile of the desired moulding.

Making Cope-and-Stick Sash by Hand (Or with a Router and Coping Saw)

If you wish to make sash by hand today, you will have to begin by finding or making a moulding plane or set of planes that suit your needs. Making your own plane is not as difficult as it may seem. Early moulding planes were made entirely of wood except for the iron and the chip breaker (Illus. 278), and you could adjust them by tapping on either the back of the iron (to advance it) or the back of the plane (to slip the iron

back) with a small hammer. A wooden wedge held the iron assembly in place.

The body of the plane was simply a sandwich of wood with the core cut out to form a throat for the iron and the passage of the shavings. The sole of a moulding plane must have a profile that's the opposite of the one you want to cut, and the iron must be ground to match the sole.

You could also do some of this work with a router. The modern, low-cost, high-performance router can easily take the place of moulding planes as a means of "sticking" or shaping the bead and rabbet along the edges of the sash pieces, but until recently it has been difficult to find router bits that will do a good job of cope-cutting the ends of the rails. Cope and stick sash-cutting bits are now available from at least one manufacturer. One method is to shape the bead and rabbet with the router, and do the cope cutting by hand, which I will discuss here. Another solution is to grind your own router bits. See the section on router-made windows, pages 219–222, for more information.

The earliest sash jointers used two separate planes for the sticking operation, shaping the bead and rabbet separately on the edges of all the pieces. Later jointers combined these planes into one that would cut the bead and rabbet at the same time (Illus. 279).

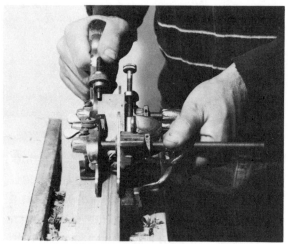

Illus. 279. Later plane makers combined the bead and the rabbet cuts in one cutter. This Stanley 55 plane can cut many different types of mouldings and rabbets.

If you are using separate planes or making separate passes with a router, experiment with your planes or router to get these cuts to match properly. For planes, take a piece of stock of about the right thickness (1½ inches), a foot or so long, and wide enough to be put in the bench vise with its edge up. Begin by planing the ovolo or bead along one edge. Then adjust your rabbet plane so that it cuts to the same depth as the deepest point of the bead cut, and wide enough so that about ¼ to ½ inch of the original edge is left between the two cuts. You may want to attach stops to the side and base of your rabbet plane, if it doesn't have built-in or adjustable stops to get it to cut consistently to just the right depth.

With the router and hand-sawn cope method, use a router table and cut the ovolo first; then set up the router with a rabbeting bit and fence so that the rabbet is the same depth as the bead and leaves the desired ¼ or ½ inch of untouched edge (Illus. 280). If you are planning on using ½-inch-wide mortises and splines or tenons, plan your bead and rabbet so that they leave the ½ inch of untouched original in the same area where the mortises will be cut. This will simplify the cope cutting.

There are several possible bits that are readily available and can be used to cut the bead. It is simplest, but not absolutely necessary, if the depth of the bead and the depth of the rabbet are identical. If one is deeper than the other, it will be much more difficult to cut the cope on the ends of the rails and muntins.

Once you have done the moulding and rabbet cuts on all the pieces, and assuming that you have cut the tenon shoulders, you can cut the mitres. This has been traditionally done with a mitring jig and a sharp chisel, and this is still a good way to do it (Illus. 281). The jig is just a piece of polished wood or metal that is held against the work by the vise, and guides the chisel in cutting a perfect mitre from the point where the tenon shoulder intersects with the bottom of the rabbet. The line where the surface of the bead cut meets the mitre cut is the line that the saw should follow when you make the cope cut (Illus. 282). A very thin-bladed coping saw (hence the name of the cut) has been used since Victorian times for making this cut, and works quite accurately and easily with the workpiece held firmly in a vise.

On the narrower muntins and mullions

where both edges are mitred and the stock is quite thin, you will have no problem getting a perfect coping cut quickly and easily by hand. On the rail ends, it is helpful to make a piece with the reverse profile of the bead and use it to scribe the outside end of the coping cut. It may also be necessary to relieve the middle parts of the coping cut with a chisel or gouge or rasp to allow the joint to fit.

A favorite shortcut of later Victorian sash makers was to chop away all but a small

ROUTING COPE AND STICK SASH

1. Cope cut

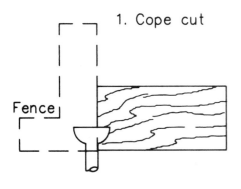

2. Cope cut

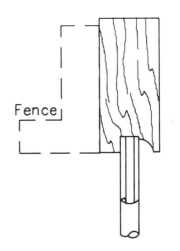

3. Mortise both stiles and rails

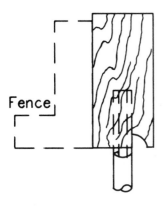

4. Stick cut

5. Stick cut

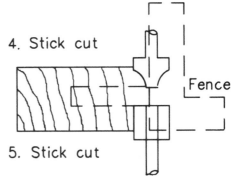

Illus. 280. Cope-and-stick sash can be made with router bits you can grind yourself, but five steps are necessary (including the mortise cut), compared to only three steps with shapers.

Illus. 281A and B. When hand-coping, make a mitre cut to reveal the line through which the cope is cut. Clamp a guide block to the work, and make the cut with a sharp chisel (upper left). Then cut the cope along the mitre line (upper right).

COPE-CUTTING FROM MITRE LINE

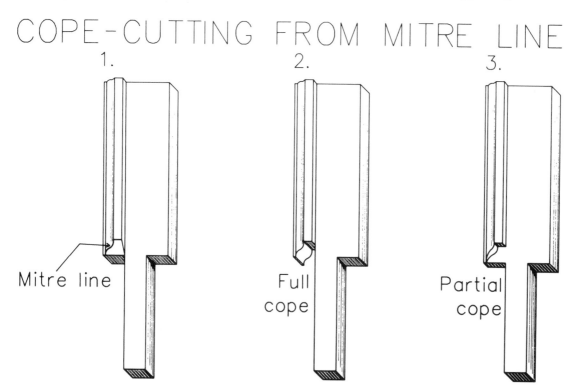

1.

2.

3.

Mitre line

Full cope

Partial cope

Illus. 282. Number 1 shows the mitre line. Number 2 is a full-cope cut made with a coping saw. The partial cope shown in 3 was a timesaving technique developed by 19th-century jointers. All but ¼ inch of the moulding was removed from the stile, and the cope was chopped quickly with a gouge.

218

portion of the moulding where the rail end contacted the stile. A small undercut could then be chopped quickly with a gouge on the end of the rail so that just a quarter inch or so of the moulding extended into the rail end. This looked like a cope-and-stick joint, was not likely to open like a mitred butt joint, and saved a good bit of time.

This joint wasn't quite as resistant to the twisting forces that a casement-type window has to withstand as the one produced using the full-cope method, but it worked just as well for the sliding double-hung sash, which came into popularity in the Victorian era.

One solution to the cope-and-stick problem that should be avoided is that of mitring the corners of both the rail end and the stile where it meets the rail, and then chopping away the moulding, as shown in Illus. 283. This leaves a mitre where the stile and rail mouldings meet that is certain to open up when the window shrinks in dry weather.

If you intend to do a lot of sash making with moulding planes, make yourself a sticking board to hold the pieces while you work. It should have the right-sized slot in it to hold the moulded or partially moulded muntins securely while you plane the other side. A screw driven partway in will work as a stop. The old sash joiners drove a small piece of knife blade into the wood to hold the piece on the other end, but an easily removable screw will also work.

Making Cope-and-Stick Sash Completely with Routers

As previously described, cope-and-stick sash can be shaped with routers on router tables with good results as long as care is taken that the separate passes needed for the various cuts are properly aligned. Furima Industrial Carbide Company now offers a set of carbide router bits designed specifically for making sash (Illus. 284). If

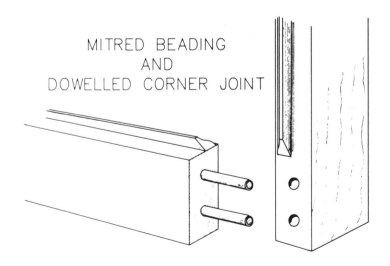

MITRED BEADING
AND
DOWELLED CORNER JOINT

Illus. 283. The wrong way. Dowels are weak and the mitred corner is sure to open up.

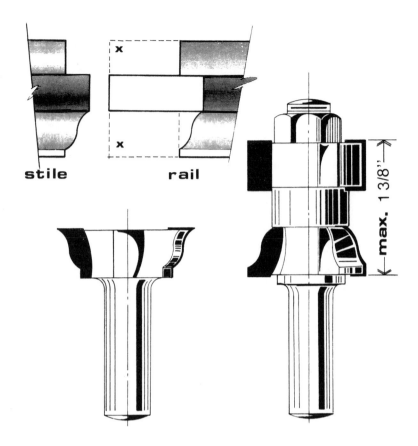

stile   rail

max. 1 3/8''

you use them, there will still be more steps involved than making sash with shapers, but the combined stick-and-rabbet cut will be faster than the method described for bits you grind yourself. Furima's bits also come with a ball-bearing guide on the stick cutter that will automatically set the depth of the cut, and will allow you to cut curved and irregular sash without making templates.

To improve the efficiency of the operation, set up Furima's bits on two separate router tables so that you won't have to change bits between cope and stick cutting. Furima's bits are available only with ½-inch shanks; so if you are using ¼-inch-collet routers, you will have to grind your own bits.

If you want to grind a set of bits, begin by buying as "blanks" any kind of high-speed steel router bit that comes close to the profile you want. The kind that have flat cutters (when viewed end on), instead of ones that look Z-shaped, are much easier to grind.

A common quarter-round bit will work for the stick cutter, but it should be no bigger than ⅜ inch in radius. The glass rabbets for most single-glazed windows are only about ¼ inch wide; so you may want to take a ⅜- or ½-inch quarter-round bit and grind it in from the outside edge or down along the bottom of the curve so that the cut is taller than it is wide.

If you are trying to match an existing moulding, cut a thin profile of it, coat the back of the router bit with machinist's blue, and scratch the profile onto both wings of the bit. Be sure and position the scratch lines the same way on both wings so that the bit will remain balanced. Use a drill press to drill $\frac{1}{4}$-inch holes very near the edges of two small blocks of wood, and use these as holders while you are grinding and comparing the two bits with each other (Illus. 285).

Illus. 286. Grinding on a slow-speed Carborundum wheel.

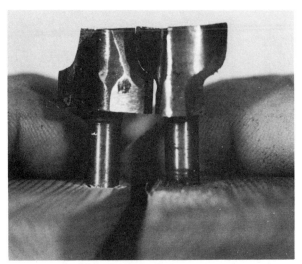

Illus. 285. When grinding router bits to match for cope-and-stick cutting, drill holes near the edges of two blocks of wood that will hold the bits squarely and firmly for grinding and so that you can compare them.

Grind the moulding cutter first, using a small, slow-speed Carborundum wheel with a tool rest (Illus. 286). Cool the bit occasionally by quenching it to avoid destroying its temper, and make sure that you have at least as much bevel as the original bit did.

Once you are satisfied with the moulding bit (test it in the router to be sure), use it as a pattern for the matching coping bit you will make next. You may want to use a straight or rabbeting cutter for the blank.

Start by grinding or sawing off the guide pin, if there is one. Then grind the shape, and set the pair of bits in their holding blocks, next to each other, in a strong light to be sure that they match perfectly. The top of the coping cutter has to be flat, with no protrusions (like guide pins), so that it can cut right up to the cheeks of your tenons.

When making sash with these bits, remember that the cope cutter must slide under the tenons; so, therefore, the bead cut must not extend down the edge of the sash further than the cheek of the tenon. You can make either the cope or the stick cuts first. I prefer to make the cope first so that I can use just a square piece as a backer to prevent chip out, and also to be sure that it is just the right height in relation to the tenon.

You will have to change the distance of

your fence from the bit to accommodate the different tenon lengths if you are using a mortise-and-tenon joint. An extra piece of scrap could also be clamped to the fence to support the ends of the muntins, and then removed for the longer tenons on the rails.

Making Noncope-and-Stick Sash with a Router

Another approach to the problem of finding router bits that will do a good job of cope-cutting the ends of rails is to avoid the cope-and-stick technique altogether and make your sash by assembling the frame before moulding or rabbeting it. Once the mortise and tenon joints have been completed on the still square sticks, you can glue up the frame. After the glue has dried, plane the joints smooth, and then simply go around both sides of the frame with the appropriate router bit to cut the bead and the rabbet. The corners on the bead side can be left rounded; so can the corners on the rabbet side, unless you are using wooden stops to hold the glass in place. If you are applying wooden stops, it will be better to chop the corners out square with a sharp chisel.

This method of sash construction is acceptable, and even enhances the design of some sash (Illus. 287), though it should never be used with anything less than a through mortises-and-tenon for the corner joints and good, solid tenons on the muntin ends. Because there is no cope-and-stick joint, but merely a butt joint at the corners (end grain butting flat-up against side grain), there is no strength in the joint, and dowels cannot be relied upon to hold it.

You may also want to try routing your

sash with it dry-assembled if you have a lot of muntins. It can be hard to hold the router steady when routing the muntins and, this way, if you destroy one of them, it will be easy to replace.

Making Sash with Shapers

The techniques for making sash with shapers are much the same as those described in the door-making section, with a few important differences (Illus. 288). Sash cutters for shapers generally come in sets that consist of a male and female bead cutter, spacers, and straight cutters for cutting the rabbet. The same bead cutters can be used with straight cutters of different cutting diameters to cut two different depths of rabbets for either single-glazing or insulated double-glazing. Single-glazed windows usually have a $\frac{1}{4}$-inch-wide rabbet, while double-glazed windows need a rabbet that is at least $\frac{1}{2}$ inch wide and $\frac{7}{8}$ inch deep.

As described in the door-making section, it is possible to cope rail ends with tenons on them with spindle shapers, but you may need a special locking nut and, in some cases, a clamp-on table to raise the work up to the very top of the spindle. The most common solution to this problem today seems to be to use dowels instead of mortise-and-tenon joints, but a better solution would be the use of splines to hold the joint together. In window sash, since the frame pieces are usually no more than 3 inches wide, it is possible to cut slots through both the rail and stile ends so that a spline can be inserted from the outside. This can be done with a dado head on the

Illus. 287A–D. You can make window sash by joining square pieces and then routing the bead and rabbet afterwards (above left), but the corners will be rounded (above right) instead of appearing mitred as with cope-and-stick sash. For some designs, a radiused corner or a router detail stopped near the corner is a pleasing effect (below left and right).

Illus. 287C.

Illus. 287D.

Illus. 288A (above left). The stick-cutting setup for modern sash cutting. Illus. 288B (above right). The matching cope cutter. Note that a ¼-inch straight cutter is stacked on top of the cope cutter to match the ¼-inch spacer in the stick cut.

table saw, or by drilling and cutting with a regular saw blade as shown in Illus. 271 on page 210, and makes for a very strong joint when done properly. The best compromise in terms of time saved and the strength of the joint may be to make splined tenons by blind-mortising both the stile and the rail end with a plunge router, horizontal mortiser, or other means, and inserting a blind spline.

Multi-paned windows are made today with no mortise-and-tenon joints where muntins meet either the frame or other muntins. This is possible because the interlocking nature of the cope-and-stick joint will hold the muntin in place, even without a tenon. Later, when you apply glass and stops or putty, the muntins are locked in place so that they cannot slide back and forth even if the glue that is applied to the ends of them doesn't hold. Applying glue to the ends of the muntins is a good idea, not so much for strength, but because it will seal the end grain against the intrusion of moisture and eventual rot.

Cutting Sequence for Shaper-Made Sash

Use the inside measurements of your jamb to determine the outside dimensions of the sash you will make. You may find it helpful to set out your dimensions on a story stick, but if you are using dowels or splines you may not need to. Cut the stiles square on both ends to the longest dimension (the outside is longer because of the sloping sill), and rip them to width. The top rail will usually be the same width as the stiles on casement windows (commonly 2½ inches) and the bottom rail is usually about an inch wider (commonly 3½ inches). The formula for figuring the length of your rails is the total width of the sash, minus the combined width of the stiles, plus twice the depth of the coping cut. So, for a 30-inch-wide sash with 2½-inch-wide stiles, and a ½-inch-deep coping cut, the rails would be cut to 26 inches. This is assuming that you are not cutting tenons on the ends of your rails.

Cut the stock for your cross-muntins to about 1/32 inch longer than the rails, but wait until you have shaped all these pieces to cut the upright mullions to length. First, take the muntins and the rails to the shaper and cut the cope on them, and then rip the muntins to a width that will leave about ¼ inch between the rabbets on both sides; then run all these pieces through the stick cutter.

Once you have a precise figure for the width of the mullions, add them up and subtract that figure from the distance between the rabbets on the top and bottom rails. Divide this figure by the number of lights from top to bottom, and you will get the length of the upright mullions (Illus. 274, page 214). It is important that the figure be precise because a small error will add up to a substantial one if it is repeated several times. Be sure to measure from bottom of

Illus. 289. With all the muntins and rails lined up evenly, mark the positions of the mullions across with a square.

rabbet to bottom of rabbet, to determine the length of the upright mullions.

Now, cut the upright mullion stock to length and "cope" it; then rip and "stick" it. Next, lay all the rails and cross-muntins out side by side with the ends perfectly even, and mark the centers of the upright mullions across them with a square, using the same method to figure the distance between them that you did to figure their length (Illus. 289).

Gluing and Truing Sash

While doors, large and unwieldy, are difficult to glue together, the technique of gluing sash is one that demands the most delicate and careful work. Even a dowel that is too tight can split a redwood stile down the middle, and the misplacement or twisting of a joint can cause a twisted and useless sash. Certainly, the greatest concern of the custom sash-maker should be proper fit; so don't forget to check everything during a dry fit before applying glue. If you are using dowels, dry-check their alignment with a couple of short dowels or dowels that have been planed down to fit a bit loosely.

The entire surface of both sides of the joints should be evenly coated with exterior-grade glue, preferably urea resin, and so should the dowels, splines, or tenons. As previously stated, even the ends of the muntins should be coated (Illus. 290). If you use wedged or pegged-through tenons, you should still cover all the meeting parts of the joints with glue—as much to minimize rot as to hold the pieces together.

Rot is the main enemy (besides boys with

Illus. 290. All parts of both sides of the joints should be covered with glue.

Illus. 291. Apply clamps on opposite sides of the work to prevent twisting of the stiles caused by uneven pressure.

baseballs) of windows, and can be controlled if you are able to stop moisture from entering the wood. Well-sealed wood, tight joints, and, whenever possible, sloped exterior horizontal surfaces will help ensure that the lumber remains solid throughout the years.

Clamps should be applied carefully on alternating sides of the sash so as to provide even pressure (Illus. 291). Be careful not to damage the ends of the muntins when clamping up your sash. If they have fallen out of place a bit, they can easily get broken or marred as the stiles are squeezed into place. If your upright mullions are loose, you may have to apply top-to-bottom clamps to tighten them up. See the section on gluing up four-panel doors, pages 109–111, for more information on this technique.

Once the rail ends have been joined with the stiles, you can begin cleaning the squeezed-out glue off the sash. A small, stiff-bristled brush and plenty of water will work well in the corners where pieces meet. A wet rag will work fine on the flat sur-faces. Be sure to get as much glue off as possible, and to get the corners completely clean, as these areas will be very hard to clean when the glue is dry. You should return to each sash a half hour or so after cleaning it to see if any more glue has oozed out, as this is often the case.

Once the glue has dried, use a sharp scraper or chisel to remove any hardened residue that may remain on the lumber. Hardened glue can dull and chip a sharp plane iron severely; so avoid planing it.

After any remaining glue has been removed from the surface, use either a jack plane or a smaller block plane to flatten the corner joints and remove any other defects before sanding. Avoid planing where muntins meet the frame of the sash because they can be broken out of the frame quite easily.

Check the squareness and straightness of the outside edge of the sash with a large framing square and a straightedge. Start by straightening one side; then measure from it to the other side at the top, middle,

226

and bottom, marking the correct measurement at each place. Connect these marks with a straightedge to verify that your second side is parallel to the first one; then plane or joint the second edge straight and to its proper width. This can be done by hand, with a hand-held electric planer, or sometimes on the jointer if the window is not too large.

When both sides are straight and parallel, plane the top so that it is straight and square to the sides. Be careful not to chip out the outsides of the stiles when you plane by planing off the end of the sash. The planing of end grain, in this case the tops of the stiles, should always be done from the outsides towards the center to avoid breaking-out the grain.

Finally, check to see that the bottom of the window is square, and make a cut on it at an angle of 15 or more degrees to match the slope of the sill. The long side of this slope is always towards the outside of the wall; so generally the cut is made on the table saw with the inside of the sash down. A clamp-on wooden fence guide will greatly help in this operation to hold the window flat (Illus. 292). If necessary, you can hand-plane the saw kerf left after this operation to smooth and straighten it, but any major unevenness should be corrected before the slope cut is made.

Depending on the sharpness of your cutters and the type of wood you are using, you may want to do some hand-sanding of the bead on the inside of the sash. You can easily and quickly sand out the flat surfaces of the sash frame with an orbital sander after you have planed and trimmed the sash. You can also use the orbital sander on any unevenness where one muntin

Illus. 292. A clamp- or screw-on fence with a notch cut out to fit around the blade will ensure a straight cut when you bevel the bottom of sash. Watch out for scrap pieces being thrown back by the saw.

meets another, or where a muntin meets the frame, but make sure you do not sand too far through these narrow pieces.

Apply a coat of sealer before installing the glass to ensure that every part of the wood is sealed; especially soak the sealer into the corners and places where mullions and muntins meet the frame. A penetrating fungicidal sealer will help prolong the life of your window.

You may want to paint your sash before installing the glass. When either the paint or the sealer has throughly dried, install the glass in a bead of silicone, butyl or acrylic caulk laid around the bottoms of the rabbets. Finally, apply the stops or glazing putty to hold the glass in place in the sash (Illus. 293). Wooden stops are preferred today, because leadless putty generally begins to fail after a few years, and must be reapplied. You can make your own wooden stop stock on the router table or shaper, and install them by mitring them with a chop saw and nailing them with small ($\frac{7}{8}$-inch × #18) brass escutcheon pins, or staples.

Building Double-Hung Sash

Special consideration must be given to the building of double-hung sash because of the way in which the meeting rails overlap to form a weathertight seal. For the building of casement windows, and most types of doors, it is standard to run the stiles the full height of the piece, and let the rails butt into them at the corners. The meeting rails of double-hung sash deviate from this rule because it is necessary for the overlapping bevels or rabbets to run the full width of the window for a good airtight seal (Illus. 294). For this reason, the best Victorian sash were made with the stile tenoned into the meeting rails, and the bottom and top rails tenoned into the stiles. A small notch was cut in the bevel at each end of the meeting rails to allow for the parting bead.

A simpler approach, which is common today, is to build both sash in the standard manner, with the rails butted into the stiles, and then to glue and nail thin wooden strips, or weather stripping, along the meeting rails to seal the space between them. If you use this method, wait until after you have mounted the sash in the jamb to apply the strips, so that you can position them perfectly for an airtight closure.

Illus. 293. Seat the glass in a bead of acrylic or butyl caulk before applying the stops.

Illus. 294. Two ways of constructing meeting rails for double-hung sash. Note that no bead cut is made on the meeting rail of the upper sash. This will make it easier to install the sash closer.

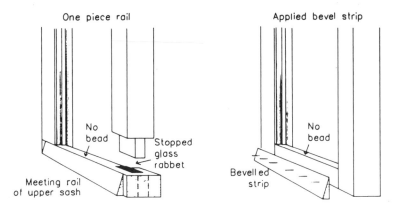

228

Unusual Projects

11
Irregularly Shaped
Doors and Windows

Walk around a nice older neighborhood in any city and note the various styles and configurations of doors and windows you come across, and you will soon realize that the designers and makers of these common, everyday objects are constantly coming up with new and different variations on old themes—whether it is a new way to align the muntins or making unusual eye-catching shapes and forms (Illus. 295). Here I describe a few of the most common variations on rectilinear doors and windows, discuss some possible solutions to the technical problems involved, and perhaps give you inspiration to try something new and different yourself.

Curved Tops
on Doors and Windows

Perhaps the most common departure from the rectangular form in doors and windows is to make some type of arch with the top edge of the structure. The arch is a very basic architectural form (the very word which we use to describe someone who

designs buildings means, literally, "former of arches"). Curved forms from a full half circle to a very slight arched segment (called an "eyebrow" by sash builders) are very pleasing to the eye in that they break up the monotony of rectangular forms and give a building a softer, smoother look that is still bold and exciting. Curves can be big or small, constant or varying, full or very slight.

You will use one of two techniques to build curved shapes for doors and windows: either join and laminate your pieces to overcome the weakness of short sections of cross-grained wood that would result if you simply cut a curved section out of a single piece of wood, or bend and laminate strips of wood to get the desired result. The first technique is generally most useful in building the sash or door itself, while the second will most often be used to form the curved parts of the jamb that holds either the door or the window sash (Illus. 296).

To build any curved topped door or window, you will have to make both the curving

Illus. 295A–D. The possibilities for creative expression are limited only by your imagination.

Illus. 295C.

Illus. 295D.

MAKING CURVED PIECES

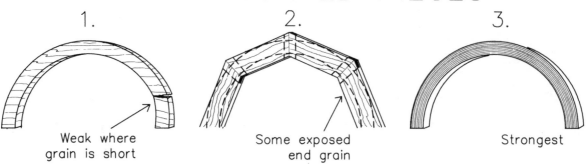

1. Weak where grain is short

2. Some exposed end grain

3. Strongest

Illus. 296. Number 1 shows where grain is weak and would be likely to break if a curved piece were cut from one piece of wood. Number 2 shows one solution, that of joining short segments to overcome this weakness. Bending and laminating a series of thin strips, as shown in 3, is the strongest method, but very time-consuming.

sash or door and a jamb head that matches it. Generally, the curved parts of the sash or door are relatively easy to make. It is often more difficult to produce a jamb or frame that matches it perfectly. Since jambs are usually at least 4 inches wide, and often as wide as 10 inches or more, brickwork laminating tends to be impractical for making this part of the structure. Bending, the preferred technique for making curved jambs, will require a form and either some very thin stock or a good steaming cabinet for steam-bending thicker stock.

Steam-bending, a common technique before the advent of reliable glues, has the disadvantage of requiring specialized equipment that you must make: a steaming cabinet long enough to hold your working stock (Illus. 297), and a heater fashioned so that it will boil water to create the steam.

"Spring-back" is also a common problem with steam-bent pieces. Because one solid piece of the desired thickness is used, the material will often retain a strong tendency to spring back towards its original flat

shape. Of course, the wall framing will eventually provide solid bracing to hold the bent piece in place, but until it is in the wall it will be difficult to work with.

Bent laminations, a more modern bending technique, are usually made by bending thin pieces of stock around an inside or convex form. Several laminations are laid up and clamped in place at once with glue between them so that when the glue dries, the lamination will tend to hold its shape. If the lamination is done properly—that is, with thin enough pieces so that the wood is not overly stressed—and is allowed to dry at least twice the normal drying time, the spring-back factor will be negligible with this type of bending. The key is in using veneers that are thin enough to easily take the desired bend and in using the proper type of glue. Urea resin glues will work for bent laminations, but epoxy resin glues are superior because of their gap-filling qualities and their ability to permeate the fibres of the wood.

Outside forms can also be incorporated into the structure of the wall as part of the

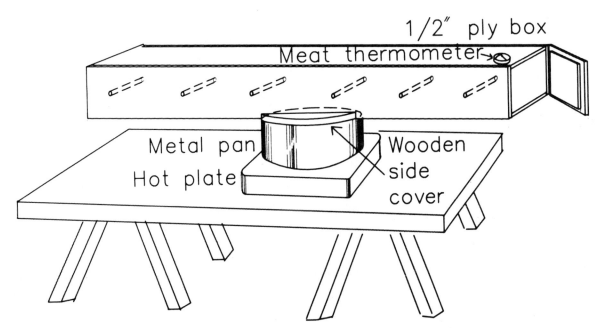

Illus. 297. A simple steaming cabinet. The box is made of ½-inch plywood with dowels through it to hold the workpieces. A large metal pan holds the water, and the wooden side cover allows for the easy addition of more water.

permanent structure. It is generally more difficult to bend a piece of wood into a outside form than around an inside form, but, once again, the thickness of the laminations and the radius of the bend are the most critical factors. If you use thin enough laminations and apply the proper pressure, you can make an inside bend (to an outside form) quite easily.

The following examples give step-by-step instructions for both these methods.

Eyebrow Door Top Made with an Outside Form

As usual, it is best to begin with the construction of the jamb or door frame, as it will be easier to shape the door tops to fit the jamb than the other way around. (Illus. 298 and 299). The sides of the jamb are built like the sides of any other door jamb, the only difference being in the construction of the top piece. This gentle arch can easily be made with a simple variation of the outside-form method. In this example, the arch is actually a section of a circle, that is, the curve is constant all along.

Start by milling a piece of clear vertical-grained wood of the proper width to a thickness of approximately $\frac{3}{16}$ inch. If you don't have the equipment to do the milling yourself, consider using $\frac{1}{8}$-inch-plywood material, called door skins, that is often available at lumberyards; this material bends easily and usually has inexpensive mahogany veneers on the surface, but is not always made with exterior-grade glues.

Determine the tightness of the curve by bending your laminating stock to whatever curvature feels and looks right for your project. Your form can be cut from a solid

Illus. 298. This gently arch-topped double-door jamb is bent against an outside form that is built into the structure.

Illus. 299. The ³/₁₆-inch veneer is bent in against the partially assembled jamb and form, trimmed to the proper length, and then nailed and glued into place against the form as the end screws are tightened. Note that the rabbeted parts of the jamb and the form are the same thickness as the framing, while the jambs and the veneer must span the full thickness of the wall, including both layers of siding.

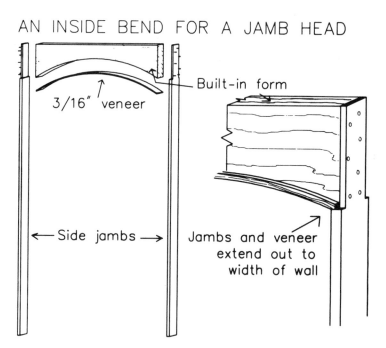

AN INSIDE BEND FOR A JAMB HEAD

3/16″ veneer

Built-in form

← Side jambs →

Jambs and veneer extend out to width of wall

piece of 3 ½-inch-thick lumber or it can be made from several thicknesses of plywood or hardboard nailed and glued together. The offset of the arch, that is, the vertical distance from the highest to the lowest point of the arch, will determine the height of your form piece. If the offset is about 12 inches, as it is in this door, then the form will have to be at least 14 inches wide. Make sure you leave room for the offset when rough-framing the doorway.

Since wood does not always bend evenly, make the actual cutting lines for your form from an easily made compass ruler rather than from a bent piece of stock. Once you have determined the radius of your curve, simply drive a nail through one end of a thin strip of wood, and make a notch in the other end at the radial distance from the nail. Lay out your form on a flat surface and project the midpoint of the arch down from the center of the form to the point where the center of the circle that the arch is a segment of would be. Now, swing the notched end of the stick across the form with a pencil tip held in the notch so that the circumference of the circle is drawn on the form. Now cut the line with a band or jigsaw to make your form.

The ends of your form should be square, and cut to the same length as the inside of your jamb (the width of the sash), plus twice the depth of the rabbet which you will cut on the top of each side-jamb piece. It helps to make the sill slots (if you are using this technique on windows) in the side jambs the same depth as the rabbet at the top.

Make the rabbet cut on the side jambs so that it extends down from the top of each piece $\frac{3}{16}$ inch farther than the height of the form for the head piece. Then screw the side jambs to the ends of the form with their ends flush to the top of the form. Use screws on at least one end so that it can be loosened a bit later when you need to get the veneer into position.

Now bevel the veneer piece at one end with a hand plane so that it fits nicely against the end of the rabbet in the jamb. Bend the veneer tightly in against the form, using clamps where necessary to pull

CLAMPING AN INSIDE BEND

Drive screws partway in to prevent clamp slippage

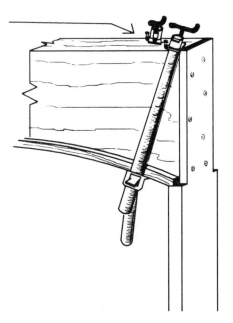

Illus. 300. Screws can be temporarily driven partway into the top of the form to give purchase for clamps if they are needed to help bring the veneer in tight against the form.

it in. (See Illus. 300 for ways to apply the clamps.) When the veneer is snug against the form all the way along, except for the last little bit, cut it carefully in place (a little long) or mark it and remove it to cut it off. Try it against the jamb, and plane the end to fit as necessary.

When you are satisfied with the fit, glue the veneer in place. Begin laying it in at the fixed end, with the screws out a little bit on the other end. When you pop in the loose end, loosen the C-clamps or short-bar clamps, as shown in Illus. 300, and tighten the screws (use bar clamps if necessary). When the jamb is tight against the end of the form, tighten the clamps again to press the veneer evenly against the form. If a little crack results between the form and the veneer, try to position it so that the curve is even from side to side, and then fill the crack with an epoxy filler or panel adhesive after the glue has dried.

Now, with the sill and form as integral parts of the window frame, install the jamb in the wall as a rectangular unit, lessening the need for special framing and trim work. Either trim out the top of the window so that it is square or make special pieces (Illus. 301) to follow the curve of the sash and jamb. You can apply the interior stops for this type of window in the same manner that the side jambs and veneer were built up. The curved stop for the head jamb may consist of several laminations, and

Illus. 301A and B. In some cases, such as an open-walled construction, you may want to cover the form or wall framing with the trim. The siding can also cover the form, and the trim simply follow the curve of the veneer.

236

should be tightly attached to the veneer with glue and filler where necessary. Use nails or staples to help pull the stop laminations in tightly against the head jamb.

Inside Forms

Bending laminations around an inside form is a more common technique that is likely to give better results with fuller or tighter curves such as the half-circle arch shown in Illus. 302. Once again, a good deal of thought and care should go into making your form, even though the form will not be a part of the finished structure when you use an inside form. Depending on the type of clamps you will be using, you may want to cut out the inside of the form (so that it looks like the letter C) or leave it solid and attach battens around the edges on which you can put the clamps. If your clamps are short use battens. You can make

clamps like the one shown in Illus. 305 that will work nicely if you hollow out the form; however, it is important not to hollow out the form to the point that it becomes weak and will deform when the laminations are being bent.

When building your form, it is best to make it ¾ inch smaller than the desired circumference of the jamb so that you can make the stops first, and then use them as part of the form when you bend the jamb. This will ensure the best matchup between jamb and stop. It is also possible to cut the form down and bend the stops after the jambs, but whichever way you do it, make sure that the form is wide enough to support the entire width of the jamb, and is very sturdy. The ends of the form should also extend out tangentially a couple of inches from the halfway points of the circle so that the ends of your jamb head will

Illus. 302. Usually a full curve, such as this arched window, is bent and laminated around an inside form.

Illus. 303A–C. This quarter-circle lamination is being made with ⅛-inch laminations bent around a form made of plywood and wooden spacers of the proper thickness. Segmented outer forms are used to reduce the number of clamps necessary. Wedges can be driven in where necessary to tighten loose areas.

Illus. 303B.

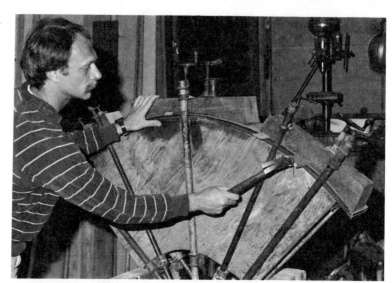

Illus. 303C.

SEVERAL BENDING METHODS

Illus. 304. Several techniques for applying pressure to bent laminations include a metal band that is tightened with bolts, inside and outside forms with pressure applied through a hose, and deflation bags which use atmospheric pressure and vacuum to apply pressure.

Steel band

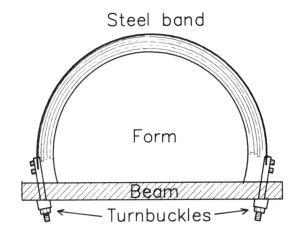

Form

Beam

← Turnbuckles →

Air pressure

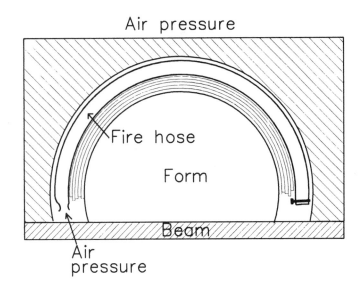

Fire hose

Form

Beam

Air pressure

Vacuum bending

Deflation bag

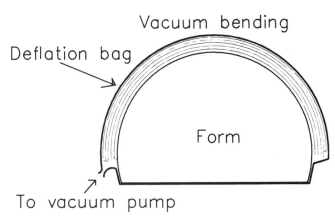

Form

To vacuum pump

Illus. 305. Lots of clamps will be needed for bending around an inside form. You can make your own clamps that will work on a hollow, or C-shaped, form from short sections of angle iron and ½-inch bolts.

AN EASY-TO-MAKE
BENDING CLAMP

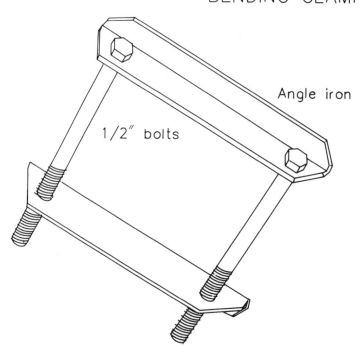

Angle iron

1/2″ bolts

be parallel for a couple of inches. This will give you some surface on which to rout or cut rabbets for a half-lap joint to attach the head to the side jambs.

As stated before, it is important to be sure that your laminations will take the desired bend. If you feel that you are forcing the wood, or if cracking occurs, then you must use thinner veneers. Drum or thickness sanders will give the best results when it comes to making veneers thinner than approximately ⅛ inch. You may be able to resaw thicker stock on either the table saw or a good band saw, and then plane it to thicknesses of ⅛ inch or more, but planers will often destroy such thin pieces. The thickness sander will also produce a better surface for gluing. If you don't have a thickness sander, check local furni-

ture makers or look through specialty catalogues for veneer makers.

Cut your veneers several inches longer than you will need them, and ¼ inch to ½ inch wider, as it will be difficult to align the edges perfectly when gluing. Remember that the outside veneer will have to be a couple of inches longer than the shortest veneer on the inside.

When you are ready to make the bend, take as many veneers as you can easily bend around the form (you can always do this in several stages if it is too difficult to get the thickness you want in one), and cover one side of each with an even coat of glue. It's easiest to work with the form by laying it down on the bench, though you could work with the form up on end if you made a stand to hold it up off the work sur-

240

face. Line up the center point of the veneers with the top center of the form, and begin clamping here. Work from the center towards both edges, placing clamps every couple of inches as needed. Make sure you have plenty of clamps on hand before starting; a typical 3-foot-diameter arch could use as any as 50 C-clamps. Only half as many of the angle iron clamps shown in Illus. 303 would be needed, since they apply pressure all the way across.

With this type of bending, there may be a small amount of spring back if the veneers are thick, but it should be minimal. If your piece springs out a couple of inches after you take it off the form, just make a brace by nailing a piece of 1 × 4 across it that will hold it in its proper shape. Since the ends of this half circle are parallel to the side jambs where they meet, they can both be rabbeted to form a half-lap joint. The overlap of the joint should be at least one inch.

Curved-Topped Door or Sash

Once again, the approach you will use will depend on the severity or fullness of the arch you are forming. For the eyebrow doors described on pages 233-241, it was possible to cut the top rails from one piece of wood and to construct the doors in the conventional manner with the rails running between the stiles. Just lay out the two stiles at the proper width, and figure the angles on the ends of the top rails and the length of the rails by marking them from the edges of the stiles. Make a pattern from the jamb to be sure that you get the tops of the doors just right, and then use a com-

pass to scribe that line down to the bottom edge of the top rails.

Make the end cuts on the top rails before making any of the curving cuts, so that you have straight edges to work from. After making the end cuts, cut the inside curve, and if you are using a shaper, also make the shaper cuts on all the pieces at this point. Now, with the door dry-assembled, mark the line for the top of the door all the way across both stiles and the top rail, and cut these lines with a band saw or jigsaw. The pieces will be easier to handle separately if you use a band saw. At this point, you could glue the door together before trimming the top if you are using a jigsaw. Either way, stay to the outside of your line when you cut. You can easily plane to the line with a block plane after assembling the door.

A fuller curve like the half-circle top in the example discussed on pages 237–241 will need some type of lamination to overcome the tendency of the wood to break easily parallel to the grain. One approach is to break the half circle into four segments (half of an octagon), and join these with splines (or finger joints) where they meet (Illus. 306 and 307). Cut the slots on the ends of each piece for the spline with a table saw or router; they should be at least 1 inch deep and one-third the thickness of the door. The grain of the splines should run perpendicular to the joint. Router bits for finger-jointing the ends of these sections are also available from Furima Industrial Carbide.

When you are ready to assemble the arch, use a solid piece of 2 × 4 lumber with screwed-on battens the proper distance apart to serve as a clamping jig. Inward

A HALF—ROUND LAMINATION

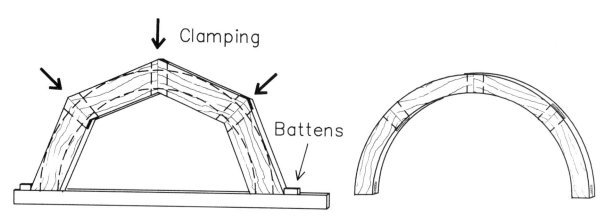

Illus. 306. *A half-round sash can be made by joining four segments with end cuts of 22½ inches. Clamping pressure is applied radially, as shown.*

Illus. 307. *To join the segments of the half-octagon shown in Illus. 306, use splines. The router bit shown here (available from Furima Industrial Carbide) will cut a finger joint, which will also make a good joint for this type of work, but remember that the segments will have to be long enough to compensate for the interlocking joint.*

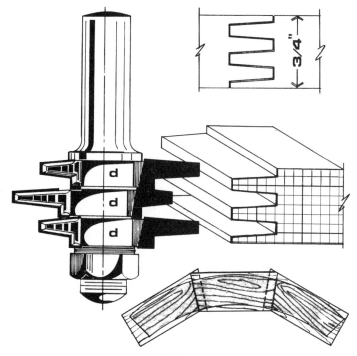

ALL PROFILES SHOWN FULL SIZE

pressure on the top pieces of the arch will force the joints tightly together. Apply battens to the 2 × 4 if angular clamping pressure is needed to help align the pieces of the arch.

A similar approach would be to build up the arch in brickwork fashion by using ½-inch thick stock and offsetting the joints of the three layers (Illus. 308). This method will produce a stronger lamination because

242

A BRICK—WORK LAMINATION

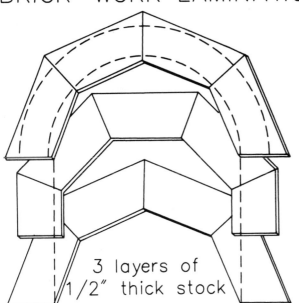

3 layers of 1/2" thick stock

Illus. 308. A brickwork-type lamination, made from three layers of ½-inch material, will give an even stronger result.

there is so much more overlap between the pieces, but it is considerably more difficult and time-consuming. You have to use a circular piece of plywood or hardboard cut to the diameter of the finished arch as part of the clamping jig.

To make the circle, find the center of a square of the same width as the diameter of your circle and drill a ¼-inch hole in it. Now, make a pivot arm like the one shown in Illus. 309 and clamp it to your band saw so that the protruding peg is positioned at 90 degrees to the cutting edge of the blade. Begin cutting tangentially to the circle until you can drop the center hole in the plywood onto the peg; it should now pivot easily to cut a perfect circle.

Nail a 2 × 4 to the circle with one edge passing through the center, and nail battens to it where the outside corners of the octagonal pieces meet the 2 × 4. Now, lay the pieces for the first layer of the lamination on the circle and clamp or tack them in place so that their joining edges are tight.

Spread glue over the whole area where the next layer of the lamination will contact the first layer, and lay these pieces out with the joints aligned so that they are at the midpoints between the joints of the first layer.

You will have to cut the two end pieces in half where they meet the 2 × 4. You can use small nails to hold this layer in place on the first layer as long as they don't go through the first layer. Do not nail near the areas you will be cutting later. Finally, apply the top layer in the same fashion, and apply C-clamps at all the joints to press the whole thing together.

When the glue has dried, leave the laminations on the circular piece of plywood, and use it as a table that pivots the lamination for cutting the waste away from the outside of the piece with the band saw. Now, fasten a block the same thickness as the lamination, with a peg running through it and extending out both sides, to the center of the plywood. To scribe the inside curve of the lamination, insert one end of

243

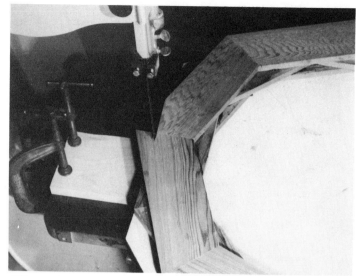

Illus. 309A (left). To cut circular pieces, clamp a pivot arm to the band-saw table. The peg in the end fits in a hole in the center of the jig which holds the workpiece. Illus. 309B (above). Cut tangentially until the hole falls onto the peg; then rotate the work for a perfect circular cut.

the peg in the center hole of the plywood and pivot a pivot arm made of ¼-inch plywood around the peg protruding from the other side of the block.

At this point, remove the workpiece from the plywood and cut it by hand with the band saw as close as possible to the line, without actually cutting the line. Now re-attach the piece to the plywood circle, and use a router on a pivot arm, pivoting around the peg in the block to trim the inside of the piece. If the pivot arm is held firmly, the result should be a perfectly smooth and even curve.

Another approach would be to make a guide template for the router by pivot-cutting it out of ¼-inch plywood. Fasten the guide template to the lamination, and trim the lamination (pages 153–155).

Once you have trimmed the lamination, attach it to the top ends of the stiles with

splines, as described on pages 241 and 242. Leave your stiles a little long until after the door is assembled, so that you will have some room to plane the upper edge of the door to match the arch of the jamb head. An adjustable compass plane is extremely helpful in fairing constant curves like this one, but if you don't have one, use a flat-bottomed plane, which also works well on the outside of a curve.

Bend-Laminating an Arched Top

Yet another approach to making an arched frame member for a door or window would be to build it up with a series of bent laminations in much the same way as that described for making an arched head jamb. For a 1½-inch-thick piece, start with 1¾-inch-wide laminating strips so that any un-evenness can be planed out later. This approach ensures that the end grain will not

Illus. 310. The same pivot-arm principle can be used to guide a router for trimming the inside of the lamination.

be exposed at all along the top of the door, and should work perfectly well as long as there are enough clamps to ensure perfect tightness all the way around when you glue the laminations. Use at least one clamp for every 2 inches of circumference of arch. Other methods of applying pressure, such as the steel-band, fire-hose, and vacuum-bag methods shown in Illus. 304, will work well for this type of lamination.

Once again, the thickness of the veneers is critical to success. Trying to work with pieces that are too thick is futile. Perfect vertical grain stock is also important for this type of bend. If the grain is vertical

and the joints are perfect, it will be nearly impossible to tell that the arched top is laminated.

Bent lamination will also work well for making a top for a door or window in the colonial or "ox-bow" style, or for any other form that demands a complex bend. Here the curve is more complex, having both concave and convex curvature in the same piece. The laminations for this bend will have to be thinner, and it is advisable that you make a bending press to help ensure that no cracks develop between the laminations (Illus. 311).

Make the bending press by marking the lines that you want for the top and bottom edges of your lamination across a block of plywood or hardboard pieces that have been stacked and glued or nailed together to the thickness of your lamination. Cut both lines carefully and clean up the edges with a rasp or sander where necessary. Now, lay up the strips of veneer for the laminations between the forms, and clamp the forms together to provide even pressure at all points on the lamination. You can also use long pieces of threaded rod with nuts and washers to bring the two parts of the form together.

A Round Window

Making a completely circular object such as a round window is only slightly more difficult than the half circles that I have already discussed (Illus. 312 and 313). It is not practical to bend laminations in a complete circle, because of the difficulty involved in getting the length of the changing circumferences accurate enough to prevent cracks from developing between the pieces.

245

The most satisfactory method is to bend two half circles, with their ends approximately an inch long, and then join the two half circles with halflaps or finger joints.

You can either band an inner circle to be made into the stops around a smaller form, or make it with the brickwork lamination at the same time that the sash is made. For a pivot-opening round window, cut the stop into two half circles and mount it as shown in Illus. 314. Then mount the sash on two pegs on opposite sides of the sash, which will fit into two holes in the jamb. Cut a small channel into the jamb for mounting or removing the sash.

Make the sash with either the brickwork or the splined-octagon method. Either way, you will need a method for cutting and join-

Illus. 311. A bending press can be made to either help with complex bends or make clamping easier.

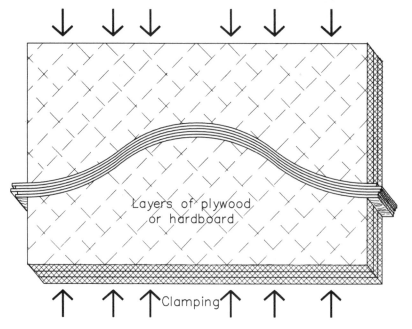

Layers of plywood or hardboard

Clamping

A PIVOT—OPENING ROUND WINDOW

Illus. 312. Round windows are beautiful and not terribly difficult to make.

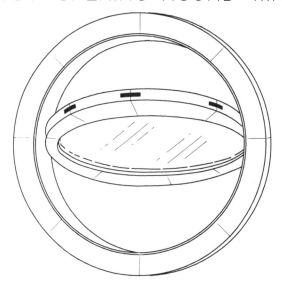

AN EIGHT-PIECE ROUND WINDOW LAMINATION

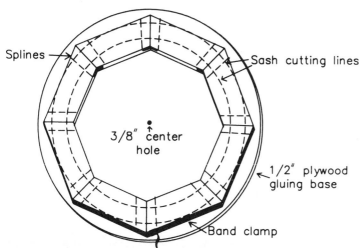

Splines →

Sash cutting lines

3/8" center hole

1/2" plywood gluing base

Band clamp

Illus. 313. Lay a round window out on a circular piece of plywood. Tighten the joints with a single-band clamp. When the glue is dry, turn the entire assembly on a pivot arm to cut the outside circle, and then use a router on a pivot arm to trim to the inner circle.

Illus. 314. Mount a pivot-opening round window on two wooden or metal pegs that fit into holes in the jamb. Mount the lower stop on the inside, and the upper stop on the outside.

ing octagons. For the best results, use a radial arm saw or table saw, set carefully at 22½ degrees, but remember, any minor error from exactly 22½ degrees will be amplified greatly by the 16 identical cuts. Make the cuts as precise as you can, and then adjust the joints where necessary with a sharp block plane; finally, use band clamps to force the joints tightly together. Trim the inside and outside of the circle using the pivoting methods for the band saw and router previously discussed.

It is important to seal the sash of a round window well because so much end grain is exposed around the outside of the sash. Also, remember that round windows do not drain well at the bottom because they do not have a sloped sill; so the area where the stop meets the jamb should be well caulked. If the window opens, make sure that the bottom stop is on the inside.

Curved Mouldings

One of the most difficult parts of making irregular doors and windows is making shaped mouldings to fit curved lights or panels. I have already mentioned some of the techniques that will be used in making curved mouldings: pivot cutting will work for cutting out pieces that are uniformly curved, and cutting to a marked line and then sanding to fit will work for most irregular curves. But how do you hold and shape such a piece once it is cut?

Though routers can also be used on this type of work, spindle shapers generally have the capacity to cut wider and deeper profiles than routers. You may be able to get the same result with a router; it will just take more time and more ingenuity. In either case, use bits with ball-bearing guides instead of rub collars. Rub collars, or guide pins, that are part of the bit tend to burn the wood as they ride over it, and will easily dig in and ruin a smooth, even curving cut if you pause too long or apply too much pressure in one place.

As previously stated, you can order many different-sized bearings that will fit on your spindle shaper through auto or machinist's supply companies. You may want to grind your own cutting knives or bits for some profiles, but you may also be able to make many of the profiles you need from combinations of standard cutters.

When using a spindle shaper without a fence, as you will want to do when shaping curved pieces, screw or bolt a support pin into the tabletop to give you something to brace the work against (Illus. 315). This will greatly reduce the danger of the cutters grabbing the workpiece, an extremely dangerous situation. For curved pieces, incorporate some type of holding jig into the construction of the piece. Sometimes this can be partially accomplished by cutting

only one edge of the curve from the block of wood to begin with and shaping it before the other side is cut away. If shaping is also needed on the other side, then you will have to use a holding jig that is curved to match the side that is not being worked.

As mentioned in previous sections, it may be necessary to laminate the stock from

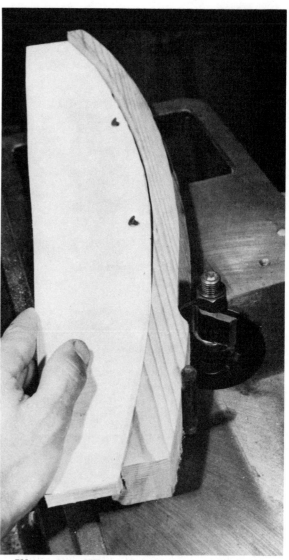

Illus. 315. When shaping curved pieces, remove the fence and screw or mount a support pin to the table to help steady the work and prevent kickback.

which you intend to make a curved moulding to avoid breaking the wood along the grain where the grain runs the short way across a curved piece. On the other hand, if you plan your pieces carefully, you may be able to avoid this extra effort by breaking or splicing the pieces in the middle of full curves or arches. The type of wood you use will also be a consideration in whether or not you need to laminate. Woods like redwood split very easily, while pine, fir, and most hard woods are less likely to split if care is taken.

Coping Curved and Irregular Joints

Making mullions fit arched rails or aligning them in unusual ways is often not as difficult as it looks. If you are working with shapers, all it usually takes is a little paring with a sharp chisel or filing to make the end of the piece fit to the rail. After that, the coping is easy if you have set up a fence with an inlaid support piece like the one shown in Illus. 223. Make sure that the muntin always has a backer to support it when you make the coping cut. This will prevent chipping and splintering as the cutter comes to the unsupported wood at the end of the cut.

If the muntin or rail itself is curved, or if it meets another piece at an angle, you may have to make a special backer block that will both support it and hold it at the right angle. If the stick cut has already been made on the muntin or rail, then you will need to make a backer that has the coping cut in it.

When muntins or mouldings meet at un-known or complex angles, the golden rule is that the angle of the mitre cut between the two pieces should be half of the overall angle formed by the two meeting pieces (Illus. 316). If the angle is not halved, the ends of the pieces where the mitre cut is made will be of different lengths, and the various elements of the mouldings will not line up.

For very complicated mitres, such as curved mouldings or places where several muntins come together, begin by making a paper model showing the lines formed by all the elements of the pieces. Snip the ends of the paper until you find the proper angles, and then transfer them to your work. With curved mouldings or muntins, the mitre line may even have to be curved to get all the lines right.

If you are fitting a narrow muntin to a convex curve, such as what would be encountered in the center of an eyebrow arch with fanned muntins, begin by cutting the muntin off straight, a little long, and then, after coping it, use a sharp $\frac{1}{4}$- or $\frac{1}{8}$-inch chisel to hollow out the center of the muntin a bit so that the outside edges fit tightly. Fanned muntins should always meet another muntin or smaller arched piece in the center (Illus. 317). Never try to bring them to a single point.

Muntins aligned diagonally to form diamond shapes are easy enough to cope, but you must lay out their patterns and cut them to length precisely. It is nearly impossible to make these muntins with tenons to hold them in place, but small nails can be driven through the part of the rabbeted side that is concealed by the stops to help keep the muntins in place until the glass and stops are applied.

Illus. 316. Number 1: The golden rule in mitring mouldings is that the angle of the mitre should be half of the overall angle between the meeting pieces. Number 2: Shows how this rule applies when more than two muntins meet. Number 3: When curved mouldings meet straight ones or other curves, this mitre is curved. For very complex mouldings, mark the various elements of each moulding on a piece of paper, and find the right mitre angle on the paper before cutting the mouldings.

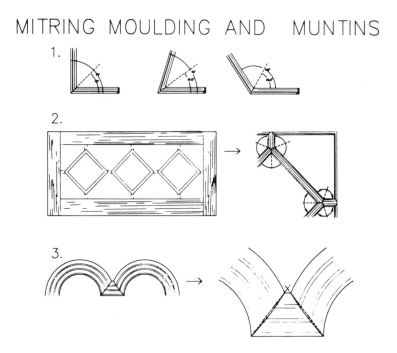

MITRING MOULDING AND MUNTINS

Illus. 317. Fanned muntins usually terminate in a small rounded piece or another rounded muntin.

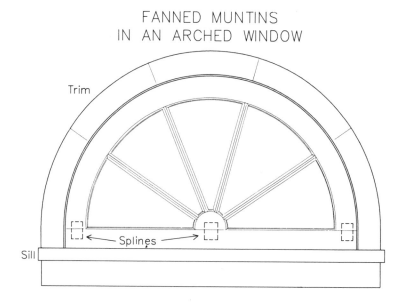

FANNED MUNTINS IN AN ARCHED WINDOW

Other Decorative Techniques

The door and window craftsmen who helped make the fine old Victorian and Georgian homes that adorn many of our cities had a bag of tricks that included appliqués, carved pieces, repetitive designs, lathe-turned pieces, and build-ups where several layers, sometimes with cutout patterns, were laminated together. These techniques were used extensively in doors and windows and in trimwork to produce a visual ambiance that gave character and uniqueness to a structure. Most of the techniques they employed are not at all difficult to accomplish with modern tools.

Grooves can be routed in either panels or trim pieces with router cutters that are designed without a guide pin for this type of cutting (Illus. 318). These router cutters can even be used with a template as a guide to cut a groove that gives the illusion of a raised panel on a flat surface such as on a plywood or solid-core door. Moulding cutterheads for the table saw can also be used for this type of work. Some cutters will leave raised beads, while other will leave grooves.

You can easily make a setup that will cut a circular pattern into a square panel or piece of trim by attaching a lathe chuck to a $\frac{1}{4}$ horsepower or larger motor that is firmly attached to a bench. Screw the panel, usually no bigger than 6 inches square, to a face plate; a machinist's screw mechanism like that used to close a vise holds a knife that is slowly advanced into the work. Then either glue two of these pieces back to back for a panel, or use them in the corners of trimwork for both the interiors or exteriors of buildings.

Appliqués were used extensively in this type of millwork (Illus. 319). Either a pattern was cut out with careful jigsaw work, and then glued to another piece which backed it and gave strength to the delicate sawwork, or a piece of moulding was chopped into short segments and glued back onto another piece with spaces between the pieces to form a repetitive pattern that gave the illusion of great complexity to a design. This was often used under sills or overhangs.

And, of course, you can spend as much time as you want carving your panels and trimwork. Much of the more elaborate Victorian trimwork incorporates combinations of carved and moulded pieces that undoubtedly kept skilled craftsmen employed for days at a time. Many of these pieces were carved only once and reproduced in plaster or cement for several buildings at once, but a surprising amount were made from wood, one piece at a time, when labor was cheap and plentiful. Many books exist

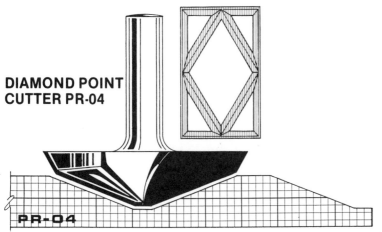

Illus. 318. Router cutters designed for decorative grooving can be used to give a flat surface the look of a raised panel.

DIAMOND POINT CUTTER PR-04

PR-04

251

on relief-carving techniques. Suffice it to say here that you should choose your wood with care for workability and solidity, and plan your design carefully.

Illus. 319A and B. Appliqués were used extensively in period millwork to make a simple door look very fancy.

Installation, Maintenance and Finishing Techniques

12
Installation Techniques for Doors, Windows, and Hardware

Doors and windows can either be pre-hung (mounted to the jamb with hinges or held in by the stops) or installed on the job. With operable windows, pre-hanging is a virtual necessity because of the difficulty of access to many windows, the fragility of windows with glass in them, and the importance of an airtight seal.

Fixed windows should also generally be installed in their jambs in the shop if the glass is held in a sash, but if there is no sash, install the jamb in the wall before putting in the glass and stops (Illus. 320). It is even possible to apply exterior trim or blind stops to a window jamb before it is installed in the wall, but this can make

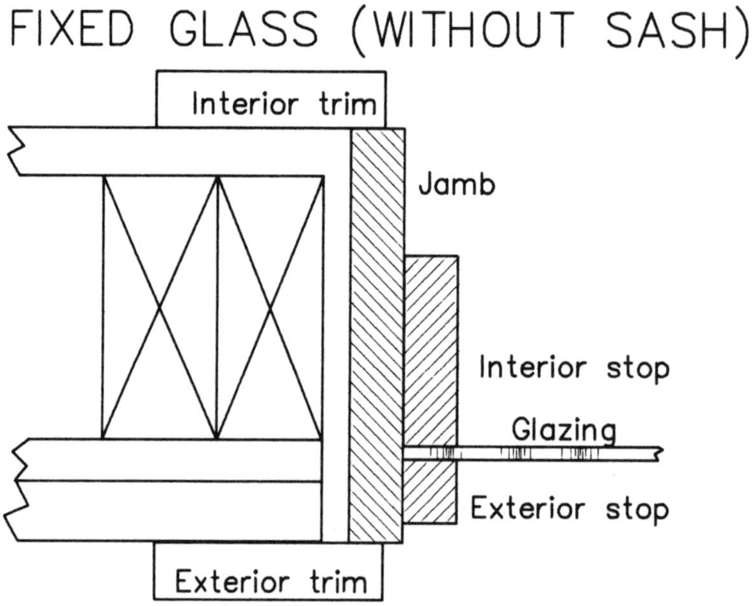

Illus. 320. Install fixed windows without sash in the wall before mounting and stopping out the glass. All other windows should be glazed before installation.

FIXED GLASS (WITHOUT SASH)

Interior trim

Jamb

Interior stop

Glazing

Exterior stop

Exterior trim

shimming the window into place a bit more difficult; so it is not often done.

With doors, the sequence is much the same. First, mortise the hinges into the door; then position the door on the jamb and transfer the hinge marks to the jamb. At this point, cut hinge mortises into the jamb and separate the hinge leaves. Mount the jamb leaf of the hinge on the jamb and tack the jamb in place in the rough opening. Finally, rehang the door for the final shimming and nailing of the jamb. The important thing with doors is to avoid getting committed (by nailing a jamb piece in place too soon) until you are sure that everything is fitting and working properly.

Sash Hardware and Sash Installation

As stated in Chapter 8, operable sash fall into two main categories: sliding sash and casement or hinged sash. The most common type of sliding wooden sash are the double-hung windows that are used throughout the world. (See Illus. 242 on page 185.) Some very specific types of hardware have evolved for these windows, and in recent years some improvements have been made in the mechanism that counterbalances the weight of the sash (Illus. 321).

The older, turn-of-the-century double-hung window was the essence of simplicity in its design, and worked well as long as it was properly maintained. The area behind the trim on both sides of the window was left hollow, and double pulleys were installed at the top of the jamb on both sides. Counterweights, called sash weights, were attached by cords which ran over the pulleys to the sash, and an ear-shaped sash

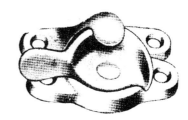

5/16"

DUPLEX ADJUSTABLE SASH BALANCE

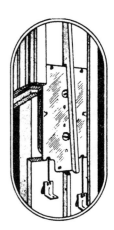

Illus. 321. Shown here are several types of double-hung sash fasteners and a detail of a modern spring-loaded sash balancer.

closer was installed at the top of the lower sash so that when it revolved into the upper part of the closer, at the bottom of the upper sash, it forced the sashes tightly closed.

Modern wooden double-hung windows are often mounted on adjustable springs fit into the jambs themselves. To do this, cut a hole in the jamb with a jigsaw, just above the place where the center rails meet. Mount the spring unit flush to the inside of the jamb. Cut a small mortise on the bottom corners of each sash to accept the clip that attaches the spring wire to the sash. The types of sash closers that are used with sash weights can also be used with the springs.

To install double-hung sash in their jambs, begin by installing the balance springs in the jambs. Next, apply the outside stop with nails and caulk. If you have designed your jambs to accept storm windows and screens, set back the outside stop from the outside edge of the jamb the thickness of the storm-window sash. Otherwise, set it flush to the outside edge. Next, with the jamb assembly laid out on the worktable, lay the upper sash in place. Then, drop the parting bead into its channel and tack it in with small nails. Now, lay the lower sash in place in its fully open position, and attach the springs or weights to both sash. Lastly, tack a temporary inside stop to the side jambs to hold the lower sash in place until the window is installed in the wall. You can usually adjust the tension of the spring units with a screwdriver to accommodate sash of different weights.

Casement windows can be mounted on regular butt hinges like those used for doors, but this will require an additional piece of hardware to hold the sash in place when it is open. Friction hinges can be used instead, but their installation requires the cutting of a long, mortise approximately 1 by $\frac{1}{2}$ inch deep on two sides of the casement (Illus. 322).

The friction hinge has a sliding arm with the right amount of friction built into it so that the casement sash won't blow back and forth when opened. These hinges, which come in various sizes, are mounted top and bottom for casement windows, and on the sides for hopper- or transom-opening windows. The size ratio of sash to hinge should be at least 3 to 1 for the best operation.

When using friction hinges, you will have to cut mortises in both the sash and the sill when these hinges are mounted on the bottom of a sash (Illus. 323). You can also use crank-operated levers to operate casement windows; these can be mounted through screens and used in conjunction with non-friction hinges where screened casements are desired (Illus. 324).

Whichever type of hinge you use, install casement windows in the jamb so that there is a clearance of $\frac{3}{32}$ inch, or about the thickness of a nickle, around the three upper sides (Illus. 325). The lower edge should fit tightly against the sill when the window is closed. It will be easiest to wait until after the window is installed in the wall to apply the stops, since the stops must fit tightly against the stool, which can't go in until the window is in the wall.

A pseudo double-hung window can be created by building the window with the look of a double-hung window, but with a fixed upper sash and a hinged, inward-opening lower sash. (See Illus. 241, page 184.) The two sash can either be offset, as with a real double-hung, or stacked one on top of the other with an interlocking rabbet to seal them. This combines the reliability of hinges, as compared to springs, with the easy exterior mounting of screens or storm windows—the major advantage double-hung windows have over casement windows. Since no inside stop is used in this type of installation, add furring to the space between the parting bead and the outside stop below the upper sash to provide a solid weather stop for the lower sash if the sash are offset.

Installing Windows in Walls

You can install windows in their rough openings either before or after the siding

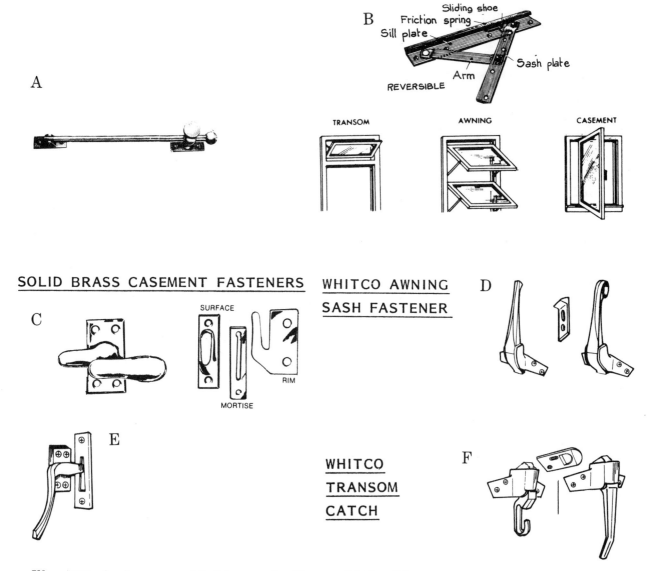

Illus. 322. A: A casement holder, used with non-friction hinges to prevent casement windows from blowing around when opened. B: Friction hinges and various applications. C–F: Various types of casement window fasteners.

Illus. 323. The areas that will have to be mortised for friction hinges. The mortises will be as long as the hinges, up to 18 inches.

FRICTION-HINGE MORTISES

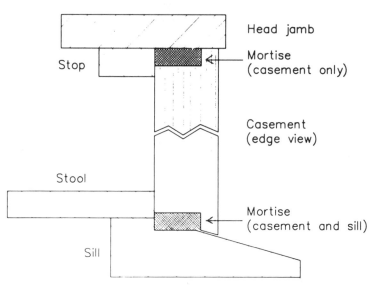

- Head jamb
- Stop
- Mortise (casement only)
- Casement (edge view)
- Stool
- Mortise (casement and sill)
- Sill

WOOD CASEMENT WINDOW OPERATOR

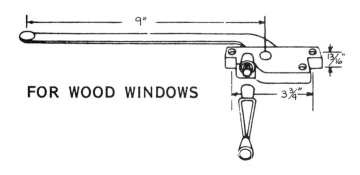

FOR WOOD WINDOWS

Illus. 324 (above left). Crank-operated levers are also used to operate casement windows when screens are to be installed. Illus 325 (above right). The proper clearance between the jamb and casement should be about the thickness of a nickel.

has been applied but you must carefully plan either way to avoid wasted effort and obtain clean results. Generally, a flashing strip of some kind is installed above windows and doors to prevent rainwater from running in under the trim and leaking into the house above the jamb. (See Illus. 107, page 76.) You can conceal or expose the flashing, but you must determine the exact position of the window before it is installed. The upper part of the flashing must be behind the siding, so the siding above the windows will have to be left unnailed if it is put up first. Apply flashing paper around the rough opening to help seal the space between the framing and the jamb, and to provide a proper vapor barrier. Perhaps the best sequence is to apply the siding, leaving the areas above the windows and doors unnailed, and then slide the flashings into place just before the windows are installed. Wait until after the window is attached in place to nail the flashing and siding down. Don't nail through the flashing near the lower edge. It is also a good idea to lap the building paper at the bottom of the window up over the framing sill.

Because of the "ears" or returns on the sill, the windows must be set into their rough openings from the outside (Illus. 326). If you install the window before the siding, tack up pieces of siding around the opening so that the outer edge of the jamb can be positioned exactly flush to the outside of the siding. Position the ears of the sill so that they are tight against the siding. Use the temporary pieces to get the spacing just right; then slide the real siding in behind the returns when you apply it.

Illus. 326. Windows must always be installed in their rough openings from the outside. This will necessitate the building of scaffolding in some hard-to-reach areas.

As you place the window in the rough opening, drive shim shingles into the cracks around the edges to square the windows up and to hold them firmly in place (Illus. 327). If the window is one of a series, be sure to check its position relative to the other windows around it; even a quarter inch up or down will be a problem when you apply interior trim. When the window is in its proper position, plumb and square, and flush to the outside of the siding; then drive a few 12d or 16d galvanized finish nails through the jamb and into the framing to hold it in place. Now, totally fill the crack between the window and the framing with fibreglass batting or urethane foam, and apply exterior trim to make the window totally weathertight.

Once you have applied the interior siding, plane the jamb down to be flush with it, if necessary, and then carefully cut the stool so that it fits tightly against both the bottom of the sash and the wall (Illus. 328). Once you have nailed the stool in place, cut and nail in the interior stops, and apply the sash closer or apply fastener.

For casement windows, run a bead of caulk along the back of the stop, and apply weather stripping to the area where the stops contact the sash. Now the window is ready for final interior trimming and completion.

Trim pieces, also called casing, are generally applied, both inside and out, so that about 1/4 inch of the edge of the jamb shows along the inside of the trim piece. The trim, therefore, overlaps the edge of the jamb by at least 1/2 inch; this overlap on the outside is very important in sealing the jamb against rain and wind; so care should be taken that these two pieces meet tightly. Use a flexible caulk and small finish nails to seal this joint, if necessary.

Trim details vary widely with the style of the structure, but a few of the more common casing profiles are shown in Illus. 329. You can either mitre or butt the joints together. It is important that you use very dry material for the interior trim, as it will

shrink and the joints will open if it is at all moist.

Door Hardware

Door hardware generally includes locksets and hinges. Many other accessories are also available to beautify your door and improve

Illus. 327. As the window (or door) is installed, shim shingles (long, low-angled wedges) are driven into the crack between the jamb and the framing from both sides of the wall to position and stabilize the window. The further the shingles are driven in, the tighter they get. When the window is properly positioned, nail through the shims and saw or break them off so that they're even with the walls.

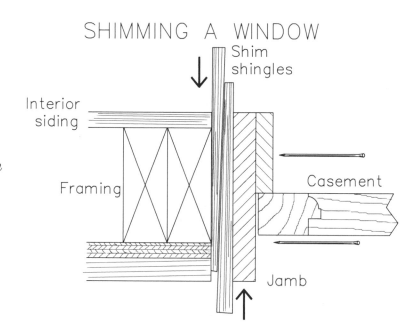

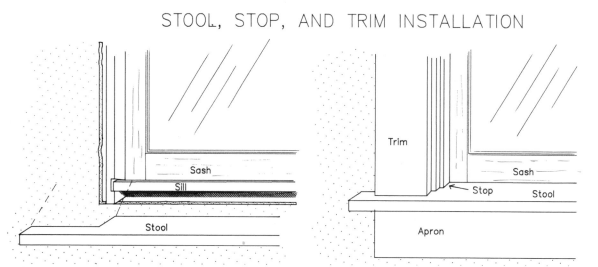

Illus. 328. The stool is usually notched on the ends so that it butts up to the inside edges of the jamb and extends out to form the base for the side pieces of trim.

CASING DETAILS

Section

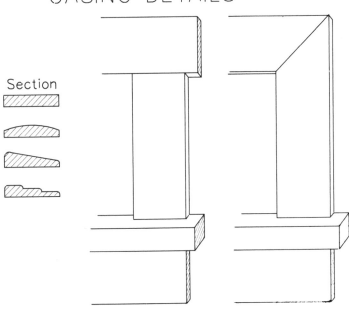

your security (Illus. 330). Butt hinges with removable pins are used for most doors, but other options do exist, including double-action butt hinges, pivot hinges, spring-loaded hinges, T-hinges and strap hinges.

A double-action hinge is actually two hinges in one, which allows the door to swing both ways. These hinges are often used on kitchen or bar doors. Pivot hinges are another form of double-action hinge that mount on the top and bottom of full-sized doors, and can be spring-loaded to always bring the door back to the closed position. Strap and T-hinges are often used for a more rustic look, or for a large swinging door such as a barn or garage door.

A large variety of locksets are available for doors, and it is important that you consider the use that the door will be put to in determining the proper lockset. For commercial or public installations, building codes often require "panic latches" that can be opened by pushing on a bar. Exterior doors in homes often have both a latch and a dead-bolt lock for security; these bolts are sometimes combined in entry sets. Interior doors can be fitted with passage latches that have no locking mechanism, or privacy latches that can be locked from one side without the use of a key.

Though many types of locksets and variations exist, their methods of installation fall into three categories. The most common type of doorknob assembly is installed by boring two holes, a large one through the face of the stile, and a smaller one from the edge of the stile into the larger hole (Illus. 331). An expandable drill bit is handy for this type of work, because the sizes of the holes vary (Illus. 332). Mount the latch assembly into the smaller hole (Illus. 333); it is held in place by two screws in the faceplate that is mortised in flush to the edge of the door. Use a sharp ¾-inch chisel to cut the shallow mortise for the faceplate. Once you have done this, mount the knob assem-

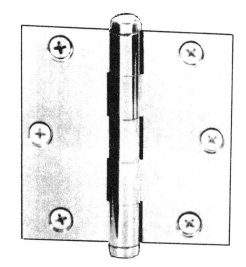

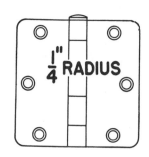

$\frac{1}{4}$" RADIUS

HORIZONTAL SPRING-PIVOT HINGE

ARROWSMITH GATE HINGES

BORDEAUX ENTRANCE HANDLE

BOMMER HEAVY-DUTY FULL-MORTISE SPRING BUTT HINGE

HERITAGE ENTRANCE HANDLE

PARKER AUTOMATIC HINGE DOOR CLOSER

SOLID BRASS DECORATOR TIPS

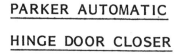

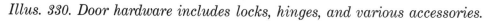

Illus. 330. Door hardware includes locks, hinges, and various accessories.

bly through the part of the latch that protrudes into the larger hole.

The distance from the edge of the door to the center of the knob is called the backset (Illus. 334); 2⅜ inches is the most common backset for cylinder locks, but many can be ordered with a 2¾-inch backset as well, making the space between the door-

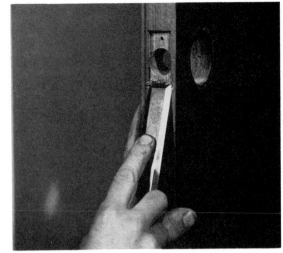

Illus. 333. Mount the latch assembly in the smaller hole.

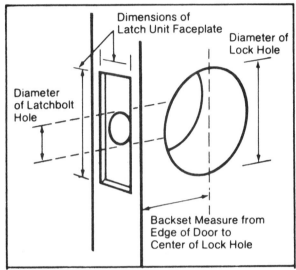

Illus. 331. A typical door-knob preparation. First drill the large hole, then the smaller one. Finally, cut the faceplate mortise with a sharp chisel.

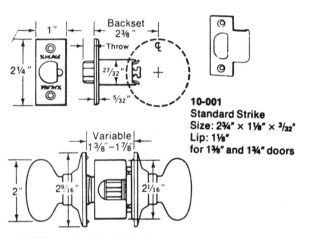

½" Throw Pin Tumbler Locks
⅜" Throw Wafer and Keyless Locks

Illus. 334. The backset is the distance from the edge of the door to the center of the actuator knob.

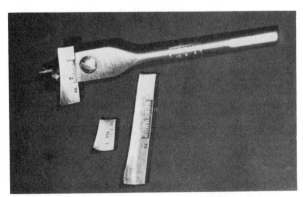

Illus. 332. An expansion drill bit with several cutting wings can cut holes of any diameter from under 1 inch to more than 5 inches.

knob and the jamb or stops a little larger.

When you have installed the lockset and it is working properly, hold it against the doorjamb to mark the position for the strike plate. Also mortise the strike plate flush to the surface of the jamb, but first bore a hole into the jamb to accept the catch. It is important not to drill or chop

STRIKE PLATE INSTALLATION

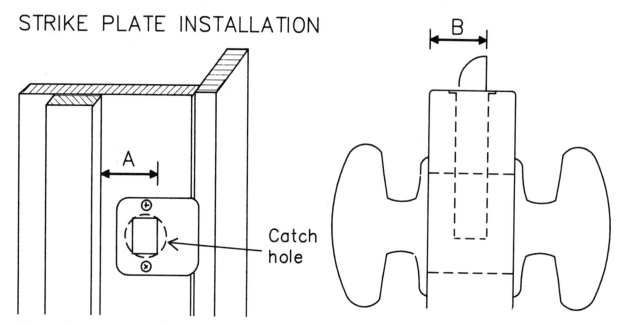

Illus. 335. It is important to drill or chop the hole for the latch under the strike plate carefully, and to position the strike plate so that the door is held tightly against the stops in the closed position.

Illus. 336. The mortises for mortise locks are very deep (4 inches or more). Care must be taken not to weaken the door by positioning the lock where it will undermine a key joint.

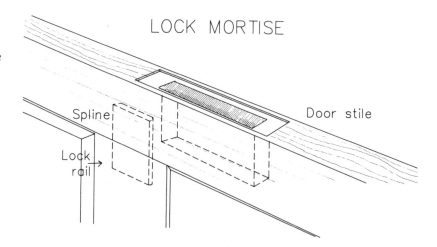

the hole any larger than necessary (undermining the screws that hold the strike plate) and to position the strike plate so that it will hold the door tightly against the stop when it is closed (Illus. 335). Most locksets come with templates and instructions for installation.

A second type of lock mechanism that is used for entryway combination locks can be installed by cutting a large mortise in the edge of the door where the lockset will go. These mortises are sometimes quite deep and as much as an inch wide (Illus. 336); you can start them with the plunge router and fence guide, but you will have to finish them with careful boring and chopping with a long mortising chisel. Then use a template to mark the positions for various holes to be bored on either side of the door for the actuating levers. Then insert the mechanism itself in the mortise, and insert or mount the levers for the knobs, dead bolts, thumb latch, and handle on cover plates that you have screwed in place (Illus. 337).

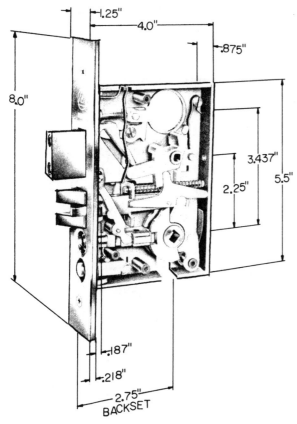

Illus. 337. Mortise locks have a very complex mechanism which combines a latch, a deadbolt, and sometimes a passage lock. This mechanism is housed in a flat metal box which must be mortised into the edge of the door.

These locksets must often be ordered left- or right-handed, depending on the side of the door they will be mounted on, and are very complicated to install. If you have never installed one before, practice the procedure on a piece of scrap before attempting the actual installation on the door. A misplaced hole could literally ruin the whole door.

The third type of lockset is surface-mounted, and is generally the easiest to install, but it is not the cleanest looking or the most secure (Illus. 338). With this type, you have to screw-mount the box-shaped lock mechanism to the interior surface of the door, and mount a catch on the interior jamb. Drill a small hole through the door for the outside knob.

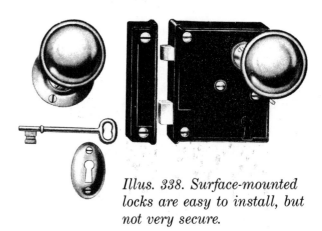

Illus. 338. Surface-mounted locks are easy to install, but not very secure.

Other locking mechanisms include hook-and-eye catches, often used for screen doors, barrel bolts, and the oldest of all, a stout bar of metal or wood held in place by sturdy brackets. For more complete information on the variety of specialty locksets and door hardware available, either ask to see the catalogues that your hardware dealer orders from or contact a locksmith who specializes in building locks.

Installing a Door

Whether you begin in the shop or on the job, the first thing to do once the door and

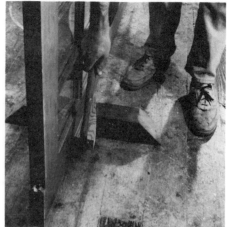

Illus. 339A and B. A length of 4 × 4 with a slot cut in it (above left) and a wedge will hold a door securely on edge for hinge or lock mortising work (above right).

jamb have been made is to mount the hinges on the door. Don't assemble the jamb until after the hinges have been mounted on it.

A piece of 4 × 4 with a slot like the one shown in Illus. 339 and a wedge will hold the door steadily on its edge. Remember that the pin of the hinge will be on the side (inside or outside) of the wall that you want the door to open to. The top hinge is usually set back 7 inches from the end of the door; and the bottom one 11 inches (Illus. 340). If a third and fourth hinge are used, they are spaced evenly between the first two.

Doors can be mounted to swing in either direction, and to open either inward or outward. An inward-opening door is considered more secure because the hinge pins are on the inside. Special screws are available that can prevent an outward opening door from being removed even if the pins are pulled. Outward-opening doors are easier to seal against the weather. Building codes often require that doors on public buildings open outward.

The width of the hinge mortise may vary depending on the size of the hinges used and the desired swing of the door. Several methods can be used to cut the mortises for the hinges. The simplest is to use a sharp chisel and a hammer. First, use a sharp knife or pencil to scribe around the hinge on the edge of the door, and then chop straight in along the inside of the line as deep as the thickness of one hinge leaf. Be careful not to split the wood when chopping parallel to the grain. Now, pare and split the waste away from end to end or by working from the side. It's better to leave the mortise a little shallow than to cut it too deep.

Hinge-mortising jigs that can be used with routers are available, but they are expensive, bulky, and time-consuming to set up. They work best if you are hanging many doors at once (Illus. 341). A simpler method is to use a small router with a fence attachment set to the width of the mortise. Chop the ends of the cut as before with the chisel, set the router to the proper depth, and remove the waste by freehand cutting up to the end lines (Illus. 342). The fence will dedermine the width of the mortise. A couple of quick cuts with the chisel will remove any waste that the router couldn't get.

When you have set the hinges, lay the door on the bench hinge pins down, and lay the hinge jamb next to it. Put the other jamb under the door to hold it up so that the pins are ¾ inch above the surface of the bench. Now, slide the jamb under the leaves of the hinges, and line the place where the head of the jamb will begin ³⁄₃₂ inch above the top of the door, and scribe around the hinges onto the jamb (Illus. 343).

Once again, chop the ends of the mortises and use the router to remove the waste. It will be necessary to change the setting on

DOOR HINGE PLACEMENT

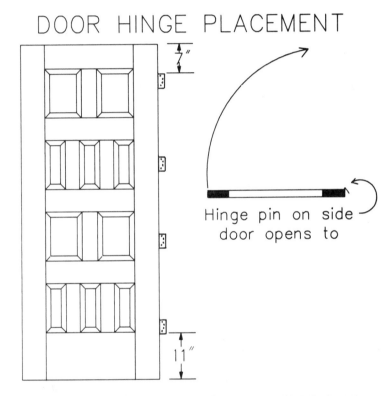

Hinge pin on side door opens to

Illus. 340. Place the top hinge 7 inches from the top of the door, the bottom hinge 11 inches from the bottom, and space additional hinges evenly between. Remember, the hinge pins are always on the side that the door opens to.

Illus. 341. Multiple hinge-mortising jigs work well when many doors are being hung. Also available are jigs that cut the outline of the hinge when it is hammered into the edge of the door or jamb.

Illus. 342A and B. A simpler method is to mark and chop the ends of the mortises with a sharp chisel (above left), and then use a router with a fence to remove the waste (above right).

Illus. 343. After you have mounted the hinges on the door, carefully mark their positions on the jamb. Be sure the top of the door is ³/₃₂'s of an inch below the place where the head jamb will be.

the fence slightly if you would like the door to sit slightly in from the edge of the jamb. When you have completed the mortises on the jamb, pop the pins on the top and bottom hinges and apply them to the jamb with the screws that are provided.

Now assemble the jamb and place it in the rough opening. You can strengthen the hinges of heavy, solid wood doors by driving the hinge screws through the jamb and into the framing (if they are long enough). If you are hanging very heavy doors, use longer-than-normal screws. In any case, first nail the jamb and head together and place the unit in the rough opening. Plumb the hinge jamb first by shimming and/or

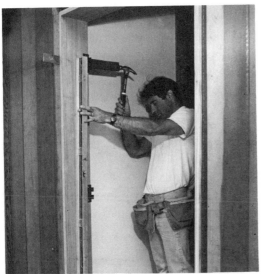

Illus. 344. Begin installing the jamb in the rough opening by shimming and nailing the hinge jamb. Once the hinge jamb is secured, reset the door on the hinges and check its fit to the head and lock jamb before securing them.

nailing as needed (Illus. 344). As with windows, it is also necessary to take care that at least one edge of the jamb is lined up flush to the surface of the siding on the wall, and that the jamb is mounted so that it is square to the walls.

When you have plumbed and securely attached (but without sinking any of the nails) the hinge jamb, hang the door on the hinges, and shim and nail the rest of the jamb into place so that the clearance is even all the way around the door. Leave slightly larger clearance along the latch side of the door when installing exterior doors, which tend to swell and shrink more.

If the door tends to spring open, it probably means that the hinge jamb is twisted or that the hinges are mortised too deeply. Check the hinge jamb for squareness with the wall and move it with shims, if necessary. If the hinges are mortised too

deeply, you can alleviate this problem by hand-planing along the hinge side of the door. You can also use a block plane to fine-tune the fit of the door to the latch jamb. On some single doors, and on most double doors it will be necessary to bevel the edge of the door, as shown in Illus. 345, so that it will close tightly without binding.

Once you have nailed the jamb with two 12d galvanized finish nails every 24 inches, apply a temporary stop to prevent damage from overswinging in the wrong direction. At this point, install the threshold.

You can either make your own threshold or purchase a variety of wooden or extruded aluminum thresholds. (See Illus. 101, page 70) For some interior doors, no threshold may be necessary, but for exterior doors a threshold is almost always needed to help drain water outward and to help obtain an airtight seal at the bottom of the door. The type of threshold that is best for a particular situation can vary widely.

A few common installation details are shown in Chapter 4. Note that space must be left at the bottom of the jamb for the threshold, and that some types of weather stripping will require over a ½ inch of space between the bottom of the door and the top of the threshold. Door bottoms can usually be cut off as much as an inch without weakening the door, but it is best to avoid this with thorough planning.

The threshold should be fitted as tightly as possible between the jambs, and should be sealed to the floor with caulk or construction adhesive. It is also important to seal wooden thresholds with a penetrating fungicidal sealer before installing them.

Once the threshold is in place, install the

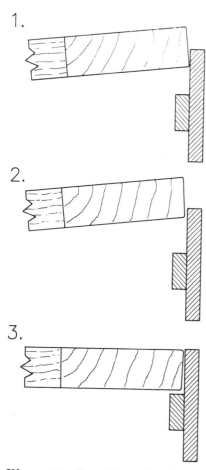

1.

2.

3.

Illus. 345. Bevelling the edge of the door will help it close tightly without binding.

lockset or latch, and finally, apply the permanent stops and trim. Apply the stops to fit to the door in its closed position; this way, any slight twist or unevenness in the door can be compensated for, making for a tight closure all around.

Most cylinder locks can be installed easily with the door in place since only a couple of holes must be bored through the door. Combination locks requiring deep mortising should be done with the door on edge. The height of the lockset installation may depend somewhat on whether there is a step up to the door, but should usually be around 36 inches from the floor to the knob. Make sure that the strike plate is positioned so that the door closes tightly against the stops; the easiest way to make sure that you are getting the strike plate in the right place is to install the lockset before applying the permanent stops. Use the temporary stop to help find the right distance from the edge of the jamb to the strike catch, and then install the finish stop with the latch held tightly against the strike catch.

If you plan to use compression-type weather stripping, such as foam stripping, apply it to the stops before they are installed. For an exterior door, make the stop detail as wide as possible, at least ½ inch thick, and apply two beads of caulk to it all around so that you can glue it to the jamb. Apply small finish nails every foot. You can use a much lighter, smaller stop for interior doors. Apply trim pieces for doors in the same manner as for windows.

Double doors and windows will require an added piece called an astragal or T-moulding between the two doors to seal the closure between them. Usually one door is fixed in place with two barrel bolts, top and bottom, and the other door which closes against it has the lockset or latch. (See Illus. 234, page 176).

Double doors are tricky to install because any twist or warping of the doors will show up dramatically where the doors meet. If one door is twisted, install the barrel bolts on the twisted door so that they will hold it straight when closed. Allow room for the astragal or overlapping rabbets when planing a double-door set. You can install the T-moulding so that it faces either in or out, and on either the opening door or the fixed door, depending on the situation.

13
Finishes, Maintenance, and Repair

Wooden doors and windows should be finished with the utmost care to enhance and preserve the beauty of your craftsmanship. Whether your creations live a comfortable life in the climate-controlled interior of your home or stand as your protection against the harsh extremes of nature, they will be subjected to more work, abuse, and scrutiny than most of the rest of your structure.

Finishing, therefore, is not the place to cut corners. The proper preparation, application and maintenance of a protective coating of stain, varnish, or paint will pay off in long years of beauty and service with minimal maintenance. Improper finishing can bring about the rapid destruction of your work.

Choosing a Finish

The wooden surfaces of doors and windows, whether they are subjected to the extremes of exterior climactic changes or not, are bound to be handled, scratched, exposed to cleaning solutions, and bleached by sun-

Illus. 346. Windows and especially doors take more abuse than just about any other part of the house except the floors.

light, as well as suffer other abuses too atrocious to mention (Illus. 346). This harsh treatment rules out altogether some finishes such as lacquers and polishes, and forces the craftsman and homeowner to choose between the advantages and disadvantages of the remainder.

A door or window's surface should be durable, easy to clean, and as easy to maintain as possible. Old favorites such as enamel paints and spar varnishes still work well and produce the smoothest surfaces, but do not necessarily give the longest-lasting protection. Synthetic varnishes are more durable, but, like all varnishes, won't hold up in direct sunlight. Properly applied acrylic-latex paints or exterior-grade stains are the longest lasting, but don't produce the kind of hard, glossy finish that many people want.

Enamel paints have always been a favorite for finishing doors and windows. They dry smooth and hard are nearly impervious to moisture and other chemical solutions, and protect the wood from ultraviolet damage. High-quality enamels come in a wide range of colors, and different colors can be applied to parts of the door to accentuate the features of your door or window. The way a door is painted can as easily be a work of art as the way it is built, and should not be overlooked a means of expression.

Though enamel paint is the most impervious, and is often preferred because it is easy to clean, tests have shown that it is not always the most durable type of paint. Latex paints, though they pass more water vapor, also remain more elastic, stretching and contracting with the wood to resist cracking and peeling longer. Tests by the Forest Service Products laboratory have shown that acrylic-latex paints, applied in two coats over an oil-based or stain-blocking latex primer, last longer than enamel paints. If you apply a coat of a water-repellent preservative before painting, you will extend even further the life of the paint, providing up to 10 years of protection without recoating.

If you want to feature the natural beauty of the woods that you have used to create your doors or windows, you will have to rely on stains, varnishes or oils to protect and maintain that beauty. Varnishes will do well in the interior of a home or in exterior areas that are not exposed to direct sunlight, but should not even be considered for work that will be directly exposed to sun and rain. Some varnishes are elastic and expand enough to withstand the normal swelling and shrinking of an exterior door, but their biggest failing is their inability to shield the wood from ultraviolet radiation. Ultraviolet radiation rapidly breaks down the lignin that binds the wood fibres together, thus destroying the foundation of the varnish and causing it to easily chip and peel; it also bleaches or discolors wood rapidly, destroying that beautiful wood color in as little as one year's time. If you simply must varnish the exterior of a door that is exposed to direct sunlight, it would be worthwhile to consider building a roof over it to protect it.

Drying oils, such as linseed or synthetic oils, soak into the wood and harden, giving a look and feel that is much like a carefully applied varnish or French polish. These oils should not be used in exposed areas either. Instead, use them for work in sheltered areas. The advantage of this type of preparation is that the oils can be poured on and rubbed with wet and dry sandpaper

Exterior wood finishes: types, treatment, and maintenance

Finish	Initial treatment	Appearance of wood	Cost of initial treatment	Maintenance procedure	Maintenance period of surface finish	Maintenance cost
Preservative oils (creosotes)	Pressure, hot and cold tank steeping	Grain visible; brown to black in color, fading slightly with age	Medium	Brush down to remove surface dirt	5–10 years only if original color is to be renewed; otherwise no maintenance is required	Nil to low
Waterborne preservatives	Brushing	Grain visible; brown to black in color, fading slightly with age	Low	Brush down to remove surface dirt	3–5 years	Low
	Pressure	Grain visible; greenish or brownish in color, fading with age	Medium	Brush down to remove surface dirt	None, unless stained, painted, or varnished as below	Nil, unless stains, varnishes, or paints are used as below
	Diffusion plus paint	Grain and natural color obscured	Low to medium	Clean and repaint	7–10 years	Medium
Organic solvent preservatives	Pressure, steeping, dipping, brushing	Grain visible; colored as desired	Low to medium	Brush down and reapply	2–3 years or when preferred	Medium
Water repellent	One or two brush coats of clear material or, preferably, dip applied	Grain and natural color visible, becoming darker and rougher textured	Low	Clean and apply sufficient finish	1–3 years or when preferred	Low to medium
Semitransparent stains	One or two brush coats	Grain visible; color as desired	Low to medium	Clean and apply sufficient finish	3–6 years or when preferred	Low to medium
Clear varnish	Three coats (minimum)	Grain and natural color unchanged if adequately maintained	High	Clean and stain bleach areas; apply two more coats	2 years or when breakdown begins	High
Paint	Water repellent, prime, and two topcoats	Grain and natural color obscured	Medium to high	Clean and apply topcoat, or remove and repeat initial treatment if damaged	7–10 years	Medium

Table 1. Exterior wood finishes.

Type of exterior wood surfaces	Water-repellent preservative		Semitransparent stains		Paints	
	Suitability	Expected life (yrs)	Suitability	Expected life (yrs)	Suitability	Expected life (yrs)
Siding:						
Cedar and redwood						
Smooth (vertical grain)	High	1–2	Moderate	2–4	High	4–6
Roughsawn or weathered	High	2–3	Excellent	5–8	Moderate	3–5
Pine, fir, spruce, etc.						
Smooth (flat-grained)	High	1–2	Low	2–3	Moderate	3–5
Rough (flat-grained)	High	2–3	High	4–7	Moderate	3–5
Shingles						
Sawn	High	2–3	Excellent	4–8	Moderate	3–5
Split	High	1–2	Excellent	4–8	—	—
Plywood (Douglas-fir and southern pine)						
Sanded	Low	1–2	Moderate	2–4	Moderate	3–5
Textured (smooth)	Low	1–2	Moderate	2–4	Moderate	3–5
Textured (rough sawn)	Low	2–3	High	4–8	Moderate	4–6
Medium-density overlay	—	—	—	—	Excellent	6–8
Plywood (cedar and redwood)						
Sanded	Low	1–2	Moderate	2–4	Moderate	3–5
Textured (smooth)	Low	1–2	Moderate	2–4	Moderate	3–5
Textured (rough sawn)	Low	2–3	Excellent	5–8	Moderate	4–6
Hardboard, medium density						
Smooth						
Unfinished	—	—	—	—	High	4–6
Preprimed	—	—	—	—	High	4–6
Textured						
Unfinished	—	—	—	—	High	4–6
Preprimed	—	—	—	—	High	4–6
Millwork (usually pine)						
Windows, shutters, doors, exterior trim	High	—	Moderate	2–3	High	3–6
Decking						
New (smooth)	High	1–2	Moderate	2–3	Low	2–3
Weathered (rough)	High	2–3	High	3–6	Low	2–3
Glued-laminated members						
Smooth	High	1–2	Moderate	3–4	Moderate	3–4
Rough	High	2–3	High	6–8	Moderate	3–4
Waterboard	—	—	Low	1–3	Moderate	2–4

Table 2. Finishing methods for exterior wood surfaces, and their suitability.

Wood	Weight (lbs/ft) at 8 percent moisture content	Ease of keeping well painted (I =easiest, V = most exacting)	Resistance to cupping (1 = best, 4 = worst)	Conspicuousness of checking (1 = least, 2 = most)	Color of heartwood (sapwood is always light)	Degree of figure on flat-grained surface
Softwoods						
Cedar						
Alaska	30.4	I	1	1	Yellow	Faint
California incense	24.2	I	—	—	Brown	Faint
Port-Orford	28.9	I	—	1	Cream	Faint
Western redcedar	22.4	I	1	1	Brown	Distinct
White	20.8	I	—	—	Light brown	Distinct
Cypress	31.4	I	1	1	Light brown	Strong
Redwood	27.4	I	1	1	Dark brown	Distinct
Products overlaid with resin-treated paper		I	—	1	—	—
Pine						
Eastern white	24.2	II	2	2	Cream	Faint
Sugar	24.9	II	2	2	Cream	Faint
Western white	27.1	II	2	2	Cream	Faint
Ponderosa	27.5	III	2	2	Cream	Distinct
Fir, White	25.8	III	2	2	White	Faint
Hemlock, Western	28.7	III	2	2	Pale brown	Faint
Spruce	26.8	III	2	2	White	Faint
Douglas-fir						
(lumber and plywood)	31.0	IV	2	2	Pale red	Strong
Larch, Western	38.2	IV	2	2	Brown	Strong
Lauan (plywood)		IV	2	2	Brown	Faint
Pine						
Norway (red)	30.4	IV	2	2	Light brown	Distinct
Southern						
(lumber and plywood)	38.2	IV	2	2	Light brown	Strong
Tamarack	36.3	IV	2	2	Brown	Strong
Hardwoods						
Alder	28.0	III	—	—	Pale brown	Faint
Aspen	26.3	III	2	1	Pale brown	Faint
Basswood	25.5	III	2	2	Cream	Faint
Cottonwood, Eastern	28.0	III	4	2	White	Faint
Magnolia	34.4	III	2	—	Pale brown	Faint
Yellow-poplar	29.2	III	2	1	Pale brown	Faint
Beech	43.2	IV	4	2	Pale brown	Faint
Birch, Yellow	42.4	IV	4	2	Light brown	Faint
Cherry	34.8	IV	—	—	Brown	Faint
Gum	35.5	IV	4	2	Brown	Faint
Maple, Sugar	43.4	IV	4	2	Light brown	Faint
Sycamore	34.7	IV	—	—	Pale brown	Faint
Ash, White	41.5	V or III	4	2	Light brown	Distinct
Butternut	26.4	V or III	—	—	Light brown	Faint
Chestnut	29.5	V or III	3	2	Light brown	Distinct
Elm, American	35.5	V or III	4	2	Brown	Distinct
Walnut	37.0	V or III	3	2	Dark brown	Distinct
Hickory, Shagbark	50.3	V or IV	4	2	Light brown	Distinct
Oak, White	45.6	V or IV	4	2	Brown	Distinct
Oak, Northern Red	42.5	V or IV	4	2	Brown	Distinct

Table 3. Characteristics of woods for painting and finishing (omissions in table indicate inadequate data for classification).

or steel wool to produce a polish that is more in the wood than on it.

You can reapply drying oils periodically without removing the previous coats of finish, and thus reduce maintenance time considerably (Illus. 347). But an oil does not even protect as long as a varnish, so that it must be maintained more carefully to avoid damage to your work.

Illus. 347. Drying oils, poured on and scrubbed with an abrasive, can give the look of hand-rubbed polish, and are very easy to maintain.

Illus. 348. Exterior-grade, semi-transparent stains may be the best choice for a natural-looking exterior finish that will provide some protection against weathering caused by ultraviolet radiation that results from exposure to the sun.

Exterior-grade, semitransparent stains offer a compromise between opaque paints and short-lived varnishes, and are long lasting and easy to maintain (Illus. 348). These stains, which soak into the wood and harden like an oil, protect the wood by repelling moisture, preventing mildew and other fungal growths, and by blocking the majority of the sun's ultraviolet rays. Though they do leave the grain and structure of the wood clearly visible, they also color it. The pigments, which are necessary to protect the wood from sun damage, are formulated to enhance and deepen the natural colors of various common woods such as redwood, cedar, teak, mahogany, pine, spruce, and fir. Generally, the darker the stain, the better the protection.

These stains are easy to apply, even on rough wood surfaces, and since they do not build up a surface film, they can be easily reapplied after a few years when the finish begins to dull. Many companies also offer similar products that will rejuvenate old weathered wood before the application of the semitransparent stains.

You can make your own stain by follow-

276

ing this recipe developed by the Forest Products Laboratory; the ingredients for the stain are shown below. The tints shown will produce a cedar-brown color, but you can vary this color by using universal tints available from most large paint dealers. Most of the other ingredients can be found at any hardware or paint dealer. The amounts shown in the table will produce five gallons of stain at a cost considerably less than that of most commercially available exterior stains.

Boiled linseed oil—3 gallons
40% pentachlorophenol solution—½ gallon
paraffin (melted)—1 pound
burnt sienna tinting color—1 pint
raw umber tinting color—1 pint
mineral spirits—1 gallon

Melt the paraffin in a double boiler, being careful not to get it too hot. Add the linseed oil/mineral-spirits solution and, when the mixture has cooled to about 70 degrees, add the pentachlorophenol solution, blending it with the other ingredients. To ensure that you don't breathe the fumes from any of these materials, especially the pentachlorophenol solution, work outside and wear gloves, goggles, and an organic-vapor respirator. If you live in a moist area where mildew is likely to be a problem, use half as much linseed oil and make up the difference with mineral spirts.

Surface Preparation

Whether you plan to paint, varnish, or stain your work, the surfaces should be clean, smooth, and free of major cracks or imperfections. Paint will stick better to vertical, tight-grained wood (Illus. 349). However, many people mistakenly think that paint will cover unevenness or coarse woodwork. Latex paints do cover the surface a bit better than enamels, but saw-kerf, scratches or rough, unsanded grain can show through even after several coats of primer and paint.

To get the best results on painted work, fill cracks or dents with a plastic or epoxy filler paste, sand them flush, and apply several coats of primer, sanding in between coats to create a smooth, defect-free surface on which to apply the paint.

When working on hard woods, you may only have to sand lightly with 120 or finer-grit sandpaper after you have planed the entire door or window to remove any unevenness at the joints or other imperfections, and have removed planing marks with a sharp cabinet scraper.

If the sanding reveals more imperfections, you may have to repeat the scraping, and then sand some more. Be careful not to work a hollow into a flat surface. Work as much on the high areas around a defect as on the defect itself.

For softer woods such as redwood, fir, pine, and others, the procedure is somewhat different. These woods will plane nicely, but they do not look good when scraped. So start sanding with a coarser-grit sandpaper—100 grit is usually coarse enough—dampen the surface of the wood with a damp rag to raise the loose grain, let the wood dry for a few minutes, and sand evenly and in the direction of the grain (Illus. 350). Orbital sanders do this type of sanding nicely, but belt sanders should be avoided because they dig in very easily and cause more damage than they remove.

After the coarse sanding, use a finer grit; usually 150- or 220-grit sandpaper is suffi-

Illus. 349. Finishes will stick better to vertical, tight-grained woods in which early and late growth are of an even density.

Illus. 350. Plane soft woods and then wet them to raise the grain, as shown, before sanding.

cient. You may have to make sanding blocks to get into some areas like corners or to sand large surfaces if you are working by hand; fold a heavy cloth like felt or velour around your sanding blocks to soften them and prevent scratching.

You can sand mouldings by hand. Fold a small piece of sandpaper into thirds. This will keep it from unfolding, and also pre-

vent it from getting under slivers and causing more damage. Sand the edges of all doors and windows to a slight roundness to make them more comfortable to handle.

Set all nails, and use a sandable wood putty or other filler to fill the holes; sand the hole until there is no trace of the putty left on the surface around the hole. Clear finishes will often accentuate the difference in color between the wood and a filler; so if you must use a filler, use it sparingly.

Another method of filling cracks, especially where joints have not come together completely, is to cut a thin, wedge-shaped piece of wood off of a large piece with the table saw, apply glue to both sides of it, and then drive it into the crack (Illus. 351). Allow the glue to dry, and then carefully pare the piece down flush to the surface with a sharp chisel. Slightly smooth it with the plane or sander to make it perfectly flush and nearly invisible.

Illus. 351. Thin wedges of wood, which taper to nothing, can be used to fill cracks where clear finishes will be used.

278

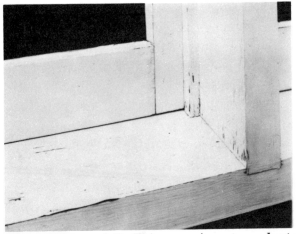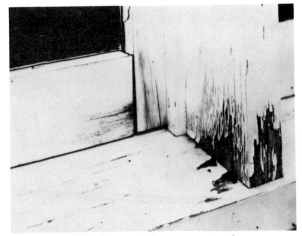

Illus. 352A and B. This experiment conducted by the United States Department of Agriculture's Forest Products lab shows the differences between using a water-repellent sealer before painting new wood (left) and not using it (right).

Dents in woods can often be removed by the application of heat and moisture. Use an iron over a wet cloth to force moist heat into the area, and then sand the grain after it has dried.

Before applying primers, varnishes, or oils, apply at least one coat of a water-repellant sealer to the surface. These sealers, which contain petroleum oils, and often a mildewcide, soak into the grain of the wood, protecting it for years from rot and mildew, and greatly prolong the life of a paint or varnish coating (Illus. 352). Soak especially well the end grain and joints where moisture can more easily enter the wood. If you plan to use a clear finish, purchase a clear sealer. Sealers containing copper napthenate will impart a greenish color to the wood.

Stripping Old Paint and Varnish

If you are renovating or repairing an older door or window, rather than building a new one, it is best to remove the many layers of cracked and chipped paint before starting anew (Illus. 353). Paint applied over too many layers of old paint will crack and peel easily. Also, trim- and jambwork tend to build up many layers of paint over the years, and often reveal fine, high-grade hard woods when stripped.

There are many methods available for stripping paints from wood, including heat, abrasion, and chemical strippers. If you're not really interested in removing the paint to get to the bare wood, but simply want to remove loose chips and prepare the surface for repainting, then abrasion may be the best approach.

Many varieties of paint scrapers are available in hardware and paint dealers. Get one that suits your job, big or small, and maintain its sharpness as you work by filing the edge so that it is flat and has very sharp corners. The paint scraper will remove the bulk of the cracked and peeled paint. Then smooth the surface further by sanding with an orbital sander, which will remove the high spots and flatten the surface. Remember that older paints contain lead,

Illus. 353. Cross-grain checking from an excessive buildup of paint.

Illus. 354. If you plan to strip all the old paint, begin by using a propane torch or heat gun to bubble the paint off. In some areas such as around glass, chemical strippers will be safer.

and the dust from them can be toxic. Always wear an organic vapor mask when stripping old paint and work outdoors if possible.

Go over the surface with a wire brush at this point; the wire brush will rough up even the low spots so that they will accept putty or paint better. You can apply body fillers or vinyl puttys with a putty knife to help fill in the low spots and further flatten the surface; several filling and sanding cycles may be necessary to totally flatten the surface before priming. The main purpose for priming over old paint is to even the color so that fewer coats of paint are needed, but primers are also chalky when dry and, therefore, can be easily sanded.

If your goal is to remove the old paint entirely, a combination of heat and chemicals may be the best approach (Illus. 354). Complete stripping is sometimes a good idea, even if you plan to repaint. Heat guns and heat plates can often be rented from rental centers. The plates will do a good job on large, flat expanses, and the guns, which blow hot air like a large hair dryer, are good for getting into corners and convoluted spots, but both can scorch the wood or surrounding materials, and the intense heat can also cause window glass to crack.

Caustic strippers are the cheapest of chemical strippers, but if they are not properly neutralized after the paint is removed, they can bleed out of the wood and destroy the new finish. Methylene chloride based, solvent-type strippers are preferred by professionals for on-the-job use because they do a quick and thorough job without harming the wood.

If possible, move the pieces that you intend to work on from the building to a well-ventilated shop area that is as warm as possible. You may even want to consider removing the interior trim and mouldings if the situation warrants it.

If you have to work in the building, protect the walls and floors, as well as yourself. Wear goggles and an organic vapor mask, as well as gloves and old clothes. Cover the walls and the floors. Test your stripper on the areas you intend to strip, and on materials that you don't want damaged.

Brush the solvent on, wait the recommended time, and check a piece to see how deeply it has penetrated. If you are removing many layers, you may have to do it in stages, because the stripper shouldn't be left on the wood so long that it dries out. A large paint scraper will work well on flat areas, but a knife, ice pick, three-cornered scraper, or other tool may be necessary to get into tight corners and ornate work.

Anything can be stripped, but if the woodwork is too ornate or too many coats of paint have been applied over the years, it may be a difficult and time-consuming job. No-rinse strippers are quite weak (30–50% methylene chloride) compared to the stronger (50–85%) brands that must be rinsed afterwards. If your job is extremely tough, try the latter. Rinsing can be done with either water or lacquer thinner. When all the paint has been removed, and the wood rinsed, let it dry overnight, sand it lightly, and it is ready for refinishing.

Priming and Painting

An alkyd (synthetic oil)-based primer is considered the best for either oil or latex paint. The best thickness for the primer coat is between .004 and .006 inch (about the thickness of newsprint). If it is applied any thicker than this, it will be more prone to cracking and peeling prematurely.

You can continue the process of sanding down the high spots and filling in the lower spots by working the primer with medium sandpaper after it has thoroughly dried, but try to do as much of your puttying or filling as possible before priming. If you have to sand or putty after the first primer coat, (the first coat will often show you defects that you couldn't see before) reprime the area and allow it plenty of time to dry before applying the finish coats.

Painting is best done on warm, dry days in a well-ventilated but dust-free area. Perhaps the biggest mistake that inexperienced painters can make is to recoat before the previous coat has dried thoroughly. If you paint, especially with enamel, over a coat of sealer or primer that is not yet dry, you will trap volatile oils under the coat and make it impossible to get the top coat to dry properly. In extreme cases, the paint will have to be removed completely because it will not dry.

If you are unsure whether a coat of paint is completely dry, scratch it with a fingernail or press a piece of tape against it and see if a chip is lifted off. If it is, the paint is not yet dry.

Do not wait too long between coats of paint. For best adhesion between coats, repaint in less than one week's time. When you paint, apply the paint to the work with one or two horizontal brush strokes, and then use long, even vertical strokes to spread that paint over as wide an area as it will cover (Illus. 355). Two thin, even coats are usually all that's needed if you did a proper job of sealing and priming.

Whenever possible, lay doors and windows out flat for painting, doing first one side and then the other. If this is not possible, watch carefully for runs and drips. Wait a few minutes after you've finished a piece, and wipe out any drips with long, even brush strokes. Avoid heavy build-ups of

Illus. 355. First apply a heavy brush of paint across the grain, and then pull it out along the grain with long strokes until the coverage is thin and even.

Illus. 356. When there is exposed end grain, moisture seeps into the door or window, making it swell and crack.

paint around mouldings, panels, and other raised edges.

When painting new windows, it will save time and trouble if you paint the sash and jamb before they are glazed or installed. Be sure to seal the entire window, especially the sill, exposed end grain, and joints with a water-repellant sealer before beginning. For the best protection, paint even the areas that won't show, such as the insides of the glass rabbets and the bottom of the sill. If you are using wooden stops instead of glazing putty, cut them to length, and then remove and paint them.

For doors and windows, the most crucial and most often overlooked areas are the top and bottom. Exposed end grain or open joints will rapidly soak up moisture and ruin the door or window if it is not completely sealed and painted (Illus. 356).

Latex paints often won't stick as well to a weathered surface or to old oil paint. If you are repainting with latex, it may be necessary to apply a coat of primer first for best adhesion. If you are in doubt about whether the paint will stick to the area,

paint a small section and allow it to dry thoroughly. Then apply a piece of tape to the area; if it lifts the new paint off, sand and prime before painting with latex.

Applying Varnish or Oil

Varnished or oiled natural-wood surfaces are always admired, and are easy to maintain on the inside of a home. Varnished interior doors will last for years without need of a recoating. Often, window frames are painted on the outside and given a clear finish inside. But getting a smooth, defect-free finish to begin with can be tricky.

The term varnish generally refers to clear (or nearly clear) finishes that build up a protective film of solids on the surface of the wood. Early 18th- and 19th-century craftsmen often made their own varnishes from recipes that were handed down from master to apprentice. These recipes were guarded and kept secret. They generally contained either alcohol or various types of oils as a solvent for resins and gums that were derived from natural sources such as trees, plants, insects, and fossil deposits.

Making these varnishes can be dangerous because the materials must often be heated, and it is very difficult to get good results with small batches. Varnishes based on the old formulas, such as sandarac, elemi, mastic, and copal varnishes, are often available through art-supply dealers today.

For our purposes, varnishes can be classified as natural and synthetic. The old favorite in the natural varnish category is spar varnish, which is made up of tung oil, linseed oil, and driers. Spar varnish has a very soft, elastic finish that can be applied undiluted with good results if the surface is completely free of dust, and if great care is taken to spread the varnish very thinly and evenly. Because of its softness, spar varnish doesn't sand well. For best results, allow as much drying time as possible, use wet and dry sandpaper, and dampen the surface when sanding.

Synthetic varnishes include phenolic-based liquids and polyurethanes which dry to form a thin plastic coating over the work. These varnishes work and feel much the same as natural varnish, but the surface is harder, more resistant to staining and moisture, and easier to sand.

Both natural and synthetic varnishes may take a long time to dry if the atmospheric conditions are damp or cold. The drying time can be improved considerably if you mix in small amounts of liquid driers that are available from most paint dealers. Synthetic varnishes will often be dry to the touch in a couple of hours if driers are used.

For the best result when applying any type of varnish, seal the wood first with a sanding sealer. This is a shellaclike sealer that dries quickly, and can be easily sanded to a perfectly smooth finish. After sanding with 220-grit paper, wipe everything down very carefully with a clean tack cloth, and make sure that the air in the workplace is as free of dust as possible. Several thin coats will always give you better results than fewer thick coats.

I like to thin the varnish about 40% with mineral spirits, add about 10% drier, and brush it on very carefully with a disposable foam-rubber brush, which will actually lay it on flatter than a bristle brush and won't cause any problem with loose bristles. Once again, the evenness of the coat is crucial. Varnish runs even easier than paint. Apply the varnish with one or two vertical strokes, and then use horizontal strokes to spread it. Soak up any extra varnish that builds up around mouldings, etc. Make each coat as thin as possible.

You can obtain a hand-rubbed varnishlike finish by thinning spar varnish with ⅓ turpentine and ⅓ linseed oil, and applying the mixture as if it were on oil. Pour it on, rub it with fine wet and dry sandpaper or a plastic steel-wool substitute (steel wool is not recommended because the metal can react with tannin in the wood to cause dark stains), and finally wipe each coat off with a clean rag. You can repeat this process any number of times to create a very polished surface that doesn't have a thick build-up of finish. The same application process can also be used with tung oil or synthetic oils; all these varnishes will give much the same result.

Maintenance of Doors and Windows

When you use the proper finish at the beginning, the maintenance of doors and windows will be minimal. Painted or stained doors or windows, especially those that are protected from direct sunlight, can be expected to last for ten years without a need for repainting. The proper finish will also prevent doors from swelling to the point where they will stick or not close, stressing the hinges and jambs, and compounding what may have been a small problem.

If you notice that a door is sticking or not closing properly, the first thing to check are the hinges. If the screws have loosened a bit, allowing the hinge or hinges to flop around, the door will sag away from the hinge jamb and bind on the lock jamb when it is closed. Often, the screws can simply be tightened to solve the problem, but if they are stripped, or the wood is cracked, you may have to fill the screw hole or crack with epoxy glue and allow the glue to dry before redrilling and resetting the screws.

If the hinges seem to be tight, then the problem is most likely the expansion of either the door or the surrounding woodwork, which is caused by moisture entering the wood. This is a danger signal, indicating either the finish has not worked or that important areas such as the end grain were not finished properly, and should be dealt with immediately. Plane down the edge of the door, checking frequently to see how it is fitting; you can usually do this with a block plane with the door in place. When the door is closing freely again, refinish any areas that are not properly sealed.

You can sometimes use shims of cardboard under one of the hinges to straighten the hang of a door relative to the jamb, thus solving problems caused by the settling of the building. If the door binds at the top,

and has a larger than necessary clearance at the bottom on the lock jamb, try to tighten the top hinge, and place a cardboard shim under the bottom hinge to straighten it out. Sometimes a 10d nail driven through the jamb in an area where the door is binding will pull the jamb back enough to solve the problem so that you will not have to plane and refinish.

As soon as signs of cracking or chipping show in the finish of an exterior door or window, it is time for you to refinish it. If you refinish as soon as possible, the damage will be minimal, and the refinishing will be easier to do; however, if possible, wait for the warmest and driest part of the year to do the work.

Old paint does not have to be removed entirely, but any loose paint should be scraped off. Putty dents, low spots where paint has been chipped off, and prime areas where bare wood shows, especially if the edge has been planed down. A few hours of maintenance can add years to the lifespan of your doors and windows.

Repairing Doors and Windows

When a window sash has rotted through, or been broken by rough use, it may be a toss-up as to whether it is worthwhile to repair it or replace it. Doors, on the other hand, can often be repaired despite quite heavy damage. The most common form of damage to both doors and windows is rot, usually in the area of the joints between the stiles and rails, near the bottom (Illus. 357).

If the repair is called for before the rot has gone too far, chisel or rout the rot out until you reach solid wood; then cut a piece

Illus. 357. Test for rot by sticking the tip of a pocket knife into the wood. If it sinks in easily, the wood is rotten.

of wood and glue it in to fill the hole (Illus. 358). Epoxy glues are the best to use for this type of work because they retain their strength even if there is a crack between the pieces of wood. You can use epoxy filler

paste to fill any cracks around the patch after it has been glued in place (Illus. 359). Once the surface has been rebuilt, plane it down flush to the rest of the door, treat it with a sealer that contains a fungicide, and prime and paint it. Rot will often run rapidly up the grain of a stile, but it won't do any serious damage as long as the wood is protected from moisture.

Broken muntins in doors or windows with multiple panes of glass can usually be reconstructed from the broken parts. Remove all surrounding glass and putty, and clean any surfaces that were previously glued. Wood that has been broken cleanly can easily be reglued. If splinters are missing, they can be patched in with wood or putty. If you must patch in a piece of wood where it will show, use a sharp chisel to flatten the surface you will be gluing it to, and then cut a piece of wood that matches as well as possible the color and grain of the piece you are fixing. Glue the patch in place first, and then shape it with

 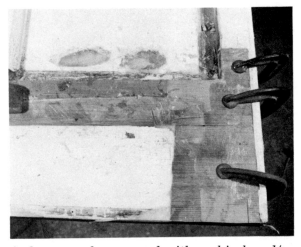

Illus. 358A and B. Rotted sections of doors or windows can be removed with a chisel and/or router and filled with new wood or plastic fillers. When damage is this severe, the new wood must be applied across the joints to strengthen them (right).

chisels, files, or planes after the glue has dried.

Another common problem is leaking, or split panels. You can sometimes remove panels by prying out the moulding on one side or the other but on a well-made door, the panel will be housed in a slot that is cut into the frame pieces. If it is necessary to remove a panel from this type of door, use a router with a flush-cutting bit with an in-board mounted bearing to cut out the moulding around the panel. If the door will be exposed to driven rain, it is probably best to cut the rabbet from the outside to allow for better drainage.

Now, to complete the reconstruction, remove the old panel and insert and mould a new panel. Bed the new panel in a heavy bead of a flexible caulk to prevent leakage and, for best results, use a bolection-type moulding securely glued to the frame members. Fill any cracks between the panel and the moulding with flexible caulk, and paint carefully with enamel or latex paint.

Illus. 359A and B. You can repair doors that have simply developed wide cracks at the joints by filling the cracks with epoxy paste and reclamping. The paste is made from epoxy glue and fillers such as Q-cell or microfibres.

METRIC EQUIVALENCY CHART

MM—MILLIMETRES   CM—CENTIMETRES

INCHES TO MILLIMETRES AND CENTIMETRES

INCHES	MM	CM	INCHES	CM	INCHES	CM
⅛	3	0.3	9	22.9	30	76.2
¼	6	0.6	10	25.4	31	78.7
⅜	10	1.0	11	27.9	32	81.3
½	13	1.3	12	30.5	33	83.8
⅝	16	1.6	13	33.0	34	86.4
¾	19	1.9	14	35.6	35	88.9
⅞	22	2.2	15	38.1	36	91.4
1	25	2.5	16	40.6	37	94.0
1¼	32	3.2	17	43.2	38	96.5
1½	38	3.8	18	45.7	39	99.1
1¾	44	4.4	19	48.3	40	101.6
2	51	5.1	20	50.8	41	104.1
2½	64	6.4	21	53.3	42	106.7
3	76	7.6	22	55.9	43	109.2
3½	89	8.9	23	58.4	44	111.8
4	102	10.2	24	61.0	45	114.3
4½	114	11.4	25	63.5	46	116.8
5	127	12.7	26	66.0	47	119.4
6	152	15.2	27	68.6	48	121.9
7	178	17.8	28	71.1	49	124.5
8	203	20.3	29	73.7	50	127.0

YARDS TO METRES

YARDS	METRES	YARDS	METRES	YARDS	METRES	YARDS	METRES	YARDS	METRES
⅛	0.11	2⅛	1.94	4⅛	3.77	6⅛	5.60	8⅛	7.43
¼	0.23	2¼	2.06	4¼	3.89	6¼	5.72	8¼	7.54
⅜	0.34	2⅜	2.17	4⅜	4.00	6⅜	5.83	8⅜	7.66
½	0.46	2½	2.29	4½	4.11	6½	5.94	8½	7.77
⅝	0.57	2⅝	2.40	4⅝	4.23	6⅝	6.06	8⅝	7.89
¾	0.69	2¾	2.51	4¾	4.34	6¾	6.17	8¾	8.00
⅞	0.80	2⅞	2.63	4⅞	4.46	6⅞	6.29	8⅞	8.12
1	0.91	3	2.74	5	4.57	7	6.40	9	8.23
1⅛	1.03	3⅛	2.86	5⅛	4.69	7⅛	6.52	9⅛	8.34
1¼	1.14	3¼	2.97	5¼	4.80	7¼	6.63	9¼	8.46
1⅜	1.26	3⅜	3.09	5⅜	4.91	7⅜	6.74	9⅜	8.57
1½	1.37	3½	3.20	5½	5.03	7½	6.86	9½	8.69
1⅝	1.49	3⅝	3.31	5⅝	5.14	7⅝	6.97	9⅝	8.80
1¾	1.60	3¾	3.43	5¾	5.26	7¾	7.09	9¾	8.92
1⅞	1.71	3⅞	3.54	5⅞	5.37	7⅞	7.20	9⅞	9.03
2	1.83	4	3.66	6	5.49	8	7.32	10	9.14

Index